Salman Rushdie

An Anthology of 21st Century Criticism

Edited with an Introduction by
Ajay K. Chaubey
Janmejay K. Tiwari
Bishun Kumar

Foreword by
Neil ten Kortenaar
Professor of English and Comparative Literature
University of Toronto Scarborough, Canada

ATLANTIC
PUBLISHERS & DISTRIBUTORS (P) LTD

Published by

ATLANTIC

PUBLISHERS & DISTRIBUTORS (P) LTD

7/22, Ansari Road, Darya Ganj, New Delhi-110002
Phones : +91-11-40775252, 23273880, 23275880, 23280451
Fax : +91-11-23285873
Web : www.atlanticbooks.com
E-mail : orders@atlanticbooks.com

Branch Office
5, Nallathambi Street, Wallajah Road, Chennai-600002
Phones : +91-44-48531784, 28411383
E-mail : chennai@atlanticbooks.com

Reprint 2019

Printed in India at Nice Printing Press, A-33/3A, Site-IV, Industrial Area, Sahibabad, Ghaziabad, U.P.

I Dedicate this book to my

Father, Late **Madhusudan Chaubey**
(1st July 1950—1st April 2015)

Papa, you have always been
A source of spur for me.
Most of the people like and get inspired
By more powerful bigwigs of the world.
However, you remain the most prevailing person,
Sailing me out from all the jeopardies
Of my life softly and smilingly.

"Papa, your son is soaring high in this cormorant
world to reach your dream.
Thank you for your selfless action throughout.
I fervently miss your perennial smiles
while the countless hurdles of life.
Love you!"

Ajay K. Chaubey

Foreword

Bill Ashcroft, Gareth Griffiths, and Helen Tiffin borrowed the title of their influential 1989 work of postcolonial theory, *The Empire Writes Back*, from an essay of Salman Rushdie. More than Walcott, Coetzee, Achebe, or Soyinka or any other candidate for the honour, Rushdie was hailed as the epitome of the literary postcolonial and his 1981 novel *Midnight's Children* as the quintessential postcolonial novel. However, no sooner did he put himself at the masthead of a literary and critical movement that sought to reverse the relations of imperial centre and periphery than Rushdie acquired a host of other, seemingly very different meanings. 1989 was also the year the Ayatollah Khomeini declared, in a fatwa, a death sentence against him as the author of blasphemous novel, *The Satanic Verses*. Rushdie has since been commonly regarded as the spokesperson for Western secularism against religious intolerance, especially Muslim religious intolerance.

The Bombay-born Cambridge-educated author has never been content to rest within a single self-definition: the Indian became British became American in a progress that he made seem inevitable. The author of the postcolonial masterpiece *Midnight's Children* became the author of the great novel of the immigrant experience in Britain, *The Satanic Verses*, and later of a novel of globalization, *The Ground Beneath Her Feet*, that folded India into a much larger contemporary world. Later still, he became the author of a New York novel, *Fury*, explicitly indebted to Saul Bellow and Ralph Ellison. The recent *Two Years Eight Months and Twenty-Eight Days* has left India far behind. The erstwhile prophet of postcolonialism has become identified with diaspora, transnationalism, or cosmopolitanism.

Part of Rushdie's restlessness can be attributed to his creativity: he has always sought new subject matter and new ways to transgress. Arguably, however, his protean versatility has not represented a journey so much as the nature of Rushdie's character already present at the beginning of his career. His novels have constantly returned to the same themes, tropes, and structural features. The violent alter ego bent on revenge who threatens the flawed hero appears in every novel, from *Midnight's Children* through *Shalimar the Clown*. So does the question of how a new idea passes from the text into the world: the Prophet in *The Satanic Verses* had one answer, Rushdie himself another. The struggle of the forces of openness and tolerance against those of narrow intolerance, of the Many against the One, has always been a concern. So is the relation of ideas, including religious ideas, to the material world. And the relation of the part to the whole has been the constant theme of the man who imagined his own circumstances as somehow linked to the nation-state and to the world. A Rushdie novel, however different from every other, is unmistakably a Rushdie novel. Arguably what is truest about Rushdie therefore is his consistency. The postcolonialist was always also diasporan and cosmopolitan. After all, the author of *Midnight's Children* could only write that novel because he stood outside India and envisaged it as a whole in a way that no one within India could. He modeled his novel of India on Gunter Grass's postmodern classic *The Tin Drum*—to the point where the chapters of the two books can almost be mapped against each other. In other words, Rushdie was always already a world author, even when he was the most identified with a national literature.

Some may feel, however, that Rushdie's great restlessness has worked against his creativity. Everything he has written since *Midnight's Children* can sometimes appear, if not a falling off, then a series of extrapolating sequels. Indian literature cannot be imagined without Rushdie, but he will never be an essential novelist of New York. The great master of the new and the surprising can seem all too predictable, a fate that echoes what has happened to postmodernism more generally. It therefore feels right that this collection of critical articles devoted to

Rushdie should take as its twin foci *Midnight's Children* and the author's entire literary output: the most significant part is a synecdoche of the whole; the whole is a working out of what was already present in the part.

Whether Rushdie is postcolonial, diasporan or cosmopolitan depends to some extent on who is reading him and what they are reading him for. It is one thing to teach him in Britain or Canada, another thing altogether to read him in India or Pakistan. It is one thing for a white critic of postcolonial literature to read him, another to read him, as several students of mine do, as a Muslim concerned with how the literary imagination can deal with Islam. Since the reader's location matters, I look forward to reading the essays in this collection located as it is firmly in India in the twenty-first century. The authors reassert the postcolonial Rushdie. Any attempt to take in Rushdie the man and his work must take into account how he looks from India (as well as how he appears to Muslims or how he appears to successive generations of writers). What doors does he open? What challenges does he pose? What do we now see that we could not see thirty-seven years ago? The mark of the living author is that he is being read afresh and in that sense this collection, *Salman Rushdie: An Anthology of 21st Century Criticism*, proves resoundingly that the author who once had a death sentence passed on him is alive, well, and living in Mumbai (and Delhi and Kolkata...)!

Neil ten Kortenaar
Professor of English and Comparative Literature,
University of Toronto Scarborough, Canada

Preface

The *leitmotif* of this volume on Salman Rushdie is to fundamentally deal with two objectives—one to update the Rushdie criticism in the second decade of the New Millennium and the other is to provide a passable break to young and vibrant scholars of India and abroad to rub their shoulders with the eminent and established scholars of 'Rushdie affairs'. Salman Rushdie is not only an author of global fame but he has emerged himself as political commentator also by giving ample place to polemics and erudition by offering his candid notion on worldwide affairs—be it release of Syrian activist, Mazen Darwish, from jail or his prompt remarks to Bhal Chandra Nemade's comment on his novels' "literary merit" or his blunt support to Sahitya Academy Award returning authors in India for dissidence and intolerance in the regime of the present Indian government.

Rushdie's literary expedition has completed span of more than four decades right from his maiden novel, *Grimus* (1975) to the latest, *Two Years Eight Months and Twenty Eight Nights* published in 2015. Rushdie adroitly situates postcolonial impressions of the Indian subcontinent and beautifully paints the canvas of fictions with multiple hues of ethnicity, Muslim imperialism, and historical blend in the post-independence politics of India. The novels of Salman Rushdie are the true representatives of postcolonial fiction. He embodies in his own life and in his writings the conundrums of the postcolonial author, writing within the traditions of Indo-English literature while concurrently appealing to the conventions and tastes globally, especially to the Western audience. The present volume offers fresh perspectives on Salman Rushdie, which contains seventeen critical essays that traverse through his literary taxonomy and bring out an incisive criticism.

We humbly concede scholarly inputs by the contributors of this volume whose enormous support and immaculate trust in us are impeccable and genuine. We warmly extend our gratitude to our teachers, PhD guides, friends, and members of our family for their unconditional and unrestricted love and support to us, which cannot and can never be returned in lieu of that. Our highest compliment and sincerest appreciation go to Mr. Harjeet Singh and his team for the Atlantic who have ocean of patience to bring this volume well in time.

No academic work seems to be perfect and flawless. Hence, we shall remain grateful to our readers who may offer their valuable suggestions, if any, to make this anthology more enriched in the next editions and your honest criticism as well as feedback is awaited at kcajay79@gmail.com.

All flaws remain to ours, of course!

Editors
Ajay K. Chaubey
Janmejay K. Tiwari
Bishun Kumar

Contents

Section–B

Midnight's Children: Fictionalizing History, Nation and Narration

Section–C

Treatment of Imagined Temporalities, Cosmopolitanism and Narrative Strategies: Recent Perspectives

Section–D

Rushdie's Diasporic Passage to the New World: Some Observations

Introduction

The Novels of Salman Rushdie
A Postcolonial Reading

> Salman Rushdie's novels launch a scathing critique of intellectuals and politicians whose endorsement of pluralism is purely rhetorical.... Rushdie shows that people who claim to promote unity are actually complicit in creating ethnic strife.... Rushdie wants a productive, inclusive cosmopolitanism...can have serious unintended consequences. (Trousdale 91)
>
> Rushdie may epitomize the migrant writer par excellence with all its potential for reinventing the world and the subject of human identity, but the Rushdie affair also places him in a position in which he seems to personify the flip side of globalization—that is, the clash of civilizations, the increasing gap between cultures, and the proliferation of fundamentalism. (Frank 132)

Sir Ahmed Salman Rushdie, one of the progenitors of the worldwide controversies till date, occupies a coveted place in the galaxy of postcolonial authors. The winner of the Booker Prize and the James Tait Black Prize both in 1981, the Booker of Bookers in 1993 and the Best of the Bookers in 2008 and, of late, the PEN Pinter in 2014, the name that has dominated the literary world since establishing himself as a leading exemplum of postcolonial, postmodern and Diaspora writings is none other than the dissident, Salman Rushdie. Perhaps, these are the reasons why "...the name of Salman Rushdie is so famous internationally that even those who do not generally read literary fictions have heard of him..." (Teverson 4). Prominent for multifarious writings, he himself is a multifaceted personality, often emerges as an unpredictable figure with an unfathomable depth of creativity and criticism. Being an iconoclast, Rushdie never chooses the trodden road; he rather plunges headstrong into the unexplored territories of literature, yet unattempted.

For the Booker, he never ran the race rather he reached the zenith of the success by bagging the same for *Midnight's Children* in 1981. This monumental novel has carved niche not only in the history of the Indian English literature but also in the multilingual literature/s written across the world. Rushdie played a groundbreaking role in new beginnings—the blending of history with fiction and magic realism. With him begins the era of new writings, new experiments giving him a new identity—the postmodern figure and a precursor of new generation—the "midnight's children". Not only his works but he himself also is a postmodern product—a blend of a god for literary aestheticians and a Satan for religious fundamentalists. He has, therefore, generated enormous interest in the intellectual circles as a vibrant writer for analysis and interpretation of his writings.

Being dissenter, he combats with his two selves—the inner and the outer, and also at the same time with the external world for his extremely controversial novel, *The Satanic Verses*. His literary authoritarianism entangles him into hullabaloos, and arrows of words penetrating his heart and mind compelling him for introspection. However, Rushdie defends himself at an appearance at 92nd Street Y, expressing his views on copyright while answering a question whether he had considered copyright law barriers (impediments) to free speech:

> No, but that's because I write for a living, (laughs) and have no other source of income, and I naively believe that stuff that I create, belongs to me, and that if you want it you might have to give me some cash. [...] My view is I do this for a living. The thing wouldn't exist if I didn't make it and so it belongs to me and don't steal it. You know. It's my stuff.[1]

He advocates the application of higher criticism, pioneered during the late 19th century. In a guest opinion piece printed in *The Washington Post* and "The Times" in mid-August 2005, Rushdie called for a reform in Islam:

> What is needed is a move beyond tradition, nothing less than a reform movement to bring the core concepts of Islam into the modern age. A Muslim Reformation to combat not only the jihadist ideologues but also the dusty, stifling seminaries of the traditionalists, throwing open windows to let in much-needed fresh air.... It is high time, for starters, that Muslims were able to study the revelation of their religion as an event inside history, not supernaturally above it, ...Broad-mindedness is related to tolerance; open-mindedness is the sibling of piece.[2]

Call him a defector or a Satan or an antireligious rabble but he bags God's blessings by asking for an apology through his *Luka and the Fire of Life*. The apology is not for having been blasphemous but for having shaken the faith of Muslims before preparing a suitable environment for developing humanist and rational thinking in them that could save them from being blind traditionalist and religious fundamentalists. Ups and downs in his journey of writing transform him into a sage of literary art and devotee of the God, the Allah. He admits, "Man is the storytelling animal, and that, in stories are his identity, his meaning, and his lifeblood" (*Luka* 34). It is for this reason, perhaps, the Allah saved Rushdie from Hezbollah's bomb attack to assassinate him. Moreover, despite all controversial condemnations, he was knighted for his services to literature on the Queen Elizabeth II's 80th Birthday on 16th June, 2007. He remarked, "I am thrilled and humbled to receive this great honour, and I am very grateful that my work has been recognized in this way."[3] Rushdie's emergence with his creative bulk has dazzled and amazed the contemporary authors and the readers for being unconventional rather than becoming enigma for both. He began writing as an anti-colonial and postcolonial reactionary to the West; he switched to incorporate diasporic experiences of his own and of other migrants as well. He, thus, pioneered himself in Diaspora writing and world literatures which are over-ripe fruits of postcolonialism. He pioneered himself as a major voice of decolonization, multiculturalism, and also of new humanism.

His works embody the stamp of contemporaneous Indian conventions and Indo-Anglian interests, which lead him to interface with the worldwide readership, especially to the Western audience. The publication of *The Satanic Verses* landed him in the labyrinth of controversy around the world and resulted him in a decree of death sentence (*Fatwa*) on him. It epitomizes the postcolonialists' flimsy and constant battle to balance the demands of conflicting cultures. Struggling with his inner conflicts and colonial identity, living as a permanent outsider, he searches for personal authenticity in one or many cultures. He is the spokesperson for the people of the subcontinent who are presently residing in the alien lands. Staying within the domains of the mainstream ideologues such as Britain and the United States, he mimics and comments on all Western ideologies and proves himself to be a representative of the East. Religious and cultural diversity of both India and Britain offers Rushdie a wealth of experiences of unnumbered issues and themes that consistently refract throughout his *oeuvre*. It is his multilevel experience that becomes valuable material for the variety of his following novels.

Every novel of Salman Rushdie deals with the thoughts of national and international theses keeping in mind his primary focus on Indian subcontinents. The opening pages of his novels evoke the themes of migration, exile, diasporic consciousness, nationalism, multiculturalism, dualism etc. His writings have become the focus of a certain kind of struggle for cultural identity in Britain and other Western states.

Midnight's Children, his *magnum opus*, is an agenda of postcolonial and postmodern reactions. The novel is a conglomeration of multifarious themes occurred in postcolonial India. It is a fantasized version of the historical reality of India that spans from the Jallianwala Massacre of 1919 to the period of Emergency imposed by Indira Gandhi in 1977. Rushdie's new venture of blending history with fiction and fiction with history, employing the technique of magic realism and supernatural elements, make the novel characteristically more different than what many other authors had already attempted. *Midnight's Children* is superficially the biography of Saleem Sinai and potentially an autobiography of Salman Rushdie himself but it is allegorically the history of India. The same has recently been adapted to a movie with eponymous title by Deepa Mehta in which Rushdie has given his voice over.

By being a great aficionado of Gabriel Garcia Marquez and Günter Grass, Rushdie amalgamates facts with fiction so artistically that sometimes it becomes a Herculean task to differentiate between truth (history) and fiction (literary invention). *Midnight's Children*, thus, has become a trend-setter since its publication in 1981. As Rajeshwar Mittapalli and Pier Paulo Piciucco put it:

> The imaginative re-working of Indian history in a culturally hybrid environment, the innovative use of literary techniques...together with a supreme command of the English language and a genius for storytelling modeled on the hoary Indian narrative traditions and cultural practices, had established *Midnight's Children* as a trend setter and classic for all times. (Preface)

The novel deals with displacement and rootlessness which are the main factors of identity crisis. Almost all the major characters whether it is Saleem Sinai, Shiva, Padma or Parvati all suffer from the psychological pangs of alienation and identity crisis. Sinai is a true portrait of Rushdie for he himself is the victim of same ailment. The hero Saleem, like his creator, wanders from place to place, from Bombay to Karachi and from Karachi to Bangladesh finally comes back to Bombay. Rushdie himself returns to India again by the time, not to the geographical India but to the "India of the mind" (*Imaginary*, 5). In view of Klaus Boerne, "*Midnight's Children* is a Copernican turning-point in the history of literature and of ideas" (23) that paves the path for other novels of Rushdie. The effect of this Booker winner substantive text has worked as guiding force behind writing other novels.

Thus, the next novel *Shame* (1984) was found to be a shorter version of its predecessor *Midnight's Children* dealing with the history of Pakistan—an "insufficiently imagined country", intermingling diasporic discourse and fictional narratives. Overtly it is a novel about political turmoil in Pakistan presenting the themes, issues and conflicts of the then conditions but covertly it deals with many major and minor political and social issues. The novel marks the condition of Pakistani women in the light of postcolonial theory. The condition of diasporic women is worse; they are doubly marginalized, and are the victims of patriarchal dominance.

In the aforesaid novels, Rushdie's representation of textualized history displays his multiple aspects that replace the uni-linear version of authorized/recorded history. Rushdie's history is the version of his memory rather than the officially written one. He never describes the past but remakes the past to suit his present purpose using memory as his tool. *Midnight's Children* and *Shame* are to some extent, the history of India and Pakistan respectively. But his novels move beyond the bounds of history for the purpose of finding universal significance of historical forces that are operating at a particular phase of time. He manipulates the truth to fictionalize it and thus, makes the real unreal and vice-versa.

The publication of *The Satanic Verses* (1988), in which Rushdie treats Quran as a literary text, open for individual perceptions dared to attempt higher criticism but its aftermath created turmoil in his mind. This is the fourth novel of Rushdie, which is influenced partly by the life of Prophet Mohammed. The book uses the technique of magical realism, with a series of sub-plots that are narrated as dream visions felt by the main character. The two protagonists, Gibreel Farishta and Saladin Chamcha, are the actors of Indian Muslim background. Farishta is a Bollywood super-star who is popular for playing Hindu deities in films, whereas Chamcha is an emigrant who has given-up his Indian identity and works as a voiceover artist in England. With the publication of the novel, Rushdie espoused worldwide controversies, which flourished in the regime of Thatcher in Britain (Teverson 145). It is the stronger socio-political satire than Rushdie's previous novels.

The fifth novel of Rushdie, *The Moor's Last Sigh* (1995) is more a postmodern than a postcolonial one. The protagonist and narrator Moor inherits the blend of races and creeds of India. His mother Aurora has the blood of Portuguese invaders as well as Catholicism in her veins whereas his father is one of the last Jews of Cochin and a descendant of Boabdil, the last Moorish ruler of Spain. The entire family mimics the chaotic diversity of South India. Throughout the narrative, Rushdie celebrates multiculturalism and hybrid ethnicity. This novel presents a family that splits on the views of nationalism and anti-nationalism and the division of the family symbolizes the divisions in the country in the name of pro-Empire and freedom loving people. *The Moor's Last Sigh* is also an attack on the parochial Hinduism led by Shiv Sena in Maharashtra who banned the novel due to its attack on Shiv Sena's supremo, Late Bal Thackeray. The people of Shiv Sena have led India towards its unwanted destination, towards a religious country instead of a secularist one. India is known for its unity in diversity—its multi-ethnicity, its multi-religions and its multi-culturalism. However, the novel delineates the postcolonial history of India, its metaphoric and linguistic divisions yet it attacks India for becoming a pseudo-secularist nation. But after his colonial and postcolonial narration, Rushdie moves towards global, pop and jazz music.

His next novel, *The Ground Beneath Her Feet* (1999), fictionalizes the fact of Ayatollah Khomeini decreed *Fatwa* on him. Rushdie begins the novel with the death of the female protagonist Vina Apsara on February 14, 1989, the very date of *Fatwa*. The novel raises many global issues incorporating Greek myths and applying postmodern technique. *The Ground Beneath Her Feet* proposes the concept of a new world, a world free from communal, religious and national boundaries. In the very text, all the aspects of Diasporas such as alienation, trauma and longing for homeland have faded out for representative migrants Ormus and Rai's love Teenage Vina Apsara, of this novel are valueless because music is beyond restraint.

With the advent of LPG (Liberalization, Privatization and Globalization), all the conflicts arising from border crossing have washed away. Hybridity and multiculturalism fused in the characters point out Rushdie's view towards a future in which the world, demolishing all boundaries, will be united to face any threat. However, Rushdie's personality differs from his theory. He himself is unable to step across the frontiers and it seems that he is still lingering within his parochial world from which he is destined not to come out.

The collision between the reactions of Islamic countries against him and his instinct for critiquing the religious fundamentalism produced a writhing fury within him. The novel *Fury* (2001) is a concrete and material form of his own abstract 'fury'. It is "his first 3-D, full volume American novel, finger snapping, wildly mind-blogging, often slyly funny, red-blooded and red toothed"[4] (*Miami Herald*). Malik Solanka, the hero of the novel, is a new version of Buddha who leaves his home for New York without informing anyone. Rushdie once again appears in the disguise of Solanka. Like his creator, Solanka also first of all flees from his academic life, then from his family and immersed into a world of miniatures. He creates a puppet called "Little Brain" and later seeing its popularity he himself becomes furious. The novel accurately deals with the darkest side of human nature.

The novel *Shalimar the Clown* (2005) is Rushdie's return to the Indian subcontinent that he had left in *The Ground Beneath Her Feet* and *Fury*. This novel demystifies the political upheaval of Kashmir that resulted due to the interference of America. The novelist delineates the story of postcolonial Kashmir and explains the reasons why the paradise became hell, how the Hindu-Muslim unity came under suspicion, why and how the citizens of paradise started becoming terrorists and what role India and Pakistan played in creating the chaos and commotion. Through the story of Shalimar and Boonyi, Rushdie displays the Hindu-Muslim harmony that existed before independence. The central theme of the novel is the making of a terrorist, as terrorism becomes a global phenomenon and a cause of concern worldwide. The effort to look into the mind and get under the skin of a terrorist becomes an artistic challenge that the novelist has dealt competently in *Shalimar the Clown*.

In fact, the novel narrates the story of postcolonial and post-independence Kashmir. Since Rushdie is a political novelist, *Shalimar the Clown* is an amalgamation of realism and magic realism. Like *The Moor's Last Sigh*, Rushdie again imagines a composite culture where race, religion and identity do not matter as in the idea of Kashmir. The novelist shows in how gradually the composite culture is destroyed by both military and militancy. Before 1947, there was no point of dispute between Hindu and Muslim. They used to celebrate each other's festivals. But the independence of India and Pakistan transformed this paradise into a battlefield where ignorant armies and citizens are being killed by their own citizens.

In his next venture, *The Enchantress of Florence* (2008), Rushdie presents adventures of colonizers. The novel is set in medieval India, at the time of the Mughal Emperor Akbar, the Great, at the time when colonizers began to arrive and establish their trade, which is customary with Salman Rushdie who never adheres to a single theme in his fictions. So is the case with *The Enchantress of Florence*. Rushdie makes the presence of the beaten past to create a better future. The novel is set in the sixteenth century India. It delineates the colonial situations and conditions in which Magor dell Amore is the representative of white colonialists, who lands on the shore of India and makes his way to Sikri to the court of Akbar and succeeds in befooling the wisest king. The female protagonist of the fiction Qara Koz seems to represent the counter discourse to the colonialism. The colonial enterprise was a product of western androcentric imperialist desire. Qara Koz, on the other hand is a woman of

Asian blood who manages to bring the whole of Florence, the epitome of western civilization of that period under her influence. She represents the subversion of the colonial enterprise. The novel has a helical structure and intertwines two stories going in diverse directions that present a beautiful picture of how Mogor comes to India and becomes closer to Emperor than his nine jewels. In the same way Qara Koz goes, from central Asia to Europe and becomes the heartthrob of Europeans. But in the end Mogor is exposed as liar and has to leave India. Mogor is a symbolic representation of the British colonizers and Koz is symbolic of Indian beauty and innocence.

Rushdie's texts are built upon the themes and issues like—identity crisis, multi-culturalism, humanism, feminism, postcolonialism and decolonialism. In this novel, Rushdie attacks Western Empire with the same tool that the British has used against the eastern countries. As a staunch de-colonialist, Rushdie takes each and every step for the "decolonization of the mind," what Ngugi demands, from psychological freedom along with the geographical and political freedom.

Joseph Anton: A Memoir (2012), the penultimate production, is an autobiography, written in third person narrative, of this "Britney Spears of literature," (13) says Meenakshi Bharat. Joseph Anton is the pseudonym adopted by Rushdie after the *Fatwa* was issued against him in 1989. Joseph is derived from Joseph Conrad and Anton from Anton Chekhov—the authors of Anglophone literature who have inspired Rushdie the most. The plight of Rushdie, post-Fatwa and his persistent attempt at making writing successful, has been excellently portrayed in this memoir.

Rushdie, of late, has released his novel, T*wo Years Eight Months and Twenty Eight Nights*, published in September 2015, which is a futuristic tale of good versus evil. Stimulated by the traditional "wonder tales" of the East, this novel is a *tour-de-force* about the age-old clashes that remain in today's world. The novel is sardonic and mordant, full of cunning and folly, conflicts and treacheries, kismet and karma, euphoria and redemption. The magic-realism has once again been employed by Rushdie, which indicates that he is a genuine literary progeny of Marquez and Llosa, the precursors and practitioners of the said term.

Mimicry of Language is one of the tools of decolonization. The West, through Macaulay's Minute, started teaching English to acculturate the Asian mind into British patterns while Rushdie and his generation started conditioning the same language to suit Asians and responded to the Empire. For this, he mixes the words of Hindi, Urdu and other regional languages in English and Anglicizes them without any reference or notes. He, in his first major novel *Midnight's Children*, exhibits the complexities and quandaries that the project of Indianising the resources of English language entails. In each of his novels, he coalesces words from several origins and tries to make them perfect. To quote Thiara: "Rushdie's novels...emphasize India's exuberant multiplicity and multi-vocality" (2009: 172). Thus, he becomes the leader of postcolonial authors who have taken the oath to "provincialize" English, and is determined to subvert the master's tool in order to make it their own.

Apart from fictionalizing the truth of India, Rushdie has a number of critical writings in the form of articles and papers and two critical treatises namely *Imaginary Homelands: Essays and Criticism 1981-1991* (1991) and *Step Across This Line: Collected Non-Fiction 1992-2002* (2002); two collections of story books *Harun and the Sea of Stories* (1990) and *Luka and the Fire of Life* (2010). Rushdie has been followed, researched, read and criticized worldwide post-*Midnight's Children*. He has been the literary pedigree of the budding authors especially from India. "He is very virtuoso and full of ideas", says Cyrus Mistry in Jaipur Literature Festival in 2014. Thus, a critical "virtuoso" is imperative in the new millennium!

Research Explorations in the Volume

Salman Rushdie, one of the pioneering voices of the "new Diaspora", progenitor of a series of controversies, what is called "Rushdie affair" in postmodern literary politics, has been superseding and has intrepid influence in literary sphere. He has written history in fiction and fiction in history by presenting the "national allegory" of the nation right from 1947 to till date. His literary journey—from *Grimus* (1975) to the latest, *Two Years Eight Months and Twenty Eight Nights* (2015)[5]—has been conspicuously rewarding via *Midnight's Children*. The present volume strives to find how Rushdie is germane in the twenty-first century politics of globalization, literary schema, and cosmopolitanism.

The book has been divided into four broad heads—the first section intrinsically deals with concurrent global issues like his Knighthood, his contentions on global affairs of literature, politics and society and worldwide controversies which he is champion of; while the second section, the lengthiest in the volume, contains exclusive essays on his most popular book till date, *Midnight's Children*. The third section, inherently grasps Rushdie's latter fictions, which have been researched and presented in the light of intertextuality, treatment of imagined temporalities, cosmopolitanism and narrative strategies, etc. The final section offers Rushdie's identity discourse, his contemplations on terrorist attacks in Kashmir and his journey towards 'new world'.

The younger and the unheard voices, budding scholars from India and abroad, candidly put forth their views in the present volume based on variegated themes explored through theoretical lenses as applied to the literary taxonomy of Rushdie. These sections have been given a suitable title followed by synopses of essays, which bring heterogeneity in the subject enunciated.

Section–A
Critiquing Rushdie's Knighthood, Authorship and Controversies: Contentions in the New Millennium

The twenty-first century is still taking shape, though we have perceived first fifteen years, so, it is difficult to pause with any conviction about its future course of development. One can only point out certain dominant trends and remain aware and attentive about how these trends change and develop. A universal aspect is challenging but several crises seem to be dogging English studies and multiple literary discourses. Postcolonial discourse was born in response to the imperial expansion of Western colonies during the nineteenth and twentieth century. Postcolonial writers such as Anand, Narayan, Rao, Achebe, Thiong'o, Lamming, Naipaul and Rushdie, therefore, arose from the experiences of colonization and their assertions were written in response to the authority exercised by the imperial powers and emphasize the differences from the budgets of the imperial centres. With the advent of such discourses on the fore, new genres of literature emerged i.e. fictional autobiography or autobiographical fiction. Rushdie, like V.S. Naipaul, has been contentious for uneulogizing remarks on contemporary socio-political, cultural and literary affairs for which he is "always controversial", writes Reder (vii) but unlike Naipaul, he has not yet bagged the most prestigious Nobel Prize, which he truly deserves for his literary contribution. However, he had again attracted the global media and academia when he was knighted in 2007 and continues to fetch controversies by his frank and forthright debates and dissidence. The papers in this section critically examine, Rushdie being Knighted; autobiographical elements in his fiction; *The Satanic Verses*, the most controversial till date and offer fresh outlooks on his self-proclaimed polemics, in the second decade of this millennium.

The first section is inaugurated with Ana Cristina Mendes's essay entitled 'Cultural Warfare Redux: Salman Rushdie's Knighthood' which is built on the premise that Rushdie's Knighthood might be addressed within the framework of a renewed nostalgia for an imagined British community, and hence construed as a symptom of postcolonial melancholia. The bestowment of this honour upon the writer, for his services to literature, to recognise his outstanding achievement in the field of literature incited, immediately, much outrage in countries with Muslim majority populations. The central aim of this essay is rather to examine the antagonism stirred up in the British press by Rushdie's honour, and to present an alternative approach to this polemic from the one outlined by commentators in the print media. The present reading is grounded on the assumption that postcolonial authors necessarily inhabit a provisional position, always prone to revision due to the dynamic interdependence between margins and centres.

Valiur Rahaman's well-researched paper 'Meta-auto-biographicity: Some Observations on Salman Rushdie's *Enchantress of Florence*' observes the hypothesis that everything—concerning with/referring to writer, reader, the presence of the writer, the absence of the author, and implicit, explicit images of author's intentions—is required at the time of reading a text. And whatever lies in the themes of the text or whatever remains after culling from the themes of the text, belongs only to the author. Rahaman holds his view that 'the text cannot exist without aspects of the author. The text without aspects of its author is a glitch.' He further expresses his view that the author lives in the realm of author's ideas through the dialogues of the characters, situations dwelt with characters, life worlds, etc.

Creating controversies is another definition of Rushdie's novels. Ramesh Tibile's paper 'Salman Rushdie: A Self-Proclaimed Controversialist' puts forth speckled rationale on Rushdie's controversy, which is his favourite legion. Tibile observes that 'the political significance of Rushdie's writing does not change from text to text not because his subject-matter changes but also because his political location changes.' He further illustrates that Rushdie proposes only one rather a tentative answer to the question of how a decentered being can work meaningfully, and that is by writing history of the particular country.

The next chapter in this segment is slightly different from the above-mentioned papers. Hetal M. Doshi in her essay entitled 'Theological Aspects and Diasporic Sensibilities in Rushdie's *The Satanic Verses:* An Analysis' offers Rushdie's attempt to fearlessly question some of the religious tenets which he finds devoid of logic. However, at the same time, Doshi also recognizes that the author has to be cautious in his presentation and execution, when his work deals with the religious sentiments of billions. Freedom of speech does not provide the license to be blasphemous. She brings the article to a close that 'the role of an art should be a reflection, not an action. It is the duty of an artist, more so of a writer to *renew* the perceptions about history, society and religion; not to *shatter* them.'

Rushdie has not only novelized his biography but also the nations he has lived in or the 'home' he envisions.

Section–B
Midnight's Children: Fictionalizing History, Nation and Narration

After the publication of Rushdie's *Midnight's Children* and its immense success, there is a general tendency among the Indian readers to see the narrative as a national allegory while the western readers mostly find it to be a fantastic *Bildungsroman* "to critique the idea of a unified personal and national narrative" (Anne Gala) with occasional peeping into the socio-political scenario of twentieth century India. Rushdie transcends the limited scope of narrating a nation from a strictly historical perspective and enchants his readers (mostly Asian) by a spell of his magic realist narration. The narrative covers a time-span of sixty years keeping the year 1947 at the centre and mostly relies on an individual's cultural memory than documented historical details. By nature, the treatment is more perspectival, and it is the basic reason behind the novel's popularity and its winning the Booker of Bookers prize. This section, the longest in the volume, deals with multitudinous aspects and approaches applied in Rushdie's trendsetter novel, *Midnight's Children*.

Suhaina Bi, in her paper, 'Presentation of a Wounded Civilization: A Cosmopolitan Perspective of *Midnight's Children*', critically analyses cosmopolitanism with that of diaspora and postcolonialism. She presents 'Cosmopolitanism as an ethos that is deduced from Enlightenment theories and values. It advocates a mode of humane thinking about the relationship between human beings without taking into consideration the geographical boundaries and a moral concern for different communities' and further holds the view that 'in his real life, Rushdie is struggling for his liberal ideals and freedom of expression and through his novels; he has raised his voice not only for a cosmopolitan but also for the whole humanity. Rushdie retells the tragedy of the minority, which usually occurs at the time of socio-political chaos in most of the nations.'

The next essay entitled 'The Dichotomous Nature of Decolonisation of India in Salman Rushdie's *Midnight's Children*' by Sutanuka Ghosh Roy aims at looking history in a new way. The need for fresh look at older historical form makes *Midnight's Children* a unique novel. Roy further explores 'how Rushdie discovers an alternative to the typical historical traditions of historical truth as merely recorded facts. He fuses memory and the process of recalling memories. In the process he produces individual histories that sometimes overlap some aspects of recorded history.' She concludes with an observation that 'his (Rushdie's) novels differ from the other Raj novels written by various authors, in so far as his vision of an Indian internationalism and multiculturalism embraces the politics of pluralism, whereas the Raj novels are more particular in the exploration of a British India'. Rushdie has shown us the dichotomous nature of India's decolonization, even in the use of language he has dislocated the English and let others into it.

Ram Bhawan Yadav's critique of *Midnight's Children* has been put in different way in his research paper 'Interfacing Myth vs. History: A Postcolonial Study of Salman Rushdie's *Midnight's Children*.' Yadav attempts to capture theoretical functioning of the myths in postcolonial English literature, in general, and Indian English novels, in particular, which play a vital role in the reformulation of natives' self and identity. In this context, his attempt is to read and examine Rushdie's said novel that blends myths with history by using postcolonial theoretical approaches. Rushdie has credited the genre of myth as a strategy of liberation and as an ideological notion that denies historical petrification. 'The way Rushdie treats the complex issues of identity and liberty makes him a central figure in Postcolonial Literature', Yadav postulates.

Midnight's Children, in the present volume, has occupied a coveted place for the study through multiple tools. But none other than T. Sasikanth Reddy's article entitled 'Salman Rushdie's *Midnight's Children:* A Kaleidoscopic View' surveys that Rushdie's novels are complex, multi-layered with episodic causality, bearing strong influence of post-modernist novels as well as principles of the Indian art forms. His exalted diction, elevated word usage and felicitous word phrases leave strong impinge on the readers. The paper ends with the conclusion that 'Rushdie presents history through the metaphor of chutnification, which gives way to his narrative. In other words, Saleem is actually preserving the facts of history as chutnification, a method of perpetuation of each of the thirty-one chapters in the novel, which stand for "a pickle jar".'

The section ends with Asis De's critique of the novel who in his paper entitled 'In Time of Narrating the Nation: Rushdie's Transcendence of National History in *Midnight's Children*.' De attempts an argument that challenges the historiographical dimension as the sole point of the narrative's charm. Alternatively, De endeavours to establish the point that a Nation could never be understood in full from any personal and perspectival version of historical reality. He clearly opines that 'a writer is usually affected by the historical milieu in which s/he lives' and the periods of an earlier time with which s/he associates his/her identity.

Section–C
Treatment of Imagined Temporalities, Cosmopolitanism and Narrative Strategies: Recent Perspectives

Salman Rushdie's novels document intertexuality, treatment of history wherein his narrative subterfuges cannot be eschewed. *The Moor's Last Sigh* focuses on the themes of Indian history and the search for identity. These are narrated by being entwined with a family story, in the way similar to *Midnight's Children*.

National history, like family story, is passed on from generation to generation. It is told from subjective point of view, and thus is subject to alteration. This section primarily deals with the major novels of Rushdie—*The Moor's Last Sigh*, *The Satanic Verses*, *Shame*, *The Ground Beneath Her Feet*, and others. Temporality and history in the works of Salman Rushdie are unfinalizable and plural. Rushdie's vindication of the 'imaginative variety of truth' and allegoric representations of nations, events and people challenge the established notions about writing history into fiction. In his novels, borderlines between the public and private spheres of experience; memory and imagination; and reality and fantasy are deliberately blurred.

In her critical essay entitled 'Chutneys, Pickles, Palimpsests and Collages: Lived and Imagined Temporalities in the Works of Salman Rushdie,' Bini B.S. explores Rushdie's multiple fiction in the light of Foucault's criticism of the conventional historiography. She further holds the view that '[H]istory in Rushdie's works takes the form of a polyphonic voice which is dappled with hues of hilarity, violence, shame, pain and caustic satire.' She concludes her paper with a notion that '[I]t is not necessary to tell apart the lived experiences and a life lived in imagination' and further 'posits that history, thus, blurs into a realm of ambivalence, indeterminacy and inconclusiveness.'

The next paper is complementary to the above-mentioned essay. The objective of this paper entitled 'Nation and Non-narration: Multiplicity, Hybridity and Heterogeneity in Salman Rushdie's *The Moor's Last Sigh*' by Manjeet Kumar Kashyap is to understand the fiction of Salman Rushdie. In Kashyap's view, the fiction of Rushdie is marked by modern historiography of India. Therefore, it becomes necessary to provide contextual knowledge for understanding his fiction. Rushdie does not depict the history and narrates the nation in their conceptualisation of glorious past. Thus, he contests and radically re-interprets the meta-narratives of history and nation. The ideas of nation and narration in his fiction are created through blend of ethnic essence and speculative narration technique. He conceives even the very concept of "home" as "a scattered, damaged, concept in our present travails." Kashyap refers to a shift from homogeneous nation-states based on the ideology of assimilation to a much more fluid and contradictory definition of nations as a multiplicity of diasporic identities.

Hetal K. Kachhia in her article 'Globalization and Cosmopolitanism: Major Themes in the Works of Salman Rushdie' studies the major novels of Rushdie. She beautifully relocates the 'globalization' and 'cosmopolitanism' in the novels of Rushdie. She writes that '(I)f we look at the terms 'globalization' and 'cosmopolitanism' as the intermingling of different cultures and its different aspects and phenomena into one another, we can say that the works of Salman Rushdie compose a global and intermingled fictional world by including the element of 'intertextuality', from his own works to the different allusions from others' works,' which makes the recurrence of characters and places possible from one text to another.

Nesha Sabar and Pramod Kumar Das also refurbish their essay with evaluation of Rushdie's narrative technique. But they chose a different novel, *Shame*, to deal with. In the paper entitled 'Salman Rushdie's *Shame*: A Study of Narrative Strategies', they focus on the various narrative strategies used in the text. In doing so, they zero in on a range of strategies such as mimicry, history, fairy-tale, magic-realism, metafiction and intertextuality employed by Rushdie to knit the narrative and these devices, in turn, help us to understand the text in better and improved way. They conclude their observation that 'Rushdie's narrative style can be viewed as a tongue-in-cheek use and 'abuse' of numerous literary narrative conventions and theoretical perspectives that include exaggerated reflections of colonial mimicry, unreliable narrator's fairytale motifs and intertextuality.'

Rushdie himself has flabbergasted his readers by collapsing the 'East-West devise' by enlivening his "imaginary homelands" and has, thus, created a new world. His diasporic itinerary has always routed through his roots, which can be divulged by his literary overtures.

Section–D
Rushdie's Diasporic Passage to the New World: Some Observations

The present segment astutely deals with Rushdie's treatment of heterogeneous themes and issues that cover a wide gamut of his intellect and ingenuity. This unit unfolds critical study on Rushdie's major novels, which have been critiqued through the rubrics of diaspora criticism, identity discourse, treatment of satire and history as well as his Indianness, which is palpable in his textual orientations.

In the very first essay, 'Journey Towards the New World in the Selected Novels of Salman Rushdie,' Ajit Kumar presents the galaxy of diasporic authors and compares with the theme, technique, matter and manner with that of Rushdie's novels and also the content and context of the postcolonial world that is adroitly presented by the author. Kumar concludes that 'in the history of Indian Literature of English, Salman Rushdie's efforts are well visible to the readers. Right from his first novel *Grimus* to *Midnight's Children*, *Shame* and *The Enchantress of Florence*, he seems to be an explorer of the human psychology being in the modern world where people long for identity and peace but they all seem wandering for it.' Kumar also opines that the effect of Diaspora is seen not only in the life of individuals but also in communities.

Vikrant Sehgal's essay 'Diasporic Identity in Salman Rushdie's *Shalimar the Clown*' underlines some of the main theories behind the postcolonial discourse, and he argues, from diasporic perspective specifically the thematic elements in Rushdie's *Shalimar the Clown*. It is his attempt, to undermine how Rushdie constructs diasporic identity and culture by specific postcolonial literary techniques such as fragmentation, plurality and language despite the influence of his emigration to England.

Indah Lestari's paper entitled 'Indianness and Satire of History in Salman Rushdie's *The Moor's Last Sigh*' observes that Rushdie's novel focuses on the themes of Indian history and the search for identity. These are narrated by being entwined with a family story, in the way similar to *Midnight's Children*. National history, like family history, is passed on from one generation to the next one. It is told from subjective point of view, and thus is subject to alteration. Through her palimpsest painting, Aurora suggests this alteration. National history is also built by foreign interference. Therefore, Indian identity is complex in racial aspect. Moreover, India is also plural in terms of language, religion, and political orientation. The paper further aims to analyze the complexity of India as a nation-state from the aspect of its history as depicted in the novel and further it enquires how Rushdie satirizes Indian history entwining the protagonist's personal life and historical events.

The next chapter titled '(W)hole in the Transition: The Problematique of Terrorism in *Shalimar the Clown*' by Javaid Iqbal Bhat in the section is about the notion of "terrorism" in the novel *Shalimar the Clown*. The paper is an attempt at looking Rushdie's literary connection with Kashmir that traces the marks of ahistoricisation and de-politicization of "terrorists" and "terrorism". It shows that the major "terrorists" are more or less lifted from context and history. The paper also looks at the motivation, if any, of the "terrorists" and the points of transition when an apparently normal individual decides to go against the authority, running away from the regular pattern of life, deciding to fight for a "cause."

Thus, the *omnibus* offers myriad minds on Rushdie's writings. The above-mentioned critical essays will certainly be proven promising contribution to the already existing vast corpus of Rushdie criticism as his works are "concerned with many connections, disruptions, and migrations between Eastern and Western civilizations".[6] The volume includes the researchers not only from India but also from abroad who are not well-known critics but have more potential for becoming duteous researchers. They have fervently participated in this book to make it worth reading for upcoming and existing scholars of the field. Since no academic work is perfect, hence, an epistemological fecundity in the very realm is always vouched for.

Ajay K. Chaubey,
Janmejay K. Tiwari,
Bishun Kumar

Notes

1. Radio show *Medierna* broadcast on Sveriges Radio P1 on 31 January 2009. http://en.wikipedia.org/wiki/Salman_Rushdie. Accessed on December 13, 2014.
2. http://www.washingtonpost.com/wp-dyn/content/article/2005/08/05/AR2005080501483.html (Para 5). Accessed on December 14, 2014.
3. http://en.wikipedia.org/wiki/Knighthood_of_Salman_Rushdie. Accessed on December 15, 2014.
4. http://www.salman-rushdie.com/blog/fury/. Accessed on December 15, 2014.
5. http://timesofindia.indiatimes.com/world/uk/Salman-Rushdie-to-publish-first-new-novel-in-7-years/articleshow/46063485.cms. Accessed on May 29, 2015.
6. https://en.wikipedia.org/wiki/Salman_Rushdie. (Para 1) Accessed on October 18, 2015.

Works Cited

Bharat, Meenakshi. "First Words." *Rushdie the Novelist: From Grimus to The Enchantress of Florence*. Ed. Meenakshi Bharat. New Delhi: Pencraft International, 2009. 11-17.

Boerner, Klaus. "The Reception of *Midnight's Children* in West Germany." *The Novels of Salman Rushdie*. Eds. G.R. Taneja, R.K. Dhawan. New Delhi: Prestige, 1992. 23-32.

Frank, Soren. *Migration and Literature*. New York: Palgrave Macmillan, 2008.

Gala, Anne. ""Specks of Voiceless Dust": *Midnight's Children* and the Impact of the Bildungsroman on the National Narrative of Postmodern India." Web. 17 Oct. 2015.

<http://www.ncurproceedings.org/ojs/index.php/NCUR2015/article/download/1346/752>

Mistry, Cyrus. "I Don't Aspire to Rushdie Writing." *Times of India*. January 22, 2014.

Mittapalli, Rajeshwar, Pier Paolo Piciucco, eds. Preface. *Studies in Indian Writing in English*. Vol. 2. New Delhi: Atlantic Publishers, 2001. 1-10.

Reder, Michael. *Conversations with Salman Rushdie*. Mississippi: University of Mississippi Press, 2000.

Rushdie, Salman. *Imaginary Homelands: Essays and Criticism 1981-1991* (1991). London: Vintage, 2010.

———. *Luka and the Fire of Life*. London: Jonathan Kape, 2010.

———. "The Right Time for an Islamic Reformation." Web. 15 Dec. 2014.

Teverson, Andrew. *Salman Rushdie*. 2007. New Delhi: Viva Books, 2010.

Thiara, Nicole Weickgenannt. *Salman Rushdie and Indian Historiography*. New York: Palgrave Macmillan, 2009.

Trousdale, Rachel. *Nabokov, Rushdie, and the Transnational Imagination*. New York: Palgrave Macmillan, 2010.

List of Contributors

Ajay K. Chaubey (PhD) teaches at the Department of Sciences and Humanities, National Institute of Technology, Uttarakhand. His key publications, *V.S. Naipaul: An Anthology of 21st Century Criticism* (Atlantic, 2015); *Transnational Passages: An Anthology of Diaspora Criticism* Vol. I and *Discursive Passages: An Anthology of Diaspora Criticism* Vol. II (Yking Books, 2015), have recently been released. Additionally, his forthcoming volume *Mapping South Asian Diaspora*: *An Anthology of 21st Century Criticism* is likely to be published by the Rawat Publications, Jaipur in 2016. He is a Life member of the research organizations viz. Indian Association for Commonwealth Literature and Language Studies (IACLALS), Association for English Studies in India (AESI) and Sahitya Academy, New Delhi. Dr. Chaubey has visited and contributed to seminars, conferences and symposia at the global forums held at Nottingham Trent University, University of Leicester and York St. John University (United Kingdom) in the previous year. He has enthusiastically imparted Anglophone literature and linguistic rules during his formative phases at Pratapgarh, Allahabad, and Jaunpur and has taught communication studies during his pre and post-doctoral research at Delhi, Lucknow and Rajasthan at the top-notch Institutions and Varsities.

Ajit Kumar has completed his PhD on Doris Lessing's selected novels from Department of English, Kurukshetra University, Kurukshetra. He has got his many research papers published in National and International Journals of English Studies. He has presented good number of research papers in National and International Conferences and Seminars. He has also been honoured with Best Research Paper Award in World Conference AIAER-2010.

Ana Cristina Mendes has been a researcher at the University of Lisbon Centre for English Studies (CEAUL/ULICES) since 2005. Her areas of specialization are postcolonial and migration studies, with an emphasis on the cultural industries and exchanges in the global cultural marketplace. She has recently been pursuing research in the subfields of poverty studies (slumming), visual arts, cinemas and literatures of the Asian emerging economies. Her publications include the co-edited book *Re-Orientalism and South Asian Identity Politics* (2011), the edited collection *Salman Rushdie and Visual Culture* (2012), and the monograph *Salman Rushdie in the Cultural Marketplace* (2013).

Asis De is Assistant Professor of English and Head of the Department of English Language and Literature (UG and PG), Mahishadal Raj College (Govt. Sponsored), Mahishadal, West Bengal, India. His research interests include the study of Identity negotiation in newer/ diasporic cultural spaces with particular reference to postcolonial Anglophone fiction (South-Asian, African and Caribbean). He has completed both his M.Phil and PhD from Jadavpur University, Kolkata. In a number of publications and conference presentations in India and in Europe (Belgium, Germany and England), he has worked on the issues of cultural identity and transnationalism in South-Asian, Caribbean and African fictional narratives. He also teaches Anglophone Postcolonial Literatures, Dalit and Tribal Literatures, Cultural Studies and Diasporic Literatures in Post Graduate level since 2010. He is a Life Member of Indian Association for Commonwealth Literature and Language Studies (IACLALS) and regular member of Postcolonial Studies Association (UK), GAPS (Germany) and European Association for Commonwealth Literature and Language Studies (EACLALS).

Bini B.S. is currently an Academic Fellow at Balvant Parekh Centre for General Semantics and Other Human Sciences, Baroda. Her PhD was an analysis of the idea of alternative history and historicity of fictional narratives with special reference to the theories of Michel Foucault. She was part of an OUP Translation Project, *An Anthology of Malayalam Literature,* which will be published this year. Her research articles, poems and translations have appeared in national and international Journals and anthologies including *Poetry Chain*, *Kritya, Samyukta*, *Dialogue, ETC: A Review of General Semantics*, *JWS: A Journal of Women's Studies*, *DUJES*, *Writing Today, South Asian Ensemble*, *Kavyabharati* and *The Virtual Transformation of the Public Sphere* (published by Routledge).

Bishun Kumar is an Assistant Professor of English in School of Humanities and Social Sciences, Babu Banarasi Das University, Lucknow. He has obtained PhD degree from University of Lucknow, Lucknow and has qualified U-SET and UGC-NET. His Area of specialization is New Humanities, Cultural Studies, Theatre Studies, Postcolonialism, Indian English Novel and Feminism. He has co-edited two books titled *Major Voices in New Literatures in English* and *Mahesh Dattani: Themes, Techniques and Issues* (both from Atlantic in 2015).

Hetal M. Doshi is an Assistant Professor of English at New L.J. Commerce College in Ahmedabad, Gujarat and has published research articles on varied subjects like poetry, translation, comparative studies and Diaspora literature. She writes both in Gujarati and English. She is pursuing her Doctorate on Indo-Canadian Diaspora Women Writers from Bhavnagar University.

Hetal K. Kachhia has been working as an Assistant Professor of English at Gandhinagar Institute of Technology, Gandhinagar (Gujarat). She has completed her M.A. and M.Phil in English Literature from Sardar Patel University, Gujarat. Her areas of interest include Indian English Literature, British Literature, and Literary Theory.

Indah Lestari was born in Singapore and lives in Jakarta, Indonesia. She completed her B.A. in English Literature from Padjadjaran University, Indonesia and M.A. in English Studies from Jawaharlal Nehru University, India. She translated J.M. Coetzee's *Disgrace* into Indonesian. She is juggling teaching with translating as well as writing travelogues, reviews of books, arts, movies, cultural performances, etc. She also writes poems, of which some have been published in *Bacopa*, *Revival* and *The White Elephant*.

Janmejay K. Tiwari holds PhD degree on Salman Rushdie from the University of Allahabad, Allahabad, UP. Currently, he is working as a freelance author and teacher based in New Delhi. Dr. Tiwari has authored several critical papers on Salman Rushdie and has interviewed Lakshmi Raj Sharma author of his debut novel, *The Tailor's Needle* (Penguin India, 2012).

Javaid Iqbal Bhat is working as Assistant Professor in the Department of English, University of Kashmir. He has completed his MA and M.Phil from the Center for English Studies, Jawaharlal Nehru University, Delhi. He has submitted his PhD thesis at the Department of English, Ohio University, USA in 2015. He specializes in Literary Theory and Criticism, British Fiction, South Asian Fiction and Romanticism.

Manjeet Kumar Kashyap is currently pursuing his PhD on "Globalization, Ethnicity and Identity in the later Fiction of Salman Rushdie" from the Department of English, Banaras Hindu University, Varanasi. He has presented research papers in several national and international seminars. He has participated in two different workshops on Research Methodology and Women Orientation Programme.

Nesha Sabar is a PhD scholar in English Literature at the University of Hyderabad. He has completed his M.Phil degree in English Literature from the English and Foreign Languages University, Hyderabad, India.

Pramod Kumar Das is Assistant Professor at the Department of English, Christ University, Bengaluru, India. He has obtained his PhD degree in English Literature from the English and Foreign Languages University (formerly CIEFL), Hyderabad. He has published research articles in various national and international journals. His translation of Oriya literary pieces into English have been published in different books. His areas of interest include Green Studies, Indian Writing in English and English Language Teaching.

Ram Bhawan Yadav is doctorate in English from Banaras Hindu University, Varanasi, UP. His areas of interests include Postcolonial Literature, Commonwealth Literature, Indian English Literature, Cultural Studies and Post Modern Literary Discourses. Currently, he is Assistant Professor in the Department of English and Modern Languages, Central University of Sikkim.

Ramesh Tibile is presently working as Associate Professor at Dr. Ghali College, Gadinglaj. His area of specializations is linguistics, Indian Literature and British Literature. He is also a recognized guide for M.Phil and PhD of Shivaji University, Kolhapur. There are three research scholars working for PhD Degree under his guidance. He has published about 25 research articles in various journals. He has completed four Minor research Projects under Distance Mode of Shivaji University, Kolhapur and one Minor Research Project of UGC. He has been invited as resource person in academic workshops, seminars etc. He is interested in creative writing in Marathi as well as English. He has visited Cape Town, South Africa for presenting a paper in an International Conference in Sep. 2011 and also chaired a session in the same.

Suhaina Bi, a doctoral candidate, is writing her thesis on the literary works of Kamala Markandaya from the Department of English, Aligarh Muslim University, Aligarh. Her area of interest is Indian Writing in English, Cultural Studies, Postcolonial literature and Feminist Theory. She has attended and presented papers in various national and international seminars. She has also participated in some of the workshops conducted by the UGC.

Sutanuka Ghosh Roy is an Assistant Professor in Tarakeswar Degree College under the University of Burdwan, West Bengal, India. She did her doctoral dissertation on Eighteenth Century British Women Poets. She is currently engaged in active research and her areas of interest include Eighteenth Century British literature, Indian English literature, Canadian Studies, Australian Literature etc. She has presented papers at National and International Seminars. She is a regular contributor of research articles and papers to national and international journals of repute.

T. Sasikanth Reddy is an Associate Professor in S.C.N.R. Govt. Degree College, Proddatur, Y.S.R. district. He completed PhD PGCTE, PGDTE from EFLU, Hyderabad. He published a book titled *Fry's Religious Plays—A Study* and published twenty-five articles in National journals, five papers in International journals, and thirty articles in books. He has six years of teaching and research experience.

Valiur Rahaman, an Assistant Professor in the Department of English, Central University of Rajasthan, Bandasindari, Rajasthan, has specialization in Literary Theory & Criticism. His published books are based on continental philosophers and contemporary literary theorists. His works include *Poetic Wollstonecraft: A Study in Aesthetics* (2009), *Liminality, Mimicry, Hybridity and Ambivalent in Literary Speculations of Homi K. Bhabha* (2010), *Interpretations: Essays in Literary Theory* (2011), *About Elaine Showalter's Theory of Gynocriticism* (2011), and *Salman Rushdie's "Joseph Anton": Words of Wounded* (2013). His forthcoming works are *The Four Great Traditions: Indian Novelists after 2005* (in press) and *Dequalification: Seven Indian Muslim Woman Writers* (in press). He is also an executive editor of international journal, *Avant Garde Responses: An Interdisciplinary Journal of Humanities & Social Sciences.*

Vikrant Sehgal is working in India as an Assistant Professor and his work in literary criticism and theory has focused on issues that are shaped by his bi-cultural background and his commitment to a vision of culture. His areas of interest include transcultural theory (between postcolonialism and globalism), the politics of disciplinary histories, cultural comparison, postcolonial neo-formalism, Indian Writing in English, Asian Studies, turn-of-the-century English literature, Anglophone and especially Francophone, Caribbean literature and theory, modern reconfigurations of antiquity, Homer. He has published seven books. His current project addresses the formation of alternative modernities in the broken link between modernism and colonialism. He is also the editor-in-chief of three international journals and member of editorial board in a number of journals.

Section–A

Critiquing Rushdie's Knighthood, Authorship and Controversies: Contentions in the New Millennium

1

Cultural Warfare Redux: Salman Rushdie's Knighthood

Ana Cristina Mendes

On June 16th 2007, on the occasion of Queen Elizabeth II 80th birthday honours, it was announced that Salman Rushdie was to be conferred a Knight Bachelor by the reigning monarch for his services to literature. The bestowment of this honour upon the writer to recognise his outstanding achievement in the field of literature incited, without delay, much outrage in countries with Muslim majority populations. The Knighthood provoked nearly as much outrage as the Rushdie affair part I of nearly two decades before, when the Iranian religious leader Ayatollah Khomeini issued a *fatwa*, or death warrant, against the writer for supposedly blaspheming Islam in his novel. In the eyes of irate Islamists, Britain's decision to honour the so-called "blaspheming apostate" was hence understood as a jingoistic ploy, coldly calculated to incite antagonism in the Muslim world. This essay is built on the premise that Rushdie's Knighthood might be addressed within the framework of a renewed nostalgia for an imagined British community, and hence construed as a symptom of postcolonial melancholia.

> I'm certainly going to somewhat find myself resisting the idea of being called a representative British figure. I think I'm flattered, but (...) I think there are certain British figures who would contest quite seriously the idea that I represented anything British.[1] (Salman Rushdie)

This rank is part of the British honours system, observable in a twice-yearly ritual and awarded for public service. Public outcry swiftly ensued in Iran and Pakistan, with hostile demonstrations and effigies of the author being burnt on the streets, while government officials accused Britain of an insult to Islam and requested an apology from the recently-elected cabinet of Prime Minister Gordon Brown. In the row over the honour—or Rushdie affair part II, as it was labelled in the print media, Pakistan's hard-line religious affairs minister went as far as to suggest that the Knighthood was justification enough for suicide attacks.[2] In the meantime, Britain's first Muslim peer, Lord Nazir Ahmed, in statements to the French newspaper *Le Figaro*, drew a comparison between Rushdie's Knighthood and the hypothetical granting of a formal commendation by the Afghan or Saudi governments to the 9/11 suicide hijackers.[3] One might speculate that such resentment provided the inspiration behind an art installation exhibited in September 2008 at the Imam Khomeini grand mosque in Tehran as part of the International Koran exhibition. Hinting at Rushdie's perceived Americanisation and endorsement of the "war on terror" in the aftermath of the 9/11 attacks, a fake coffin bearing a US flag was on display, featuring skulls instead of the customary stars, as well as an Israeli flag accompanied by images of the writer, one where he is behind bars and fittingly dressed in an American flag, and the other where he is seen holding a copy of his novel, *The Satanic Verses*, published in 1989.

On June 19th, 2007, only three days after the news of the honour was released, Mohammad Reza Bahonar, first deputy speaker of Iran's Parliament, declared:

> Salman Rushdie has turned into a hated corpse which cannot be resurrected by any action. The action by the British queen in knighting Salman Rushdie, the apostate, is an unwise one. The British monarch lives under this illusion that Britain is still a 19th century superpower and that bestowing titles is something still deemed important.[4]

At this point, a question arises regarding the cultural meanings attached to a reward structure that is conditioned by its institutional dynamics and, most importantly, by its imperial past. Currently seen by many as a quaint remnant of a defunct era in the context of a post-imperial society, the honours system has been at the centre of a contentious debate over the urgency of its reformation or even complete eradication. Bahonar's inflammatory statement discloses one of the issues this essay focuses on—if only incidentally—, namely, the function and significance of the British honours system today. Indeed, based on its colonial connotations, this system has been included in a broader set of demands for radical reform going on in Britain. The purpose of this essay is not to delve into the furore in the Islamic world over the awarding of an Order of the British Empire (OBE) to Rushdie, nor to address its impact in global politics; in other words, it does not intend to deal with the worldwide political and religious storm brought about by the Knighthood. The central aim of this essay is rather to examine the antagonism stirred up in the British press by Rushdie's honour, and to present an alternative approach to this polemic from the one outlined by commentators in the print media. The present reading is grounded on the assumption that postcolonial authors necessarily inhabit a provisional position, always prone to revision due to the dynamic interdependence between margins and centres. Following this reasoning, Rushdie's own standing in the field of postcolonial cultural production cannot be adequately charted on an exhausted two-dimensional map which relies on centre/periphery and left-wing/right-wing dichotomies. Beyond a consideration of how *The Satanic Verses* controversy was reignited by the awarding of the Knighthood, this essay addresses the potential of the Rushdie affair part II for questioning such binary oppositions.

Paul Gilroy contends that, at the turn of the millennium, British attitudes to racial issues are constrained by the ambivalence of a "postcolonial melancholia", that is, by a "cultural disorientation that accompanies the collapse of imperial certainties into postcolonial nihilism".[5] Not unrelatedly, in a 1982 essay Rushdie bluntly remarks that four centuries of loot and plunder, of assuming superiority to "the Fuzzy-Wuzzies and the wogs", must of necessity leave its imprint on British society.[6] He quotes E.P. Thompson's depiction of Britain as the last remaining colony of the British Empire[7] to sustain the argument that Britain is in the early 1980s a "new colony" with Asian and black immigrants as colonial subjects, and the British police force as colonising army.[8] "This is how", Rushdie contends, "the new Empire was imported".[9] While the Indian-born writer sees the popular appeal of "television series, films, plays and books all filled with nostalgia for the Great Pink Age"[10] as incontrovertible evidence of a nostalgic longing for a "new Empire", Gilroy detects in the early 2000s an analogous postcolonial melancholia, which manifests itself in an incapability or unwillingness to accept the demise of the British Empire. As Gilroy notes:

> The consolidation of postcolonial melancholia suggests an even more disturbing possibility, namely that many people in Britain have actually come to need "race" and perhaps to welcome its certainties as one sure way to keep their bearings in a world they experience as increasingly confusing. (…) The loss of empire—and the additional loss of certainty about the limits of national and racial identity that result from it—have begun, ironically, to sustain people, providing them with both pleasure and distraction.[11]

This essay is built on the premise that Rushdie's Knighthood might be addressed within the framework of a renewed nostalgia for an imagined British community, and hence construed as a symptom of postcolonial melancholia. Bearing in mind Bahonar's statements, one of the after-effects of what Gilroy identifies as postcolonial melancholia might well be the "illusion that Britain is still a 19th century superpower and that bestowing titles is something still deemed important". This leads us to different, yet related, reactions to Rushdie's Knighthood, coming mostly from left-wing intellectuals in Britain, centred on these thorny questions: Why would a postcolonial author, committed to undermining imperial hegemonies, accept an OBE? How could he be, in his own words, "thrilled and humbled to receive this great honour", and "very grateful that [his] work has been recognised in this way"?[12] Does this excitement and appreciation betray the writer's conversion to establishment values? Why would a self-styled leftist be so willing to accept an honour that annihilates his "leftist credentials"? This essay poses a few interrogations of its own: After all, what compels critics to constantly account for Rushdie's political views (misinterpreting, most of the times, its marked complexities)? How could his acceptance of the OBE, apparently in keeping with the status quo, be explained? Has indeed Rushdie shifted from a position of autonomy to one of subordination towards the British establishment, or is this act in any way subversive?

For some detractors of Rushdie's Knighthood, the authoritative precedent of the refusal of an OBE by the Indian author Rabindranath Tagore stands as a reminder that the bestowment (and repudiation) of a British Knighthood is not exempted from political implications. Writing in Bengali during the period of the British Raj, Tagore was awarded the Nobel Prize in Literature in 1913 and was knighted in 1915 by King George V but, following the Jallianwala Bagh massacre four years later, he renounced the honour in protest against colonial repression in India. In a letter published in the reputed English-language Indian newspaper *The Statesman*, addressed to the then Viceroy, Lord Chelmsford, and dated June 3rd, 1919, Tagore asks to be "relieve[d]" of the title and explains his reasons at length:

> The enormity of the measures taken by the Government in the Punjab for quelling some local disturbances has, with a rude shock, revealed to our minds the helplessness of our position as British subjects in India. (...) The time has come when badges of honour make our shame glaring in the incongruous context of humiliation, and I for my part, wish to stand, shorn, of all special distinctions, by the side of those of my countrymen who, for their so called insignificance, are liable to suffer degradation not fit for human beings.[13]

Besides the authoritative example of Tagore, a more recent high-profile case of a prospective recipient the Order of the British Empire who publicly turned it down concerns Benjamin Zephaniah, the African Caribbean British activist and poet. Similarly to the example set by the Indian writer, who returned the Knighthood through an open letter published in the Indian press, Zephaniah made public his reasons for refusing to accept from Queen Elizabeth the honour in a polemical article—with the suggestive title "Me? I Thought, OBE Me? Up Yours, I Thought"—published in *The Guardian* in November 2003. The Rastafarian poet justifies his attitude, describing the OBE as a legacy of the inhumanity of colonialism:

> Me? I thought, OBE me? Up yours, I thought. I get angry when I hear that word "empire"; it reminds me of slavery, it reminds of thousands of years of brutality, it reminds me of how my foremothers were raped and my forefathers brutalised. (...) Benjamin Zephaniah OBE—no way Mr Blair, no way Mrs Queen. I am profoundly anti-empire.[14]

The declared intention behind declining the award is to protest against the institution of monarchy "that still refuses to apologise for sanctioning slavery". Furthermore, the poet's attack is also directed at British Government policies, including the pro-US stand on the war in Iraq, and in particular at the then Prime Minister Tony Blair who he deems accountable for "pour[ing] the working-class dream of a fair, compassionate, caring society down the dirty drain of empire". Zephaniah jokes that "Whoever is behind this offer can never have read any of [his] work", or his name would not have been submitted to the Queen for approval. He even suggests that, instead of the Knighthood, he be given "some of those great African works of art that were taken in the name of the empire and let [him] return them to their rightful place".

More than two years previous to his rejection of being made a Knight, Zephaniah readily repudiated being given such an honour. In the aptly-entitled poem "Bought and Sold", formerly published in his poetry collection *Too Black, Too Strong* (2001) and reprinted in his article published in *The Guardian*, he denounces black writers who compromise their work by accepting "smart big awards and prize money", and who consent to being decorated at Buckingham Palace:

> It's not censors or dictators that are cutting up our art.
> The lure of meeting royalty
> And touching high society
> Is damping creativity and eating at our heart. (...)
> The empire strikes back and waves
> Tamed warriors bow on parades
> When they have done what they've been told
> They get their OBEs.

Refusing to join what he dubs "the oppressors' club", the poet chastises fellow writers who, in his perspective, have sold out their artistic integrity by accepting such accolades. Zephaniah regards the bestowment of honours upon black artists as part and parcel of Blair's "cool Britannia project" that "gives OBEs to cool rock stars, successful businesswomen and blacks who would be militant in order to give the impression that it is inclusive". He does not mince words in condemning what he perceives as the selling out by black artists:

> I think OBEs compromise writers and poets, and laureates suddenly go soft (...). There are many black writers who love OBEs, it makes them feel like they have made it. When it suits them, they embrace the struggle against the ruling class and the oppression they visit upon us, but then they join the oppressors' club. They are so easily seduced into the great house of Babylon known as the palace (...).
>
> I have even heard black writers who have collected OBEs saying that it is "symbolic of how far we have come". Oh yes, I say, we've struggled so hard just to get a minute with the Queen and we are so very grateful– not.

Besides the ambivalence of the OBE itself, the perception that postcolonial artists might at times be co-opted by the establishment is a persistent anxiety. Zephaniah himself confesses to having been "called a sell-out for selling too many books, for writing books for children, for performing at the Royal Albert Hall, for going on Desert Island Discs, and for appearing on the Parkinson show". In the self-reflexive shift of the last decades, postcolonial critics have denounced the progressive evacuation of resistance to renovated forms of western imperialism in postcolonial cultural artefacts. Arguably, these have become not only institutionalised, but also inescapably commodified and some even turned into multicultural staples. For instance, the critic Mita Banerjee contends that September 11, 2001 marks the emergence of the "post-ethnic postcolonial"[15] and that, in a related conservative turn, postcolonial literature has been converging with "post-leftist politics"; in this context, she questions if the post-9/11 Rushdie might adequately be regarded as "the Tony Blair of postcolonial studies".[16] Against this backdrop, it should come as no surprise that the writer underwent a fierce attack when he accepted the OBE. Indeed, leftist critics felt that the ideologically oppositional agenda of postcolonialism was necessarily compromised when one of the most high-profile—and much defamed—British postcolonial authors chose to accept the honour.

As Boyd Tonkin notes, "More than any other writer alive", Rushdie "has found himself transformed into a character—ogre, joker, beast and, just occasionally, hero—in other people's scripts and stories".[17] Even for a polemic writer, he has been for an uncommonly long time the object of controversy on both left and right. It might be relevant to recall here that throughout the Thatcher era, the writer was a renowned adversary—and definitely not a supporter—of the British establishment. At the time, both Rushdie's fictional work and essays reproached the policies of Margaret Thatcher, the then Prime Minister and leader of the Conservative Party, and exposed the pervasiveness of British institutional racism, as when he denounces that "British thought, British society, has never been cleansed of the filth of imperialism. It's still there, breeding lice and vermin, waiting for unscrupulous people to exploit it for their own ends."[18] To some right-wing commentators, Rushdie is an ungrateful rabble-rouser who, by vilifying Thatcher—or "Torture. Maggie the Bitch", as one of the characters refers to her in *The Satanic Verses*[19]—, bit the hand that during the Rushdie affair part I provided the writer with costly police protection, estimated to amount to £1 million a year.[20] The debate around Rushdie's police guard and his (in)gratitude is resurrected on a regular basis.[21] For instance, in 2001 the Labour peers Lord Nazir Ahmed and Lady Manzila Pola Uddin called for the removal of the protection on the grounds that the writer was obsessed with egocentric self-promotion, "whether it's with a model [Padma Laksmi, who later became his wife] or saying his life is in danger".[22] In Baroness Uddin's perspective, "Public money should be used for someone who is grateful. We should not pay for this protection when he has so little gratitude. It is a mockery of democracy."[23] As expected, after his polemic non-refusal of the OBE nearly two decades after the Iranian fatwa, conservatives blamed again the self-centred troublemaker for allegedly threatening Britain's internal security (Cohen).[24]

To some leftist critics, Rushdie's caustic comments on press freedom in Denmark or Islamic dress were read as treason to the tenets of cultural relativism, and these controversies were only to be reinforced in light of the Knighthood the writer was "thrilled and humbled to receive".[25] The OBE did not sit well with some parts of the British press, with a few commentators labelling it as a retribution for Rushdie's apparent backing of the Iraq invasion and his pro-establishment attitude towards the US-British "war on terror". Previous to this acceptance, left-wing commentators had already claimed the writer had gone right-wing—they had taken issue with the writer's "American turn" and apparent endorsement of US foreign policy. Newspaper reporters and editors alike were swift to offer their insights on the political implications of a postcolonial writer accepting an award bestowed by the reigning monarch of Britain and head of the Commonwealth. Rushdie was expected to refuse the Knighthood, as Zephaniah and Tagore did; instead, he accepted it and the consequences of the writer's apparent realignment—or perceived reallocation of ideological positioning from the standing he held in the 1980s and early 1990s—are traced in various comments in the print media, by and large to the left of the political spectrum. A few reactions published in the newspaper *The Guardian,* the self-described "world's leading liberal voice",[26] are significant in this respect: on the same day of the announcement of the OBE, Esther Addley, a senior reporter on the broadsheet newspaper, comments that the honour "signals a belated endorsement by the British establishment";[27] a few days later, Michael White, a former political editor of *The Guardian*, confesses his perplexity in the face of the writer's actions: "I still don't understand why a leftie like Salman Rushdie, who abandoned Britain for New York in a huff, would want an honour from the British establishment."[28] These reactions somehow replay the earlier furore in the British press around the publication of *The Satanic Verses*. In the late 1980s, as Sanjay Subrahmanyam recalls in an article marking the 20th anniversary of Khomeini's *fatwa*, "Rushdie-bashing was (...) a low form of journalistic sport, including unpleasant puns on his name ('Salmonella' Rushdie and so on)."[29]

The most heavily-quoted and extensively reprinted piece from *The Guardian* in the aftermath of the writer's award was penned by Priyamvada Gopal. From a position Rushdie might well characterise as "sanctimonious moral relativism" and regard as representative of "a *bien-pensant* anti-American onslaught",[30] Gopal reads Rushdie's acceptance of the Knighthood as the culmination of a career trajectory that began as radically opposed to the British establishment, with work imbued with an "uncompromising ethical vision", and then slid into conservatism. She states that the writer's honour is "a reward for abandoning the anti-establishment stance he once espoused".[31] Gopal contrasts what she perceives to be Rushdie's current right-wing, aligned political positioning with his prior critique of "tyrannical forces in both west and non-west", recognition of these forces "as twinned", and a pronouncement of "a plague on both their houses". Now the writer is seen as the unthinking spokesperson for US political, military and cultural domination. Gopal charges Rushdie with ideological betrayal and concludes the article lamenting "the mutation of this relevant and stentorian writer into a pallid chorister is a tragic allegory of our benighted times, of the kind he once narrated so vividly". The critic notes the irony of accepting an award from the queen regnant of a nation the writer likened to "a peculiar-tasting smoked fish full of spikes and bones".[32] In *The Satanic Verses*, the Indian boy Saladin Chamcha is sent by his father to an elite boarding school in England where, only after a few days in the country, he is presented with a kipper when he comes down for breakfast. Unacquainted with grilled herring, Chamcha "sat there staring at it, not knowing where to begin".[33] He eats it whole, while his fellow students watch him in silence without any intention of helping him. This adversity taught Chamcha a valuable lesson, and, being "a bloody-minded person", set his mind to conquer England: "'I'll show them all', he swore. 'You see if I don't.' The eaten kipper was his first victory, the first step in his conquest of England. William the Conqueror, it is said, began by eating a mouthful of English sand."[34]

In pointing out inconsistencies in the ideological standing of the post-*fatwa* and post-9/11 Rushdie, commentators risk diverting attention from the bigger picture. Assuming that the writer *should* and *must* be an unequivocal standard-bearer of a fixed and unchanging political agenda, either leftist or right-wing, only serves to prove that he has been trapped in a discursive dilemma for a couple of decades. Critics should instead be concentrating on moving the debate forward: what is needed here is to displace the primacy of the *fatwa* years, by drawing attention to this predicament. James English and John Frow argue that the Rushdie affair part I was sparked by "the attempted conversion" of the writer's pre-existent literary capital in the early 1980s, "by means of the whole apparatus of his celebrity, into a special kind of political standing"; this ignited controversy in Britain because it was, "from the standpoint of the local religious leaders who first attacked the novel [*The Satanic Verses*], a threat and an affront".[35] Likewise, the left-liberal onslaught, or Rushdie affair part II, that the writer faced in the British media following his non-refusal of the OBE seems to be motivated by feelings of "threat and affront". Ever since the *fatwa* placed upon the writer in 1989, his name has become a political battleground, a site of conflict where commentators on the left and on the right struggle over the label—either progressive or conservative—to attach to the writer's shifting ideological positions. As Tonkin asserts,

> Symbol, victim, blasphemer, target—Salman Rushdie, it seems, is anything people need him to be. (...) Everyone, fan or foe, invokes their own imaginary Rushdie. We dream him up, and he duly takes shape: as blaspheming apostate for many still-outraged Muslims; as cocky subcontinental pseud for old-school British racists; as martyr to free speech for liberal literati. With the announcement of his Knighthood (...), this parade of straw men swelled to a seething carnival of prejudice and projection.[36]

Even if Gopal is one the "kneejerk-leftist haters" in this "seething carnival of prejudice and projection",[37] she is correct in pointing out that what is ultimately at stake in the issue of the Knighthood is not "one man's oddly bathetic 'gratitude' or even the meaning of being knighted in this day and age".[38] Conceptualising Rushdie as a liminal cultural actor allows for a fresh understanding of the seemingly paradoxical acceptance of an OBE. In fact, his position as a postcolonial critic and fictional writer should not be grounded on a terrain artificially constructed around a centre/margin binary. Following the logic of the centre/margin dichotomy, the acceptance of the Knighthood might well be construed as an example of the numerous symbolic ways Rushdie has written himself into the metropolitan centre, or, alternatively, as a critical intervention from the margin. These have proven to be incorrect readings, because partial and incomplete. The line dividing centre and periphery—upon which commentators in the British print media relied for guidance in their analyses of the Knighthood polemic—has been blurred by globalisation and postcolonialism. In the end, the binary centre/margin should be construed as relational. Besides, such dichotomy had already been disturbed and dismantled through the postcolonial performative acts of eating kippers by the Indian-born writer, a former schoolboy at Rugby.

Notes

1. W.L. Webb, "Salman Rushdie: *Satanic Verses*", in *Conversations with Salman Rushdie*, ed. Michael R. Reder (Jackson: University of Mississippi Press, 2000), 93.

2. David Batty and Peter Walker, "Rushdie Knighthood 'Justifies Suicide Attacks'", *The Guardian*, June 18, 2007, http://www.guardian.co.uk/world/2007/jun/18/books.religion [accessed September 2, 2008].
3. Commenting on the honour bestowed upon Rushdie, Lord Ahmed argues: "This honour is given in recognition of services rendered to Great Britain. Salman Rushdie lives in New York. (...) He is a controversial man who has insulted Muslim people, Christians and the British. He does not deserve the honour. (...) Two weeks ago, Tony Blair talked about building bridges with Muslims. What hypocrisy! What would one say if the Saudi or Afghan governments honoured the martyrs of the September 11 attacks on the United States?" (Translated from Rémi Godeau, "Lord Ahmed: 'Son Titre Doit Lui Être Retiré,'" *Le Figaro*, October 14, 2007, http://www.lefigaro.fr/international/2007/06/21/01003-20070621ARTWWW90263-lord_ahmed_son_titre_doit_lui_etre_retire.php [accessed September 2, 2008].)
4. Robert Spencer, "Death to Rushdie, Again," *FrontPageMagazine.com*, June 20, 2007, http://frontpagemagazine.com/Articles/Read.aspx?GUID=A81DD5BC-CAA8-4E1F-A867-4DF059F2B3DF [accessed September 30, 2008].
5. Paul Gilroy, *After Empire: Melancholia or Convivial Culture?* (London: Routledge, 2004), 125.
6. Salman Rushdie, "The New Empire within Britain," in *Imaginary Homelands: Essays and Criticism 1981-1991* (London: Granta, 1991), 130.
7. Rushdie, "The New Empire Within Britain", 130.
8. Rushdie, "The New Empire Within Britain", 132.
9. Rushdie, "The New Empire Within Britain", 133.
10. Rushdie, "The New Empire Within Britain", 130.
11. Gilroy, *After Empire*, 116.
12. Emily Dugan, "Queen's Birthday Honours Recognise Famous Names and Private Deeds", *The Independent on Sunday*, June 16, 2007, http://news.independent.co.uk/uk/this_britain/article2663239.ece [accessed October 23, 2008].
13. Rabindranath Tagore, "Letter from Rabindranath Tagore to Lord Chelmsford, Viceroy of India", 1919, 2001, http://www.

calcuttaweb.com/tagore/knighthoodrej.shtml [accessed June 19, 2008].

14. Benjamin Zephaniah, "'Me? I Thought, OBE Me? Up Yours, I Thought,'" *The Guardian*, November 27, 2003, http://www.guardian.co.uk/books/2003/nov/27/poetry.monarchy [accessed September 2, 2008].
15. Mita Banerjee, "Postethnicity and Postcommunism in Hanif Kureishi's *Gabriel's Gift* and Salman Rushdie's *Fury*", in *Reconstructing Hybridity: Post-Colonial Studies in Transition*, ed. Joel Kuortti and Jopi Nyman (Amsterdam and New York: Rodopi, 2007), 313.
16. Banerjee, "Postethnicity and Postcommunism", 321.
17. Boyd Tonkin, "Salman Rushdie: 'Fiction Saved My Life,'" *The Independent*, April 11, 2008, http://www.independent.co.uk/arts-entertainment/books/features/salman-rushdie-fiction-saved-my-life-807501.html [accessed September 20, 2008].
18. Rushdie, "The New Empire Within Britain", 131.
19. Rushdie, *The Satanic Verses* (New York and London: Viking, 1989), 269.
20. Sarah Womack, "Rushdie Does Not Need Police Guard Say Asian Peers", *The Telegraph,* June 19, 2001, http://www.telegraph.co.uk/news/uknews/1372442/Rushdie-does-not-need-police-guard-say-Asian-peers.html [accessed September 20, 2008].
21. In December 2008, Rushdie declares: "It's been a decade now since I had any police protection, since all those things that I'm supposed to be guilty of. That the country spent so much money protecting me and so forth. Well, the country hasn't spent any money on me in the last 10 years, during which I've faithfully paid my taxes. So it's possible that I have paid it back. In a way it's been a good investment—keep me alive and my taxes will pay for it." (Quoted in John Preston, "Salman Rushdie: Provoking People is in My DNA", *The Telegraph*, December 29, 2008, http://www.telegraph.co.uk/culture/books/4015303/Salman-Rushdie-provoking-people-is-in-my-DNA.html [accessed December 30, 2008].)
22. Quoted in Womack, "Rushdie Does not Need Police Guard say Asian Peers."

23. Quoted in Womack, "Rushdie Does not Need Police Guard say Asian Peers."
24. Patricia Cohen, "Now He's Only Hunted by Cameras," *New York Times*, May 25, 2008, http://www.nytimes.com/2008/05/25/books/25cohe.html [accessed September 20, 2008].
25. Cohen, "Now He's Only Hunted by Cameras."
26. Check the official website of *The Guardian* (http://www.guardian.co.uk/).
27. Esther Addley, "Literary World Applauds Rushdie Knighthood," *The Guardian*, June 16, 2007. http://www.guardian.co.uk/society/2007/jun/16/books.politics [accessed October 23, 2008].
28. Michael White, "Why Did Rushdie Even Accept a Knighthood?" *The Guardian*, June 20, 2007. http://blogs.guardian.co.uk/books/2007/06/why_did_rushdie_even_accept_a.html [accessed September 2, 2008].
29. Sanjay Subrahmanyam, "The Angel and the Toady", *The Guardian*, February 14, 2009. http://www.guardian.co.uk/books/2009/feb/14/salman-rushdie-ayatollah-khomeini-fatwa [accessed February 14, 2009].
30. Salman Rushdie, "The Attacks on America", in *Step Across This Line: Collected Non-Fiction 1992-2002* (London: Vintage, 2003), 392.
31. Priyamvada Gopal, "Sir Salman's Long Journey", *The Guardian*, June 18, 2007, http://books.guardian.co.uk/comment/story/0,,2105445,00.html [accessed June 19, 2008].
32. Rushdie, *The Satanic Verses*, 44.
33. *Ibid.*
34. *Ibid.*
35. James F. English and John Frow, "Literary Authorship and Celebrity Culture", in *A Concise Companion to Contemporary British Fiction*, ed. James F. English (Malden, M.A.; Oxford: Blackwell, 2006), 54.
36. Tonkin, "Salman Rushdie: 'Fiction Saved My Life'."
37. *Ibid.*
38. Gopal, "Sir Salman's Long Journey."

Works Cited

Addley, Esther. "Literary World Applauds Rushdie Knighthood." *Guardian*. June 16, 2007. Web. 23 Oct. 2008. <http://www.guardian.co.uk/society/2007/jun/16/books.politics>

Banerjee, Mita. "Postethnicity and Postcommunism in Hanif Kureishi's *Gabriel's Gift* and Salman Rushdie's *Fury*." *Reconstructing Hybridity: Post-Colonial Studies in Transition*. Eds. Joel Kuortti and Jopi Nyman. Amsterdam and New York: Rodopi, 2007. 309-24.

Batty, David and Peter Walker. "Rushdie Knighthood 'Justifies Suicide Attacks'." *Guardian*. June 18, 2007. Web. 2 Sept. 2008. <http://www.guardian.co.uk/world/2007/jun/18/books.religion>

Cohen, Patricia. "Now He's Only Hunted by Cameras." *New York Times*. May 25, 2008. Web. 20 Sept. 2008. <http://www.nytimes.com/2008/05/25/books/25cohe.html>

Dugan, Emily. "Queen's Birthday Honours Recognise Famous Names and Private Deeds." *The Independent on Sunday*. June 16, 2007. Web. 23 Oct. 2008. <http://news.independent.co.uk/uk/this_britain/article2663239.ece>

English, James F. and John Frow. "Literary Authorship and Celebrity Culture." *A Concise Companion to Contemporary British Fiction*. Ed. James F. English. Malden, M.A.; Oxford: Blackwell, 2006. 39-57.

Gilroy, Paul. *After Empire: Melancholia or Convivial Culture?* London: Routledge, 2004.

Godeau, Rémi. "Lord Ahmed: 'Son Titre Doit Lui Être Retiré'." *Le Figaro*. October 14, 2007. Web. 2 Sept. 2008. <http://www.lefigaro.fr/international/2007/06/21/01003-20070621ARTWWW90263-lord_ahmed_son_titre_doit_lui_etre_retire.php>

Gopal, Priyamvada. "Sir Salman's Long Journey." *Guardian*. June 18, 2007. Web. 19 June 2008. <http://books.guardian.co.uk/comment/story/0,,2105445,00.html>

Preston, John. "Salman Rushdie: Provoking People is in My DNA." *Telegraph*. December 29, 2008. Web. 30 Dec. 2008. <http://www.telegraph.co.uk/culture/books/4015303/Salman-Rushdie-provoking-people-is-in-my-DNA.html>

Rushdie, Salman. *The Satanic Verses*. New York and London: Viking, 1989.

———. *Imaginary Homelands: Essays and Criticism 1981-1991*. London: Granta, 1991. 129-38.

———. "The Attacks on America." *Step Across This Line: Collected Non-Fiction 1992-2002*. London: Vintage, 2003. 391-93.

Spencer, Robert. "Death to Rushdie, Again." Web. 30 Sept. 2008. <http://frontpagemagazine.com/Articles/Read.aspx?GUID=A81DD5BC-CAA8-4E1F-A867-4DF059F2B3DF>

Subrahmanyam, Sanjay. "The Angel and the Toady." *Guardian*. February 14, 2009. Web. 14 Feb. 2009. <http://www.guardian.co.uk/books/2009/feb/14/salman-rushdie-ayatollah-khomeini-fatwa>

Tagore, Rabindranath. "Letter from Rabindranath Tagore to Lord Chelmsford, Viceroy of India." Web. 19 June. 2008. <http://www.calcuttaweb.com/tagore/Knighthoodrej.shtml>

Tonkin, Boyd. "Salman Rushdie: 'Fiction Saved My Life'." *Independent*. April 11, 2008. Web. 20 Sept. 2008. <http://www.independent.co.uk/arts-entertainment/books/features/salman-rushdie-fiction-saved-my-life-807501.html>

Webb, W.L. "Salman Rushdie: *Satanic Verses*." *Conversations with Salman Rushdie*. Ed. Michael R. Reder. Jackson: University of Mississippi Press, 2000. 87-100.

White, Michael. "Why Did Rushdie Even Accept a Knighthood?" *Guardian*. June 20, 2007. Web. 2 Sept. 2008. <http://blogs.guardian.co.uk/books/2007/06/why_did_rushdie_even_accept_a.html>

Womack, Sarah. "Rushdie does not Need Police Guard say Asian Peers." *Telegraph*. June 19, 2001. Web. 20 Sept. 2008. <http://www.telegraph.co.uk/news/uknews/1372442/Rushdie-does-not-need-police-guard-say-Asian-peers.html>

Zephaniah, Benjamin. "'Me? I Thought, OBE Me? Up Yours, I Thought.'" *Guardian*. November 27, 2003. Web. 2 Sept. 2008. <http://www.guardian.co.uk/books/2003/nov/27/poetry.monarchy>

2

Meta-autobiographicity: Some Observations on Salman Rushdie's *The Enchantress of Florence*

Valiur Rahaman

> My reader then is not to be surprised, if, in the course of this work, he shall find some chapters very short, and others altogether as long; some that contain only the time of a single day, and others that comprise years; in a word, if my history sometimes seems to stand still, and sometimes to fly. For all which I shall not look on myself as accountable to any court of critical jurisdiction whatever; for as I am, in reality, the founder of a new province of writing, so I am at liberty to make what laws I please therein.
>
> (Fielding in *Tom Jones*)

I

The author lives in every words, ideas, dialogues of the characters, situations dwelt with characters, life worlds he describes, characters of the story within the story—he writes and his characters has told in that story—and all other concerns related to the text of an author, belong to the author himself particularly. The text cannot exist without aspects of the author. The text without aspects of its author is a glitch. Even a fragment—a literary glossolalia in a mature work or a text—an unconcerned dialogue, or awkward situation to the narration or story, subjoins the mind of the author. *The Enchantress of*

Florence, for example, is the result of fuzzy narrative technique. However, Rushdie narrates the story and let one of his narrators of that very story to tell his story; his creative leitmotif unties the Rushdie at each narrative mystification.

The creative leitmotif is an unexplainable phenomenon; however, it can be illustrated by observing the cases occurred in the lives of the authors. It is often observed that the author always keeps his leitmotif alive with works. The leitmotif of the author is his signature, the signpost of his works. No author, no artist can achieve the goal of artistry paramount if he or she does not drive him/herself with signet leitmotif; is not driven by the same. Those who drive his leitmotif are may be a successful historian or social worker. Those who are driven by the leitmotif, they outreach the limitation of time and space, they may speak about the past, present and the future at a time of narration; they always conjugate the different, uncommon gauzy periods, situation or history. Thus, there are two kinds of leitmotif: first, factual, straightforward, and dead; and second, devious, creative and alive. The first one is devoid of imaginative force. The other is remainder of imaginative force. The other is more powerful writing than the first one. The first is originated whereas the other originates in the process of creation and offers itself to the author. I will call the result of this process creative leitmotif of the author. Every creative artist or author lives with it in all odd and even situation of his life. He cannot keep it aside and go a pace ahead without it. Kālidās[1], Shakespeare, Milton, Johnson, Locke, Rousseau, Wordsworth, Shelley, Keats, Kant, Coleridge, T.S. Eliot, Kafka, Sartre, Samuel Beckett, Paul Celan,[2] Blanchot, Aurobindo, Tagore, Levinas, Derrida, Foucault, Jürgen Habermas and so on are examples of men possessing their own creative leitmotif singularly. They are categorized under types of discourses based only on representation of their leitmotivs.

The first responsibility of readers is to find out and observe these leitmotivs of the authors in texts. The most complex will turn, then, into simple and vice versa. The poststructuralist theorists have either waylaid, waymarked, waysided, waypointed or made the leitmotivs way-out. Thus the poststructuralist texts are wavicles of leitmotivs of the authors. It is worth notice, why we have started observing the name of an author, a noun as an adjective. We often leave our sentences with a trail adjectival phrase like '...Other in Hegelian sense'; '...trace in Derridean sense'; '...being in Heideggerian etc. etc.' These are the examples of semantic representation of author's leitmotif. Perhaps, Rushdie is very much right writing: We live in ideas. Through images we seek to comprehend our world. And through images we sometimes seek to subjugate and dominate others. But picture-making imagining can also be a process of celebration, even of liberation. New images can change out the old (Salman 2010). Prof. Devy also contends that,

> When one writes, it is not merely to express oneself. Every act of culturally significant writing is necessarily an experiment with the medium of expression. And, in the process of the medium too acquires new tonalities. An actor will not only communicate a certain play or a story; he also addresses a body in such a way that the body's ability to express undergoes a radical change. This self-reflectivity allows human animals to change the world that is given to them. The aesthetics and the ethical belong to this power of creativity. (Devy 45)

Aristotle emphasized on attribution of highest mind to author. He looks for the power of author to produce "pity and fear" in the audience. Coleridge appreciates the unique vision of the author who sees "the images rose up before him as things... prose words in their best order; poetry, the best words in the best order" (Coleridge 1827). T.S. Eliot's contention challenged the traditional viewpoints of god-like image of author. "The more perfect the artist, the more completely separate in him will be the man who suffers and the mind which creates, contends T.S. Eliot" (Eliot 1923). This additional qualification of the author 'the more completely separate in him' dangerously misunderstood by W.K. Wimsatt. Wimsatt with Monroe C. Beardsley attacked on impressionist criticism and proposed "Affective Fallacy" which arises from judging a poem by the emotional effect that it produces in the reader. He argues that the reader's response to a poem is the ultimate indication of its value.[3] For example, 'the murder of Duncan by Macbeth', say Wimsatt and Beardsley, 'whether as history of the eleventh century or chronicle of the sixteenth, has not tended to become the subject of a Christmas carol.' The implication is that murder tends to be seen in much the same way in different cultures at different periods and that it therefore has a certain stable significance when used in a literary work. However, one should not make too much of this argument. Murder in *Macbeth* is a horrid crime because Shakespeare makes it so by introducing a host of suggestive symbols and a complex apparatus of evaluation which enable the reader to place the murder on a moral scale (Olsen 1978; 2008).

Roland Barthes, a leading expert in semiology and cultural theory, "believes that the author dies at each writing because it (writing) is that neutral, composite, oblique space where our subject slips away, the negative where all identity is lost, starting with the very identity of the body writing" (Barthes 1977: 142). The author is no one to be interpreted through/ across his works. He cannot be the implication for his works. If reader is influenced by the temperament of the author; and if he elevates the very influence at reading the text, he cannot justify his reading. The contents of the text are not the command of its author-god, as Roland Barthes postulates:

> We know now that a text is not a line of words releasing a single 'theological' meaning (the 'message' of the Author-God) but a multi-dimensional space in which a variety of writings, none of them original, blend and clash. The text is a tissue of quotations drawn from the innumerable centres of culture...the writer can only imitates a gesture that is always anterior, never original. His only power is to mix writings, to counter the ones with the others, in such a way as never to rest on any one of them...life never does more than imitate the book, and the book itself is only a tissue of signs, an imitation that is lost, infinitely deferred. To give a text an Author is to impose a limit on that text, to furnish it with a final signified, to close the writing. (Barthes 1977: 146-47)

Dana Anderson's *Identity's Strategy* (2007) reviews the role of the author how he formulates his self into what he termed as "rhetoric self" (Anderson 2007). Anderson argues for the presence of the author founding on Kenneth Burke's idea of the 'Dialectic of Constitutions' based on 'rhetorical strategy and symbolic acts' (Burke 1945; 1969: 323).

For where nostalgic literature is concerned, the work may be, not a portrait of the times in which it was produced, but compensatory or antithetic to its actual context of situation. Or there arises a related consideration: The work may be a portrait of its author, but the author himself may not have been representative of his period. The vexing consideration in this case is that, *without adequate biographical data, we might not be able to judge whether the work should be taken as consistent with the author's temperament or as antithetical to it* (Burke 2003: 111) [italics mine].

Dana Anderson analyses how the author's self converts itself into the rhetoric-self and how the readers notice the presence of the author through reading words symbolically implies for the author's identity, and how this identity formulates responses to texts. To this he calls 'identity's strategy' as a persuasive force in the writing's 'textual making' process (Anderson 2007: 163). Foucault concedes that even if the author's presence in the text is rejected, the space made of the absence of the author needs to be interpreted, and that interpretation leads the reader to the world of discourse. Thus the absence of the author causes the presence of new discourses. The presence of the author may be biographical or subjective to the author's temperament but his absence transgresses biographicity and turns by itself into a meta-autobiographic world where everything, everybody, every fiber of human psychological, sociological, historical, non-historical being seems 'other' to the author yet belongs finally with him.

The narration of such a meta-autobiographic world is textured by transgressing the author's subjectivity. It does not mean to die or to kill or to negate the significance of the author from his writing. An Author's subjectivity may have an analogy with Derrida's 'transcendental signified' which causes infinite play—play of interpretation, as Derrida puts forth: "The absence of the transcendental signified extends the domain and the play of signification infinitely" (Derrida 1967; 1978: 354). Then the author and reader will alike know the mystery of literature. For knowing the power of the secret of literature, for literature's sake, the author must transgress his presence from his art, step across his aspects, and liberate the reader from his prophecy to the interpretation and perspectives of his art to envisage the meta-autobiographic world where his art is temporarily destined to go. Perhaps for this very reason, Foucault in his "What is an Author?" asks us to 'locate the space left empty by the author's disappearance, follow the distribution of gaps and breaches, and watch for the openings that this disappearance uncovers' (Foucault 1984: 104-05). He does not characterize author as an 'intelligible being", an individual with a "deep" motive, a "creative" power, or a "design", a "reformer" but as a culture embalmed and imbued with discourse. He located the 'author-function' at the space left by the author's disappearance from his writing. The fourth characteristic of the author function may be understood in analogy with what I called meta-autobiographic world. Salman Rushdie is much infatuated with this world which he calls *the* anti-world, but that unwonted texturing of such worlds gives a pavonine[4] effect on us—the effect which erects the life world similar to the mind of the author, reader and the world both belong to. Rushdie's world refers to the fourth important characteristic traits of Foucault's idea of author-function which 'does not refers to purely and simply to a real individual, since it can give rise simultaneously to several selves, to several subjects-positions that can be occupied by different classes of individuals' (Foucault 1984).

Salman Rushdie's world belongs to his alter-ego as Shiva ("incomplete, muddled and hybrid"), Dr Aziz's wife ("I am falling apart"), Padma, and Saleem, in *Midnight's Children* in which banal becomes tragic. Rashid Khalifa, Nobodaddy, Luka, Captain Aag and their anti-characters in *Luka and the Fire of Life* (2010) represent his alter-ego. Indeed. But, these alter-ego(s) is/are the results of the process of revision which tells what

Collins has called 'desire to understand our culture and ourselves as products of previous codings'.[5] The story is a series of Harun Stories. The inspiration of this story is, as Rushdie conceded, "the world of video games" wrote as a gift for his 13-year-old son. How lightly the author has accepted these unacceptable truths. The narration technique may challenge greater readers and serious professor's mind, but, Rushdie accepts the book as a gift for his immature son. The reason why I am concentrating on telling these facts behind the creation of Rushdie's novels is that the literary text or any art deconsecrates omnipresence of the author when reader deconsecrates his rude perspectives to biographic elements in the text, and author writes transgressing his self.

II

The power of Salman Rushdie's writing is his art of storytelling. It underlies human truth though it seems much fictitious, submerged with fantasy, dream, unreal and impossible world. Storytelling, for Rushdie is a language of what makes us human. Rushdie's tenth novel, *The Enchantress of Florence* (2008), seems a historical fiction from formalist point of view but its thread unties the mystery of the art of storytelling. It reexamines the art, its function and effect. It discusses the function of stories and the significance of the storyteller.

As the power of Shakespeare lies in his art to manipulate world perception in the words of imagination picturizing the historical icons and alluding to philosophy of art and artistry —the metaphor of modern world, so Rushdie's power lies in interweaving multiple stories for exposing the single impact on the audience. His *Harun Stories*, *Luka and Fire of the Life*, and *The Enchantress of Florence* are examples for how to become the creative narrator and the master of language. His power as a novelist lies in the art of imbricating multicoloured live-narratives to make a roof of his room where world exists imbued with its realities with, rather shadowy impressions.

Rushdie always depicts two worlds and put together asking us to see and observe them at a time. It is also observed that his two worlds are never ending existence and unnamed, unknown. His characters are shown complex as hang on creature looking for that never ending existence.

The Enchantress of Florence runs on his two leitmotivs: 1. free speech is banned even when the period celebrates Renaissance; 2. the strange or any uncommon, unusual thing, innovative, reformative, radical subject is not easily envisaged or practised, conceded in the society even after achieving Independence, Democratic and Enlightenment world. People do not accept transgression of tradition. They blindly believe on what they do not want it to believe. They do not envision. Before *fatwa*, Rushdie poured out his migrated self through glasses, glosses, and imaginings for bringing out a radical world where everybody can share pain of the same indecent incidences. After *fatwa* he wrote and published *The Moor's Last Sigh* (1996) in which he depicts grim world of an unheard man, Moraes Zogoiby, a character's death 'under the cover of darkness'; under 'wretched disoriented state'; 'stood in darkness, lost'. The novel echoes: "A door—a whole life, a whole way of understanding life—closed behind me. I stood in darkness, lost" (Rushdie, *The Moor's Last Sigh*, 1995; 1996: 285-86).

But, Rushdie's grimness, unlike Kafkaesque, outreaches the pessimism developing the sense of assertiveness, forceful, and stubborn critique of faiths which justify man as tool or secondary being; sense of refusal to be frightened. "Fear... rules your life with a stupid blinding omnipotence, or else you overthrow it, and its power vanishes in a puff of smoke" (Rushdie, *The Moor's Last Sigh*, 1995; 1996: 164). *The Ground Beneath Her Feet* (1999; 2000) and *Fury* (2001) maybe called transitional novels after the *fatwa* period, because it includes travelogue elements, as Rushdie has journeyed from Bombay to London to New York and to Manhattan (during writing *Fury*). Critics and reviewers have observed Clarrisa Laurd, first wife as Pamela Lovlace in *Satanic Verses*, Uma Marianne, second wife as Wiggins in *The Moor's Last Sigh*, Elizabeth West, the third wife and Padma Lakshmi as Neela in *Fury*, yet these characters locate themselves beyond such biographical territories.

III

The best example of texturing the period of the world golden era, great romances, Calvino's Invisible Cities, and Arabian Nights in *The Enchantress of Florence* (2008).

The Enchantress of Florence sets in the Renaissance Italy and Akbar's India, exposes mythogram of ancients and that of moderns. The scenes are neither European nor Indian, just as the characters are not quite historically accurate, nor would we want them to be. The novel begins with the arrival of a mysterious yellow-haired stranger who called himself Mogor dell'Amore, the Mughal of Love, at the palace of Fatehpur Sikri—the city built by the Mughal emperor Akbar the Great in the sixteenth century—claimed to tell bewitching stories and secret recounting only to the emperor. His real name is Niccolo Vespucci—cousin of Amerigo and namesake of Niccolo Machiavelli. He reported that he has journeyed from his birthplace in the New World via Florence to Mughal Hindustan with a desire to tell a secret story.

Mogor dell'Amore bold stratagems, artistic and magical narration bewitched Akbar. His art of telling the digressive, weaving and unweaving of a story that captivates the emperor's attention, is the art of author's own. The author has articulated the art of narration artfully. Mogor dell'Amore's stories told in the novel recalls Shaharzad and Saharyar of the *Arabian Nights*. Apart from stories he told the story involves three childhood friends: Antonio Argalia, Niccolo "il Machia" (Niccolo Machiavelli), and Ago Vespucci, who happens to also be the storyteller.

At the heart of *The Enchantress of Florence* is a mysterious woman named Qara Köz, who has the bewitching power to place all those who behold her under the power of her charm. What is most interesting about this novel is the examination of storytelling, particularly the role of the storyteller in our lives. Rushdie has stated that this novel is an attempt to finally distance himself from his fiction, yet the novel bears the storyteller as political threat is a central theme.

The Enchantress of Florence is an allusive novel. The depth of complexity and artistry of intertextuality determines the characteristics of postmodern fictional narrative. As Eliot composed *The Waste Land* (1922), by alluding to many literary, mythological and theological sources to present his view to modern world, so Rushdie did. He followed Calvino in his own style with a particular motif to reflect culture as an unfinished project. Calvino's explorer Marco Polo introduced cities consisting in desire, culture, civilization and people, exhibiting an imaginative quality of Calvino, but textual artistry of Rushdie's fiction affects the postmodern world. It cannot be taken negatively, there is nothing wrong with this if this artistry of texturing and storytelling keeps the reader enchanted. This is what a peculiar charm one may trace out in Rushdian narratology. There is Derridian 'closure' of narration. It affects unfinished narrative projects. At end, one may feel, there is yet telling a new story—an unpublished story. Complexity of narration of this novel maybe regressed in case one reads *The Enchantress of Florence* with Calvino's *Invisible Cities* (1972: 74).

In the novel, Salman Rushdie weaves a multilayered, multicentred, and multivocal story in which historical events and adventures of wonder promiscuously intermingle, defying any clear-cut boundary between reality and fantasy.

Since the novel sets in the fifteenth and sixteenth centuries, this maybe simply categorized as a historical novel. But, to me, it is ahistorical novel. Rushdie ahistoricised the cited history by admixing narrative artistry and history. It is ahistorical because it mirrors contemporary sensibilities and apprehensions "before the real and unreal were segregated forever and doomed to live apart under different monarchs and separate legal systems" (Rushdie 2011: 153). It depicts the quest of belonging to home which never ends even after all ending. In Florence the Renaissance is in full swing; in India the Mughal Empire is at its height under Akbar the great; Elizabeth I is Akbar's contemporary; the Ottoman Empire is at its most expansive; the Safavi empire is established under Shah Ismail; and the New World is "discovered", mapped, and named by an Italian mapmaker named Vespucci (Ganapathy 2009).

As the greatest master of intertextuality and postmodern artistry, Rushdie dissolves the ethnocentrism of the West, linking these contemporary moments with profound imagination. By interconnecting them he enlightens the root cause of human suffering. Most of the larger events in the novel are quite close to historical record. There was an inescapable hybridity and productivity to all these worlds—great movements of people, ideas, art, and knowledge brought about through violent conflict and conquest, but also by trade, alliances, and pilgrimage. This was a moment of great beauty, art, philosophical advancement, and wonder facilitated and made possible by movement/ migration.

Rushdie seamlessly and sensuously connects tale and historical worlds by personalizing moments of exchange and encounter, situating interpersonal relationships against the historical backdrop, and inventing fictional characters or fictional relationships between historical characters as intermediating devices—personalized agents of diffusion, discussion, hybridity—migrants across time and space. Despite the complicated multicultural and multilingual dramas that are behind the stories, we follow easily, drawn deeper into the lives and passions of the characters by the magic of the storyteller, who reminds us that "witchcraft requires no potions, familiar spirits or magic wands. Language upon a silvered tongue affords enchantment enough" (Rushdie 2011: 35).

Since *Midnight's Children* (1981) Salman Rushdie has often visited the *Arabian Nights* as a source for inspiration, and its trace remains a potent generative force behind the Enchantress as well: the outer frame introduces us to the Mogor dell'Amore, also known as Uccello di Firenze, or Niccolo Vespucci, the blond-haired, counterfeit "English ambassador" who arrives at Akbar's court by virtue of his tales of wonder. His story is the central puzzle of the book. He conjured Akbar, his city, suspending the eventual verdict on the veracity and possibility of his claim that he, the Mogor dell'Amore is Akbar the Great's uncle. Like Scheherazade, the Mogor's ability to draw his audience into his tale world is a life-and-death matter. As in the *Arabian Nights*, this outside frame encloses the stories of countless other interrelated characters, each with their own stories, which unfold throughout.

In addition to Akbar and the Mogor dell'Amore, the most important of these include the Enchantress of Florence herself—Angelica, or Qara Köz—and Argalia/Arcalia. These four central characters are themselves related, and relate all the events and stories in the novel to one another in a dynamic matrix in which narration is made equivalent to and dependent on movement. Angelica, the hidden Princess Qara Köz, is the lost great-aunt of Akbar, lover of Argalia, the Florentine orphan turned Ottoman Janissary commander; and the Morgor dell'Amore is, years after both their deaths, presenting himself to Akbar, claiming to be not only Angelica/Qara Köz's son, but, thereby, Akbar's uncle. It is this claim that constitutes the outer frame, motivating the generation of all the stories within it.

The movement and interrelationships of these main characters, their histories, and the histories of those whose lives they move through, reinforce the dual themes of the book: the inevitability of movement and transformation, and the impossibility of stasis and cultural "purity". Movement defines these characters as much as it defines Akbar's empire (the nomadic legacy of Genghis Khan, Timur, and Babar is only a few generations deep), and yet each of these characters is motivated by the narrative of the "return", dream of the imaginary homeland, and frustrated by their failure to achieve it.

After traveling from East to West across the then-known world, and finally running out of options, Angelica started her final voyage to the New World where people blindly live after gaining enriched culture. Angelica went on, "into a world of fantasy which men were still dreaming" (331), hoping that the suggestions of passage to India were true, and yet, "[d]reaming of finding her way back to her point of origin, of being rejoined to that earlier self, she was lost forever" (331). Antonio Argalia, characterized as a native son of Florence, orphaned at an early age, goes on a quest to become a soldier of fortune, a member of a troop of mercenaries. Ottoman kidnaps Argalia, he is inducted into the Janissaries, converted to Islam, and rising through the ranks of the Janissaries to become the commander in chief of Mehmet II (Mehmet the Conqueror) and his successor, Beyazit. Under Beyazit, he routs Shah Ismail and saves Angelica, Ismail's war prize, in the battle of Chaldiran. He ultimately found loneliness, "Loneliness is the wanderer's fate; he is a stranger wherever he goes, existing only through the power of his own will" (Rushdie 2011: 89).

The Enchantress of Florence, Qara Köz, also suffers of loneliness, though she has power to do anything. The narrator discloses the inner self:

> As for Qara Köz, however, when the door closed behind her and her Mirror she found herself unexpectedly drowning in a flood of existential dread. These sadnesses came over her from time to time, but she had never learned to be on her guard against them. Her life had been a series of acts of will, but sometimes she wavered and sank. She had built her life on being loved by men, on being certain of her ability to engender such love whenever she chose to do so, but when the darkest questions of the self were asked, when she felt her soul shudder and crack under the weight of her isolation and loss, then no man's love could help her. As a result she had come to understand that her life would inevitably ask her to make choices between her love and herself and when those crises came she must not choose love. To do so would be to endanger her life. Survival must come first.

This was the inevitable consequence of having chosen to step away from her natural world. The day she refused to return to the Mughal court with her sister Khanzada she had learned not only that a woman could choose her own road, but that such choices had consequences that could not be erased from the record. She had made her choice and what followed, followed, and she had no regrets, but she did, from time to time, suffer the black terror. The terror buffeted and shook her like a tree in a storm and the Mirror came to hold her until it passed. She sank onto the bed and the Mirror lay with her and held her, tightly, her hands hard upon Qara Köz's biceps, held her not as a woman holds a woman but as a man does. Qara Köz had learned that her power over men would permit her to shape her life's journey but she had also understood that that act of shaping would entail great loss. She had perfected the arts of enchantment, learned the world's languages, witnessed the great things of her time, but she was without family, without clan, without any of the consolations of remaining within one's allotted frontiers, inside her mother tongue and in her brother's care. It was as if she were flying above the ground, willing herself to fly, while fearing that at any moment the spell might be broken and she would plummet to her death (119-20).

Babar also encounters the pain of failure:

> Babar had set his heart on Samarkand but in spite of the defeat and death of Shaibani Khan, Lord Wormwood, the Mughal forces didn't seem able to hold on to the fabled city for any length of time. So Babar, too, was homeless, Khanzada was homeless, and the family had no permanent foothold on any patch of God's earth. (Rushdie 2011: 120)

Intrigue and Treachery at the Ottoman

Turkish Empire court forces the couple, Argalia and Angelica, to seek a return to Florence, where the Medici has dissolved the republic, reestablished papist regime. Medici tortured and exiled his boyhood friend Niccolò Machiavelli, who had led the republican militia against the papal theocracy and armies. In one of the most intriguing subplots of the novel, the fictional characters of the Morgor dell'Amore, Angelica, and Argalia serve as interlocutors between Machiavelli and Akbar, allowing for discourses across time and space on the nature of power, morality of men, despotism, and enlightened rule. Niccolò Machiavelli tried his best to regain his blissful seat but failed. Argalia fails in his return to Florence as well: at the service of the Medici, maintaining a distant relationship with Machiavelli, he, at last, is caught under the treachery of the court. He remains alone to listen silently his own retainers, and the superstition and petty fickleness of blind people. Akbar's empire policies and regulations of the court at Sikri failed to maintain human relationship and unity. His empire falls to the thanatos: jealousy, gossip, pettiness, superstition, and mental eeriness. Although the East and West are now commonly described as locked in a "Clash of Civilizations", what Rushdie tragically lays bare is the improbability.

The narrator explicitly describes the causes of the failure republicanism and its leader Machiavelli. Rushdie condemns people who never speak against fanatic craziness like papal authorities and people against radical enlightener. He thinks the power drives the people. Power is all.

After fourteen years of loyal service the people had shown that they did not care about loyalty. The people were fools for power.... Such a people did not deserve to be cared for. They did not deserve a republic. Such a people deserved a despot.... The pain that had coursed through his body was not pain but knowledge. It was an educative pain that broke the last fragments of his trust in the people. He had served the people and they had paid him in pain, in that lightless subterranean place, that place without a name in which nameless people did nameless things to bodies that were also nameless because names did not matter there, only pain mattered, pain followed by confession followed by death. The people had wanted his death, or at least had not cared if he lived or died. In the city that gave the world the idea of the value and freedom of the individual human soul they had not valued him and cared not a fig for his soul's freedom, nor his body's integrity neither. He had given them fourteen years of honest and honorable service and they had not cared for his sovereign individual life, for his human right to remain alive. Such a people were to be set aside. They were incapable of love or justice and therefore did not signify. Such a people no longer mattered. They were not primary but secondary. Only despots mattered. The love of the people was fickle and inconstant and to pursue such a love was folly. There was no love. There was only power (Rushdie 2011: 110).

Akbar abandons Sikri, he agonizes envisaging that:

> In the present he was invincible. He could build ten new Sikris if he pleased. But once he was gone, all he had thought, all he had worked to make, his philosophy and way of being, all that would evaporate like water. The future would not be what he hoped for, but a dry hostile antagonistic place where people would survive as best they could and hate their neighbors and smash their places of worship and kill one another once again in the renewed heat of the great quarrel he had sought to end forever, the quarrel over God. In the future it was harshness, not civilization that would rule. (Rushdie 2011: 116)

The novel repudiates linear, Eurocentric histories of the Renaissance and conjures in their stead a synchronous world of parallel realities in which the seeds of secular humanism flower not once but twice—once in northern Italy and simultaneously in northern India (Ganapathy 2009: 9-22). But, proliferation of that seeds is yet to grow.

Allusion

Rushdie has woven together strands from historical and literary sources, and yet the read is short, swift, and light, never ponderous or didactic. There are complexities and intertextual, inter-linguistic depths to plumb...or not, detours that only enrich the reader's pleasure in the whole (Ganapathy 2009).

In addition to the influence of the *Arabian Nights*, Rushdie alludes to style, theme, and characters of Ludovico Aristo's *Orlando Furioso* (1532) and Matteo Boiardo's *Orlando Innamorato* (1495). In *Orlando Furioso*, Angelica and Argalia are brother and sister, but Argalia's entourage, including four giants, is retained. Rushdie's fanciful cities, Fatehpur Sikri, Florence, Samarkand, Herat, Istanbul, and the recounting of such cities by the Western visitor to the court of Akbar are reminiscent of Calvino's *Invisible Cities* (1972: 74); and the Mogor, polyglot interlocutor is a reminiscent of Umberto Eco's protagonist Baudolino (2000). He also alludes to implications for his own fantastical tale of the sea-stories, particularly *Haroun and the Sea of Stories* (1990). These allusions along with suitable nature of narrative specifying the human tendency fabricates reality show of this present world. History is the history of clashes, wars, battles, social struggles based on religion-state conflict and treachery. Man is picturised as helpless creature struggling for survival resulting failure. The feat of relationship is less than desire to survive.

The novel invites us to reconsider axiomatic tenets about modernity, secularism, and humanism—chief among them the relation between the ethos of modernity and the rejection of an enchanted world where there is nothing but pain and treachery, falsification and blind imitation of falsified imitations; where there is no respect of loyalty, no reward to trust, no reciprocation at all; where there nothing remains but tales of failure civilization. Rushdie always favor radicalism in religion and republicanism in the state. He describes Machiavelli as one who, "held popes responsible for most of the wars of the period, and thought of many bishops and cardinals as criminals, but cardinals and popes liked what he had to say about the nature of the world better than princes (Rushdie 2011: 114).

But, the trauma of punishment repeats itself as centre of Rushdie's narrative. Here, I quote some key lines telling about the mind behind man as object to punishment for nothing but imagined radical thought. These lines express the very thought which he has penned in many articles and narrations after *fatwa*.

> Once a man has been in a torture chamber his senses never forget certain things, the wet darkness, the cold stink of human ordure, the rats, the screams. Once a man has been tortured there is a part of him that never stops feeling the pain. The punishment known as the strappado was among the most agonizing torments that could be inflicted on a human person without killing him outright. His wrists were fastened behind his back, and the rope that bound them passed over a pulley hanging from the ceiling. When he was lifted off his feet by that rope the pain in his shoulders became the

> whole world. Not just the city of Florence and its river, not only Italy, but all God's bounty was erased by this pain. Pain was the new world. (Rushdie 2011: 110)

The Enchantress of Florence, the Emperor, Akbar, Machiavelli's republic dream, individuals' dreams lead nowhere but "to roam, to scavenge, to depend on others, to fight without success, to be lost".

Notes

1. The greatest Sanskrit Indian poet, dramatist and visionary who wrote plays such as *Mālawikāgnimitra* ("Mālavikā and Agnimitra"), *Abhijñānashākuntala* ("The Recognition of Shakuntala"), and *Vikramorwasheeya* ("Pertaining to Vikram and Urwashi"). His epic poems include *Raghuvamsha* ("Dynasty of Raghu") and *Kumārasambhava* ("Birth of Kumar Kartikeya"), and the lyrical *Meghadoota* ("Cloud Messenger") and *Rutusamhāra* ("The Exposition on the Seasons").
2. Paul Celan (1920-70), German language postwar-poet and translator, wrote on death-theme.
3. See W.K. Wimsatt and M.C. Beardsley, "The Affective Fallacy", *Sewanee Review,* 57 (1949), reprinted in Wimsatt, *The Verbal Icon,* p. 21.
4. It refers to Latin 'pavoninus, from pavo, pavon' standing for 'peacock'. Pavonine effect, I used for universality of the iridescent effect produced after reading the presence of the author's absence and presence in the text. Peacock, be it Asian or African, green, golden or blue, is always characterized with resplendent trains of long upper tail coverts, concealing their relatively short tails, raising and spreading in scintillating manner. The feathers produce iridescent effect on seers.
5. Jim Collins, "Post-modernism as Culmination" in *The Post-Modern Reader*, Ed. Charles Jencks. London: Academy, 1992: 108.

Works Cited

Anderson, Dana. *Conversion, Identity's Strategy: Rhetorical Selves in Conversion*. Columbia: Univ. of South Carolina Press, 2007.

Barthes, Roland. *Image-Music-Text: Essays Selected and Translated by Stephen Heath*. Trans. Stephen Heath. London: Fontana Press, 1977.

Burke, Kenneth. *A Grammar of Motives*. California: University of California Press, 1969.

———. *On Human Behaviour: A Gathering While Everything Flows 1967-1984*. Ed. William H.

Derrida, J. *Writing and Difference*. Trans. Alan Bass. London: Routledge and Kegan Paul Ltd., 1967; 1978.

Devy, G.N. "The Being of Bhasa." *The G.N. Devy Reader*. New Delhi: Orient Blackswan, 2009. 44-45.

Eliot, T.S. "Tradition and Individual Talent." Eliot, T.S. *Selected Essays*. London: Faber and Faber, 1923. 17-18.

Foucault, M. "What is an Author?" *Foucault Reader*. Ed. Paul Rabinow. Trans. Josue V. Harari. New York: Pantheon Books, 1984. 105.

Ganapathy, Doré Geetha. "Shakespeare in Rushdie/Shakespearean Rushdie/Shakespearean Rushdie/Rushdie." *Atlantis,* Vol. 31, No. 2 (2009): 9-22. Web. 27 Aug. 2013. <http://www.jstor.org/stable/41055361>.

Olsen, Stein Haugom. *The Structure of Literary Understanding*. London: Cambridge University Press, 1978; 2008.

Rueckert and Angelo Bonadonna. London: University of California Press, 2003. Coleridge, S.T. "Table Talk." 12 July 1827.

Rushdie, S. *The Enchantress of Florence*. London: Vintage, 2011.

———. *The Moor's Last Sigh*. 1995. London: Vintage, 1996.

———. *Imaginary Homelands*. 1991. London: Vintage Books, 2010.

3

Salman Rushdie: A Self-Proclaimed Controversialist

Ramesh Tibile

Salman Rushdie is one of the most controversial novelists listed in the Third World Literature. He is known as the fearless commentator upon the state of global politics today. His novels, *Midnight's Children* (1981), *Shame* (1983) and *The Satanic Verses* (1988) were admired by worldwide readers and critics. His above works depict the religious situation and especially the prophet Muhammad. For this depiction, he has received strong protest from some Muslim groups. In February 1989, Ayatollah Khomeini issues a *fatwa* that demands the execution of Rushdie and his publishers. The Iranian cleric, Hassan Sanei offers a reward for Rushdie's murder. These events made him to hide himself. After long diplomatic negotiations, Iran's Foreign Minister, Kamal Kharrazi withdraws punishment that made him to move in public life. Still the complete threat is not yet removed. His works had an impact on the literary world. And so, besides the *fatwa*, he remained studied in universities, negotiated by other writers, read by readers across the globe. Salman Rushdie here invites the protest being controversial in his depiction about well-established religious beliefs particularly in Muslim Community.

The keen reader or observer of Salman Rushdie's work may easily experience his combined personality as migrant intellectual who is identified with Western metropolitan elite in terms of class, literary preferences and educational background with his typical identity as the interpreter and authentic public voice of the Third World. His migration extends him a chance for fresh thinking about the nation. On the other hand, this migrant position imposes them to write about nationhood at a distance. Besides Salman Rushdie's prominence as a writer, it is harder to establish what it is precisely that he is famous for his writings, or the 1989 *fatwa* in which the Ayatollah Khomeini demanded his execution for blasphemy. His readers observed his comic style with which he used to tackle political and religious issues with levity, irreverence and humour. His deliberate habit of treating sacred subject matters with irreverence provoked anger among some fundamental Islamic groups. Though he has acquired a somewhat mythical reputation with the publication of his most controversial novel, *Satanic Verses*, he himself invited worldwide anger from Islamic group. His interest in depicting political life in Pakistan brought him into difficulty. His novel, *Shame*, depicts the contemporary political situation in Pakistan, revering to the two important architects of Pakistan history—Raza Hyder and Iskander Hirappa (based on General Zia and Zulfikar Bhutto, respectively) provoked anger in fundamentalists. He observes the repressive situation of Pakistani society which is authoritarian in its social and sexual codes. He objects the women's critical situation being under the intolerable burdens of honour and prosperity.

He invoked the anger of his own community for depicting untold reality that dishonours their people in his novel, *Shame* which cannot recover his reputation. The novel *Shame*, based on contemporary politics in Pakistan, was also popular, but Rushdie's fourth novel, *The Satanic Verses*, encountered a different reception. Some of the bizarre adventures in this book depict a character modeled on the Prophet Muhammad and portray both him and his transcription of the *Quran* in a dubious light. After its publication in the summer of 1988, *The Satanic Verses* was denounced as blasphemous by outraged Muslim community leaders in Britain, and public demonstrations against the book spread to Pakistan in January 1989. On February 14, the spiritual leader of revolutionary Iran, Ayatollah Ruhollah Khomeini, publicly condemned the book and issued a *fatwa* (legal opinion) against Rushdie; a bounty was offered to anyone who would execute him. He went into hiding under the protection of Scotland Yard, and—although he occasionally emerged unexpectedly, sometimes in other countries—he was compelled to restrict his movements.

His book, *The Satanic Verses,* encourages everyone to create or choose his/her own life irrespective of the authority and tradition. Here, he tries to deconstruct the certainties of Islam as well as Western liberalism. He believes that the debate he proposed can be helpful to reduce the sufferings caused by Islamic fundamentalism and insularity. The title refers to a disputed Muslim tradition that is related in the book. According to this tradition, Muhammad added verses (*sura*) to the Qur'an accepting three goddesses who used to be worshipped in Mecca as divine beings. According to the legend, Muhammad later revoked the verses, saying the devil tempted him to utter these lines to appease the Meccans (hence, the "Satanic" verses). However, the narrator reveals to the reader that these disputed verses were actually from the mouth of the Archangel Gabriel. The book was banned in many countries with large Muslim communities. The publication of the book and the *fatwa* sparked violence around the world, with bookstores firebombed. Muslim communities in several nations in the West held public rallies, burning copies of the book. Several people associated with translating or publishing the book were attacked, seriously injured, and even killed. Many more people died in riots in some countries.

Rushdie is originally from a Shia Muslim family. The influence of his religion is not seen in his writing as he seems to be an atheist. In 1990, in the "hope that it would reduce the threat of Muslims acting on the fatwa to kill him", he issued a statement claiming he had renewed his Muslim faith, had repudiated the attacks on Islam in his novel and was committed to working for better understanding of the religion across the world. However, Rushdie later said that he was only "pretending". His books often focus on the role of religion in society and conflicts between faiths and between the religions and those of no faith. He aims a reform in Islam. He expects a move of Muslims beyond tradition and asks to accept the modern way of living. According to him, the core concepts of Islam need to be reformed and made suitable to the modern age. His idea of reformation in Muslim philosophy means nothing but to reject the dusty, stifling seminaries of the traditionalists and allow much-needed fresh air letting the windows open. He demands his youngsters to study inside the history forgetting the apparent side of it. He points out that broad-mindedness is related to tolerance; open-mindedness is the sibling of peace. Here, we feel that Rushdie is called for reform in Islam in a guest opinion. He was supportive of the US-led campaign to remove the *Taliban* in Afghanistan, which began in 2001, but was a vocal critic of the 2003 war in Iraq. He has stated that while there was a "case to be made for the removal of Saddam Hussein", US unilateral military intervention was unjustifiable. In 2006, Rushdie stated that he supported comments by the then-Leader of the House of Commons Jack Straw, who criticized the wearing of the niqab (a veil that covers all of the face except the eyes). Rushdie stated that his three sisters would never wear the veil. He said, "I think the battle against the veil has been a long and continuing battle against the limitation of women, so in that sense I'm completely on Straw's side." The Marxist critic Terry Eagleton, a former admirer of Rushdie's work attacked him for his positions, saying he "cheered on the Pentagon's criminal ventures in Iraq and Afghanistan". However, Eagleton subsequently apologized for having misrepresented Rushdie's views.

Salman Rushdie's following comments on other writers indicates his initiative in fighting with the world ideas related to religion: Most of the writers have lost hope and ambition, all desire to wrestle with the world. Their books dealt with tiny patches of the world. Very few writers had the courage or even the energy to bite off a big chunk of the universe and chew it over. His bile-spewing satires on South Asian political leaders in *Midnight's Children* and *Shame* and anger at institutionalized racism in the British police force in *The Satanic Verses* are his daring activities that gave open challenge to political leaders. He objects the idea that the function of writing is to find a new ways of describing the world. According to him, re-describing the world is the necessary first step towards changing it. He adds further that it is the fiction maker's capacity to use unusual, fantastic, surrealistic effects that gives a work its political power. Rushdie points out that the unreality is the only weapon with which reality can be smashed, so that it may subsequently be reconstructed. Through writing the author is expected to speak truth to power which may cause the power to change. Here, he objects that the book is able to change the world. But he expects that the writer should try to change something small inside the minds of a few people with so you may lead to change world slowly. So the writer must be firm with his thoughts and ideas, though they are controversial to power or tradition.

We can observe very easily the reflection of critical view of party politics (Marxist party politics) in his two works—*Grimus* (P.S. Moonshy) and *Midnight's Children* (Qasim the Red). His first novel, *Grimus* is a fine example of science fiction in which he employed the technique of fantasy. His second book, *Midnight's Children* brought him into focus as it helped him to bag the Booker Prize Award (1981) as well as Booker of Bookers—a special award (1993). The protagonist of this novel, Saleem Sinai, is one of the midnight's children, born during the freedom struggle as well as the story of partition of India and Pakistan. Through this character, Rushdie displays his identity. He comments on political, social, religious world of India as well as Pakistan. His novel, *Shame* depicts the contemporary political situation in Pakistan. His two characters—Raza Hyder and Iskander Hirappa resemble with General Zia and Zulfikar Bhutto, respectively. In this novel, he depicts the Pakistani repressive society under the social and sexual codes that crushes Muslim women beneath intolerable burdens of honour and propriety. In the novel, *Shame*, Rushdie deliberately comments on the social structure of Pakistani society that grows upon a diet of honour and shame. Here, he lists the shameful activities such as—Failure in loving one's national flag, malpractice during voting, extra-marital sex, smuggling, etc. being practiced in Pakistani society that hampers the real progress of the society. Repression and humiliation of women result in violence. Rushdie's invites social attack on him by depicting unwanted picture that is honoured and considered ethnic on religious ground. He also tries to explore political, social and cultural defects of Pakistan society in general and Muslim religious life in particular. His mythical novel, *The Satanic Verses*, steps ahead in his criticism on issues like, migration, racism, sexism and modernism. Here, Rushdie provides alternative of the lovely life rejecting the authority. Rushdie challenges the certainties of Islam and English liberalism.

The resistance to such perceived political resignation is apparent in almost all of Rushdie's writings. His bile-spewing satires on South Asian political leaders are easily observed in his *Midnight's Children* and *Shame*. He expressed his serio-comic eructations of anger on institutionalized racism in the British force very strongly in *Satanic Verses*. His *The Ground Beneath Her Feet*, *Fury* and *Shalimar the Clown* are his interrogations of the global power of the United States. In all these cases, Rushdie strongly demonstrates his purpose to bite off big chunks of the world and chew them. For Rushdie, politics is central to his art, but his art is also central to his politics.

This is not a site for polemics about the novel or the "Rushdie Affair". To many Western readers *The Satanic Verses* appears as a brilliant attack on religious bigotry. To too many Muslims, east and west, it appears as a vicious series of insults to many of their most cherished beliefs. There are other positions: liberal and conservative non-Muslims deplore his irreverence, and liberal Muslims deplore the *fatwa* against Rushdie and support his right to publish, or even admire his work; some American and British non-Muslim critics have been critical of him. But the important debate, the one that makes a difference in the real world, is the one between the extremes and between those extremes there remains a seemingly unbridgeable gulf. It is not my desire to exacerbate the tensions surrounding this novel, or to delve in any depth into the controversy.

To a conservative Muslim, Islam is not just a religion in the sense that most Westerners use the term, a private faith which provides hope and consolation within a secular world. Islam is a way of life, a body of law, an all-embracing cultural framework within which novels are distinctly unimportant and potentially troublesome. That a mere novelist should dare to satirize fundamental religious beliefs is intolerable. Salman Rushdie dared to do that, so brought himself into difficulty. To understand his position as a political novelist, we must abandon the idea that he is or sets to be, a politically transformative writer, and accept instead that he is, a reactive writer, satirizing what is, without attempting to offer any coherent blueprint for what should be. The political significance of Rushdie's writing does not change from text to text not because his subject matter changes but also because his political location changes. In his work, Rushdie proposes only one rather tentative answer to the question of how a decentred being can work meaningfully, and that is by writing history of the particular country.

Salman Rushdie does not like to accept if he finds something wrong in it. Therefore, he suggests the random reformations in it. Through his writing, he challenges the years' long tradition and the cultural practices. He fails to suggest a particular remedy over these wrong or any suitable substitutes to them. He initiated the challenge to his native practices being influenced by the metropolitan systems. Hence, he can be interpreted as self-proclaimed controversialist.

Works Cited

Cundy, Catherine. *Salman Rushdie*. Manchester: Manchester University Press, 1996.

Harrison, James. *Salman Rushdie*. New York: Twayne, 1992.

Rushdie, Salman. *Midnight's Children*. London: Jonathan Cape, 1981.

———. *Shame*. London: Picador, 1984.

———. *The Satanic Verses*. 1988. Delaware: Consortium, 1992.

Sanga, Jaina. *Salman Rushdie's Post-colonial Metaphors: Migration, Translation, Hybridity, Blasphemy and Globalization*. Westport: Greenwood, 2001.

Teverson, A. *Salman Rushdie*. New Delhi: Viva Books, 2010.

4

Theological Aspects and Diasporic Sensibilities in Rushdie's *Satanic Verses*: An Analysis

Hetal M. Doshi

Introduction

Just as goods, services, capital and technologies have flown from one nation to another, people too have moved from the countries of their origin to other countries under the influence of Globalization. Such a flight of people from their homelands to altogether alien lands is popularly known as the phenomenon of 'Diaspora'. Diaspora, thus, is an offshoot of the rapidly growing process of globalization. It is indeed perplexing that the Eastern countries have accepted the Western products and technologies with open arms but have failed to accept the Western influence and views on their culture and religion. Globalization and the resulting diasporic movements are bound to have such all-pervasive influences, including those on religion and culture.

The views of Indian diasporic writers, writing from the Western world, on the issues of culture and religion have undergone a significant change and are clearly visible in their fresh writings. Rushdie's *Satanic Verses* is a magnificent specimen of this influence.

This paper has been classified into four sections. 1. Objective, 2. Information, 3. Analysis, and 4. Conclusion.

The section on information is further categorized into three parts:

A. The Abstract of the Novel, *The Satanic Verses*

B. The History and Origin of the Term: "*Satanic Verses*"

C. *The Satanic Verses*: Controversial Elements.

The section on Analysis, which addresses some of the more subtle issues of the story, is divided into two parts.

A. Rushdie: A Hero and a Villain

B. The Role of Diasporic Sensibilities in Shaping the Novel.

1. Objective of the Paper

Most of the research about Rushdie's *The Satanic Verses* (1988) has not dealt with some of the fine, delicate and subtle aspects of the novel. Unfortunately, these theological aspects were eclipsed by the controversy about the blasphemous nature of the book. The extremely captivating and creative portrayal of the character of Gabriel Farishta, his thrilling dream sequences and the implications of the novel as a modern way of thinking among Muslim youth (under the influence of cultural-globalization) has not been analyzed systematically by too many scholars.

The current paper strives to investigate such philosophical contexts of the novel. It also tries to examine the impact of migration on the writer's perception of his religion and culture.

2. Information

A. The Satanic Verses: An Introduction

This is the fourth novel of Rushdie which is influenced partly by the life of Prophet Mohammad. The book uses the technique of magical realism, with a series of sub-plots that are narrated as dream visions felt by the main character. The two protagonists, Gabriel Farishta and Saladin Chamcha, are both actors of Indian Muslim background. Farishta is a Bollywood super-star who is popular for playing Hindu deities in films, whereas Chamcha is an emigrant who has given-up his Indian identity and works as a voiceover artist in England.

At the outset of the novel, both are trapped in a hijacked plane during a flight from India to Britain. They are magically saved. Then comes an incredible transformation where Farishta becomes Angel Gabriel whereas Chamcha transforms into a devil. Farishta's transformation was the symptom of his mental illness. Chamcha, on the other hand, is arrested and passes through a torment of police abuse as an alleged illegal immigrant.

Both the leading characters struggle to sail in the exile waves. Farishta is happy as he finds his lost love; the English mountaineer Allie Cone, but this love relationship is hampered by his mental sickness. Chamcha's main mission is to take revenge on Farishta for having deserted him after their falling from the hijacked plane. He does this by fostering Farishta's jealousy against his girl and thereby breaking his relationship with Allie. When Farishta realizes what Chamcha has done, he forgives him and even obliges him by saving his life.

The story also implants a series of magical dream vision narratives, attributed to the disturbed mind of Farishta. These dreams are chronicles of revelations; religious faiths and fears. One of the dream sequences which triggered the controversy and was offensive to Muslims described the life of Mohammad (the name in the novel—Mahound) in Mecca (Jahilia). The main focus is on the episode of the satanic verses in which Mahound first proclaims a revelation in favour of the old polytheist deities but later renounces this as an error induced by Shaitan. The second sequence tells the story about Aayesha, an Indian peasant girl who claims to be receiving revelations from archangel Gabriel. A third sequence presents a figure of a fanatic expatriate religious head, the 'Imam'. Through these dream series, Rushdie attacks some of the tenets of Islam, which he finds to be unscientific and inexplicable.

Ultimately, both the characters return to India. Farishta, a chronic schizophrenic, kills Allie in an outburst of jealousy and then commits suicide. Chamcha, after finding forgiveness from Farishta and reunion with his father and his Indian self, decides to remain in India.

Thus, the novel besides giving hullabaloo to Muslim faith is a simple record of the migrated experiences of two Indians in Britain's soil.

B. The Satanic Verses: History and Origin of the Term

According to a popular folklore, an angelic messenger named Gabriel sent by Allah revealed and conveyed various tenets and doctrines of Islam to Prophet Mohammad in the form of verses which were eventually recorded as text in Quran by a poet-friend of Mohammad called Salman. There is a controversial incidence in the Prophet's biography which points out at the existence of three goddesses Al lat, Al Azza and Mannat in the *pre-Islamic* Mecca. When the prophet divulged his revelations from the Allah and appealed the Meccans to accept the principles of Islam and Allah's sole existence, they were reluctant to accept it.

Disappointed and dejected by the fact that his appeal to embrace Islam was not acceptable to certain groups, Mohammad became a bit flexible. In order to entice such groups to Islam, he admitted the existence of their three goddesses as the daughters of Allah. However, he later realized, by doing so, he has accepted the polytheism, pluralism of gods, something against the essence of Islam; a grave violation of Islam's absolute monotheistic requirement. As an afterthought, he abrogated these verses from Quran saying that the *Satan* had misled him to speak so and they were not the messages from the Allah. These messages which are said to be stirred by the Satan and which were later on aborted from Quran are known as the "*Satanic Verses*".

This incidence was such that it could raise the doubts on the credibility of Mohammad's revelations in Quran. Some would feel that there could be other instances as well where the Prophet might have instilled some of his personal biases and views. Some would even doubt the fact that did Allah really reveal all that the Prophet claimed he had. As the centuries passed by, this issue and the controversy were forgotten and no one found it appropriate to re-open it. Most people in the modern world were unaware of the so-called *Satanic verses* and their implications.

C. *The Satanic Verses*: The Rudiments of Controversy

Rushdie's books are notoriously famous for triggering controversies. Portrayal of Indira Gandhi as an ambitious political woman in *Midnight's Children* and underscoring an assumed tiff between Zulfikar Ali Bhutto and Zia Ul Haq in *Shame* are some of the famed instances. The *Satanic Verses* is not an exception. What exactly was so controversial in the book?

Some of the issues in the novel resulting into the world-wide resentment are as below:

- *The title*: It bears the reference to an assumed incident in the life of Prophet Mohammad when a few verses were evidently spoken by Mohammad as a part of Quran and then withdrawn afterwards on the basis that the devil had sent them.
- *Permission of polytheism*: These dubious verses sanctioned prayers to be made to three goddesses Al'lat, Al Azza and Mannat, an unpardonable violation of the Islamic belief in monotheism.
- *Portrayal of Prophet Mohammad*: Rushdie's delineation of the Prophet in the guise of his character Gabriel Farishta is derogatory. Mohammad's portrayal as a lustful man having twelve wives is excruciating.
- *Farishta's dream sequences*: His dream that he is actually a receiver of God's messages meant for the humans is offensive to the popular Muslim belief. His fear that he is becoming more lunatic due to the force of dreams suggests that the Prophet was, in reality, an insane man.
- *Choice of the names of characters*: The name Mahound, which is the name given by Rushdie to his Prophet, was insultingly used for the Prophet during the crusade. Jahilia (the name for the holy city of Mecca in the novel) suggests the time of ignorance before Islam.

The character named Saladin (originally a Muslim protagonist of the crusades) is portrayed as a villain. Ayesha (originally name of the wife of Mohammad) is shown as an Indian girl leading her fellowmen to the pilgrimage. Jahilia's prostitutes had taken the names of the wives of Mohammad.

- *Goddess's visit on the death of Gabriel*: As Gabriel Farishta dies in the novel, Allat pays a visit at the end. This visit suggests that such goddesses do exist.
- *Frequent usage of abusive words*: "Nigger eats white man's shit" (*TSV* 461), "White women—never mind fat, Jewish, non-deferential. White women—were for fucking and throwing over" (*TSV* 261). The recurrent use of words like 'Bastard', 'Bloody', 'Fucking' etc. are disparaging for divine personas.

3. Analysis of the Hullabaloo

A. Rushdie: A Hero and a Villain

What Rushdie did through his novel was, unnecessarily, as some would feel to bring back the controversy to the notice of the people, most of whom did not even know about it. The main character of the novel, Gabriel Farishta was depicted as resembling to Prophet who used to get similar dreams of revelations from Allah. But his dreams were just the absurd imaginations of a schizophrenic and not the revelations from the God. This actually was an attempt to question the credibility of the Quranic preaching and pointing out the possibility that the Prophet wasn't sinless.

Rushdie has depicted his main character, Gabriel Farishta as a false prophet, who is away from reality, living in his own self-construed dreams. He perceives himself to be divinely inspired, but everyone else around him believes that he is crazy, just as the Prophet's contemporaries thought of him in Mecca. The author has also challenged the stringent and rigid tenets of Islam through this character. By using magical realism, Rushdie has portrayed Farishta as a split personality. When in his dreams, he assumes himself to be a receiver of Allah's messages and during the phase of his human consciousness, he acts as an ultra-modern Muslim.

When Gabriel Farishta falls seriously sick, he pleads to Allah for quick recovery, the plea which goes unheard and unnoticed. As the God did not respond, Farishta gradually started losing faith in Islam and in fact developed hatred towards the religion. The novel mentions that gradually when Farishta started believing in himself instead of that in the religion, he started getting well. He felt better and recovered faster. This further drove him away from Islam and he started doing exactly all that was prohibited in the religion. He ate pork and had an affair with a white woman, both of which were prohibited in Islam.

Further, at places in his fiction, Rushdie had raised doubts about the sincerity of Salman, the poet who had penned down the verses in Quran which were revealed by the God's messenger to Prophet. He has suggested that Salman might have played some mischief while doing his job. Rushdie as a modern Muslim has also questioned the tradition of going to Mecca for every Muslim. Making Saladin Chamcha, the second significant character of the novel his mouthpiece, Rushdie observes,

> He stood at the window of his childhood and looked out at the Arabian Sea. The moon was almost full; moonlight, stretching from the rocks at Scandal Point out to the far horizon, created the illusion of a silver pathway, like a parting in the water's shining hair, like a road to miraculous lands. He shook his head. He could no longer believe in fairy-tales. Childhood was over, and the view from this window was no more than an old and sentimental echo. To the devil with it! Let the bulldozers come. If the old refused to die, the new could not be born. (267)

By the "illusionary silver pathway" and the "road to miraculous lands", the author means the path which leads to Mecca. He then asserts that this age-old path of tradition no longer appeals him. He finds it a mythical fairy tale. He then adds, 'let the bulldozers come' and destroy all such myths.

Because only when such old myths will die, the new and modern thinking will evolve 'if the old refused to die, the new could not be born'. The implication is clear. Just as the holy and sacred *yatras* in Hindus are no guarantee for obtaining the salvation; neither is going to Mecca for Muslims.

May be the author is indicating that the good deeds are more important than all the rituals and pilgrimage. Indeed, a noble thought. Unfortunately, Rushdie was never credited for being an ultra modern, postcolonial and post religious Muslim writer, who dared to think beyond and challenge the religion. The novel is an insight into his unusual personality. Some personalities like him are an outcome of such a family upbringing, educational training and social conditioning that they would not accept any religious dogmas, scriptures, traditions and conventions before putting them to the acid test of logic and reasoning. If certain tenets and doctrines seem to be unscientific, inhumane and devoid of any credible justification, they would vehemently challenge them. The chances of such religious criticism coming from the people belonging to the same faith are very high because they have known that religion inside-out, read and practised it for years and continuously thought about it critically. Gautam Buddha and Mahavir Jain pointed out serious limitations in Hinduism, especially the inhumanity involved in the caste-system and the unfair dominance of Brahmins prescribed in Hindu scriptures; Rajnish Osho challenged various canons of Jainism and many catholic scholars have confronted various dimensions of Christianity.

It is the blind and unshakable faith of some narrow minds, which are obstinately reluctant to listen any view and argument against their beloved religion, no matter how convincing and logical it is. The religion for them is beyond science and logic. These are the people who term such rebellious thinkers as atheist. If Buddha and Mahavir became the figures of worship, if Osho earned respect of billions, why should Rushdie is singled out as an atheist for his criticism of Islam?

Criticism of the select aspects of a certain religion need not be treated as a controversial piece of writing, if it is independent of pre-conceived notions and biases, purely based on sound logic and aimed at educating the people about the unscientific dimensions of various faiths. Unfortunately, Rushdie became over-sarcastic and at times extremely derogatory in his description of Mohammad and Islam. Giving the names of Mohammad's wives to the prostitutes and pimps is certainly unacceptable. Similarly, the use of abusive language at times was uncalled for. Had Rushdie been a bit more prudent in selection of his words, more scholars would have defended him and kept him in the category of a social reformer.

If a Hindu writer challenges the highly discriminatory caste system in Hindu religion (as described in *puranas*), there is nothing wrong in it. On the contrary, he should be credited for educating the society and spreading the awareness, compelling the people to think. Rushdie almost did the same. He made the people aware about some of the controversies surrounding Islam and Mohammad. He made people think scientifically and logically. He pointed out the importance of self-belief versus the blind faith in religion. He had the guts and courage to criticize some of the religious tenets which he found to be unnecessarily stringent and rigid.

B. The Role of Diasporic Sensibilities in Shaping the Novel

The novel offers interesting evidence that the diasporic state of living especially in the Western world indeed influences one's interpretation of one's own religion and culture. One tends to identify and challenge the rigid tenets and irrational beliefs of one's own religion under the influence of western liberalism. The novel can also be seen as a frustrating collision of two religious ideologies, the uncompromising eastern religious standards and the tolerant and moderate Western credos and author's reactions to both. The sudden and inexplicable outburst against religion and its proponent in the novel might be an outcome of the constant rejection by the Western world to whole-heartedly assimilate the migrants from the Third World countries and the resulting frustration.

Initially in the novel, Saladin Chamcha, an aspiring actor, is just consigned to voice-over roles because 'his face is the wrong colour' for British television (61). During his meeting with media executive Hal Valance, the later utters that advertising is a trade in which the people of 'the tinted persuasion' (267) do not charge well. Hal's statements are the archetypal representation of the racial prejudices of a white man.

> Within the last three months, we re-shot a peanut-butter poster because it researched better without the black kid in the background. We re-recorded a building society jingle because T' Chairman thought the singers sounded black.... We were told by a major airline that we couldn't use any blacks in their ads. (*Ibid.*)

The author and his characters eventually end up blaming their (own) origin, religious values and culture as a major cause for their failure in the economic and social life. The alien culture seems more attractive and appealing. The strong desire to please those in power and position makes them rebellious against their own faith and validate those of the former. In the process, they may dig deep and indeed come out with some remarkable conclusions, several of which may be actually controversial but thought-provoking at the same. And when the author is an ultra-modern creative genius, he is bound to give altogether new dimensions to religion and spirituality.

4. Conclusion

All in all, it can be concluded that if we forget about the belittling style of presentation, we can credit Rushdie for his attempts to make a generation more scientific, the attempt which mainly failed due to over-aggression and sarcasm. The novel teaches another important lesson. No matter how important and logical the message is, if it confronts a particular religion and its well-accepted principles, it has to be presented in humble and polite words; as an appeal and not an assertion. When dealing with the faith of billions, you need to use words with discretion and wisdom. Freedom of speech does not mean freedom of hurting the sentiments. Truly speaking, the role of an art should be reflection, not action. It is the duty of an artist, more so of a writer to *renew* the perceptions about history, society and religion; not to *shatter* them.

Works Cited

Rushdie, Salman. *The Satanic Verses*. London: Penguin Viking, 1988.

———. *Imaginary Homelands: Essays and Criticism 1981-1991*. New York: Granta Books, 1991.

Ruthven, Malise. *A Satanic Affair: Salman Rushdie and the Rage of Islam*. London: Chatto & Windus, 1990.

Suleri, Sara. *The Rhetoric of English India*. Chicago: University of Chicago Press, 1992.

Section–B

Midnight's Children: Fictionalizing History, Nation and Narration

5

Presentation of a Wounded Civilization: A Cosmopolitan Perspective of *Midnight's Children*

Suhaina Bi

Salman Rushdie has helped the Indian Writing in English to gain a reputation in World Literature in addition to win the prestigious prize of Booker of the Bookers for himself in 2008. He is the foremost writer who presented the sub-continental Diaspora with all its geographical and psychological pros and cons both in real and virtual sense. Most of the characters of his novels suffer from the disease of alienation and rootlessness because of their frequent and forced displacements. This is perhaps the reflection of his own personality for he had to leave his home, not once but several times; sometimes at will and at other occasions by force. Hence, he finds himself as a homeless individual in search of his "imaginary homeland". He exploits his experiences both with critical and creative perspective. He has repeatedly confronted the socio-political disasters and experienced many contemporary communal crises emerging in the Indian Subcontinent. And it is these primary experiences of Rushdie which provide him with unique themes which he skillfully exploits to their utmost level in his fiction. Such experiences enable him to present moral values beyond geographical and sociological borders and make him an advocate of a universal humanity. His novels present themselves through the eyes of a cosmopolitan or a rootless individual; because it is the cosmopolitan individual who can best analyze the civilization which gets continuously wounded in the name of patriotism and nationalism or because of the loyalty concerned only to a specific community, doubtlessly happening on the cost of one's own conscience in this age of multiculturalism and globalization.

Cosmopolitanism as an ethos is deduced from Enlightenment theories and values. It advocates a mode of humane thinking about the relationship between human beings without taking into consideration the geographical boundaries and a moral concern for different communities. It supports the idea of "*weltbürgerlich*" (qtd. in Niesen 1) or the concept of 'the world citizenship'. Cosmopolitanism is "globalist understandings of universal citizenship" (Niesen 2) and an intellectual and aesthetic stance towards divergent cultural experiences and it requires an ability to see oneself from the perspective of others that is often developed through psychological disposition and is a structure of feelings evaluated through the geographical changes of an individual. According to the anthropologist Ulf Hannerz, cosmopolitanism is a "willingness to become involved with the Others, and the concern with achieving competence in cultures which are initially alien" (239-40). Cosmopolitanism is developed among ordinary individuals because of the changes of their practices of everyday life that leads traversing emotional ties with strangers beyond geographical and sociological borders. Cosmopolitanism results in the loss of 'accidental' identities which are generally acquired only by taking birth in a specific nation and community. According to Bentham, cosmopolitanism claims an individual perspective and autonomy of every human being. He says that cosmopolitanism refers to the moral universalism, i.e. "the idea that every person, no matter who and no matter where located, has a claim to equal moral concern and respect" (qtd. in Niesen 5). Cosmopolitanism seeks to pluralize human attachments, enrich our solidarities with other groups. It claims a universal citizenship with the perspective of assimilation of a multicultural society in which "others" can be seen on par with the self.

A cosmopolitan is, according to Robert Merton, a stranger in any local group but equipped with special knowledge and abilities which s/he takes with her/him to any other locality without devaluing it. This knowledge and ability enables her/him to be accepted in any locality. S/he has a social status that is acquired in another society. Though there is lack of the knowledge of acquaintance which makes her/him rootless, but s/he possesses an ability to make her/himself at home in every new locality while moving throughout the world (qtd. in Hannerz 5). Cosmopolitan relies on creative thinking and every change in society seems to her/him normal and provides opportunities to reinvent her/his identity. S/he easily learns the new ways of an alien society. Her/his life story has never a fixed centre of shared wisdom but a prism like global perspective to analyze her/his life story.

The approach of *Cosmopolitanism* is very often applied and presented in Indian writing in English for the negotiation of English language has provided the authors of Indian literature a large cosmopolitan English-speaking audience—whether Indian or non-Indian. Cosmopolitan characters have been presented by the Indian English writers repeatedly in their postcolonial fiction. Sahgal's *A Time to be Happy* (1958) and *The Day in Shadow* (1971), Kamala Markandaya's *The Coffer Dams* (1969), Khushwant Singh's *Train to Pakistan* (1956), and Bhabani Bhattacharya's *Shadow from Ladakh* (1966) may be presented as some of the examples of such works. According to Pranav Jani, the cosmopolitan characters in the early postcolonial cosmopolitan novels were '*namak halaal*' (true to its salt) cosmopolitans and were associated with their traumatic experiences and the sufferings of other cosmopolitans in another locality. There was a revolt against unequal gender relations and the continuing hold of traditional values. Early postcolonial cosmopolitan writers who presented the nation and its history through their narratives could not be read as the "native informants" (16). But the novelists of the 1980s and 1990s, such as Amitav Ghosh in *The Shadow Lines* (1988), Shashi Tharoor in *The Great Indian Novel* (1988), Vikram Chandra in *Red Earth and Pouring Rain* (1995), Rushdie in *Midnight's Children* (1981) and *The Moor's Last Sigh* (1995), and Rohinton Mistry in *A Fine Balance* (1995) are regarded as "native informants" and they attempted to speak for the hierarchical problems of socio-political subversion and oppression of all Indians. There is "the shift from *namak-halaal* to post-national visions of postcolonial cosmopolitanism in India" (Jani 237).

Rushdie is the most distinguished postcolonial cosmopolitan writer. In almost all of his novels, he presents a cosmopolitan individual as the narrator of the story, e.g. in *Grimus* (1975) the narrator Flapping Eagle is alienated and marginalized in his own tribe because of his auspicious birth, in *Midnight's Children* there is a search for imaginary homeland by its narrator Saleem Sinai and *The Ground Beneath Her Feet* (1999) is preoccupied with the issues of globalization. Rushdie's *Midnight's Children* is the most distinguished novel in this range because of its presentation of radical and overt cosmopolitanism. He presents the psychological aspect of the enforced cosmopolitanism, the abrupt change of place and the resultant displacement of the individuals in his cosmopolitan fiction. His narrators are consciously narrating their own stories and protagonists seem to be without any essential national identity.

The present paper attempts to present the cosmopolitan experiences of the repeatedly displaced narrator Saleem Sinai of *Midnight's Children* (*MC*) and his direct as well as indirect confrontation with the socio-cultural crisis and political conflicts of his age. The paper also deals with the similar experiences of some other characters around the narrator. The narrator Saleem Sinai is the illegitimate son of Vanita and William Methwold and is brought up by a Muslim family. Born at the midnight of 15 Aug. 1947, when the nation (India) also gets a new lease of life from the shackles of the foreign rule, his birth is celebrated because he is born with the nation and he is greeted by the first Prime Minister of the nation Pt. J.L. Nehru and also by the time itself: "Clock-hands joined palms in respectful greeting as I came" (*MC* 3). He is the most celebrated child of the 1001 'midnight's children' because he belonged to an elite family of a minority community. His birth was publicly announced by his mother. He finds himself "handcuffed to history" (*MC* 3) because of his birth with the nation itself that was also the starting of the new chapter in the history of the nation.

This novel is an autobiography of its narrator for his infant son, Aadam Sinai. Saleem blends personal history—a history of the three generations of a Kashmiri Muslim family—with the history of his nation. He is self-consciously narrating the story in which he, sometimes, addresses directly to his readers as he says: "I should speak plainly, without the clock of a question mark" (*MC* 206). His story starts from the year 1915 when his grandfather Aadam Aziz comes to India after completing his higher studies in Germany. At that time, Kashmir was an independent state. Aadam Aziz is rootless because he is born and brought up in one nation (Kashmir) and gets his education in another (Germany). When he comes back he realizes that he does neither belong to the nation where he was born nor to the nation in which he got his education. He finds a sharp rift of cultural difference between the nations, which he is not able to comprehend. When he moves to Amritsar with his newly married wife, Naseem Ghani, Jallianwala Bagh massacre of 1919 takes place in front of his own eyes and he witnesses the spill of the blood flowing on the ground like the red medicine, mercurochrome. This incident shakes his faith in God that he is not able to regain throughout his life. He could not stay there and moved to Agra with his family.

The above incident makes him staunch secular and an anti-colonialist. He has three daughters and two sons. Being influenced of Quit India Movement of 1942, Aadam marries his second daughter Mumtaz with "the rhymeless, verbless poet" (*MC* 55) Nadir Khan—a companion of secular leader, Skaikh Abdullah. Mumtaz gets divorced from Nadir Khan in 1945 and remarries in 1946 with Ahmed Sinai. It is her second husband who names her as Amina Sinai. Ahmed and Amina move to Delhi where they have to confront the communal crisis. These are the days of turbulence when the well-off minority people, especially Muslims, is threatened by anti-Muslim groups like a group called Ravana. Ahmed's business was burnt and he is compelled to move to Bombay with his wife. He gets a home in Buckingham Villa. The owner of the Villa William Methwold restricts the new residents from bringing any kind of change in the Villa until the political power of the nation is formally transferred into the hands of the indigenous political leadership.

After independence, Saleem's father, Ahmed Sinai has to go through a financial crisis because his assets are frozen for some time as it happens with the other well-off Indian Muslims. This is a very tough time for Indian Muslims who are seen as the advocates of Pakistan in spite of their decision of not migrating to Pakistan. They are considered as if they are the disloyal citizens of India. In some cases, it was thought that "the Indian Muslims were hostages to be held in security for the treatment of Hindus in Pakistan" (Hasan 52). When Mahatma Gandhi was assassinated on 30 January 1948, it was doubtful whether a Muslim was the assassinator or a Hindu. This suspense created an atmosphere of utter confusion and horror especially for Muslims for "if a Muslim did this thing there will be hell to pay..." (*MC* 196). Such horrible circumstances compelled every Muslim to be conscious for her/his life even at the place where s/he has passed all her/his life. The narrator's family was terrified and they "remained [confined] within the walls of Buckingham Villa (put furniture against the doors...)" (*MC* 197).

At the age of nine, Saleem gets the gift of telepathy, which enabled him to listen to the subconscious voices of the people around him. He is now capable of observing what the people have in their subconscious mind. Through the introduction of the gift of telepathy, Rushdie enabled Saleem Sinai to present the cosmopolitan's traumatic experiences which remain neglected for a long time. With the help of this gift Saleem is able to record and latter on narrate the simultaneous events in a *heteroglossial* manner. Various voices intermingle with each other at a single time and became a sort of 'All India Radio', which could observe heterogeneous experiences of the other cosmopolitan individuals in heterogeneous societies and give voice to such experience.

When Saleem Sinai is ten years old, his ayah, Mary Pareira discloses the secret that he is not the son of his present parents but of Hindu parents. After the discovery of his birth he never finds himself at home while he is at his own home and amidst of his own people. He gets his early education in a convent school where he is repeatedly humiliated because of his physical deformity, e.g. the scares on his face, a big nose and a bald patch on his scalp. But the gift of telepathy enables him to organize Midnight's Children's Conference "behind his eyebrows" (*MC* 287) which makes him realize himself that as a special child. In 1958, he and his family leave India to go to Karachi (Pakistan), where they reside for four years. In these years, he and his family are treated as inferiors in comparison to the indigenous people of the city. They are regarded merely as the poor relatives of General Zulfikar Ali or else as "*Muhajir*".[1] In Pakistan, he loses his contact with the other midnight's children. But Saleem is after all capable of making himself to be identified as a special boy and better than Saleem is after all capable of making himself to be identified as a special boy and better than Zulfikar's own son, Zafar. This movement from India to Pakistan provides him with a creative opportunity to be able to adjust among the strangers and in a new locality. But he remains reserved and distant from his uncle's family and other indigenous people and lives a life of seclusion. General Zulfikar trusts him and keeps him as a companion in some of his secret missions.

Saleem and his family come back to India in 1962 after getting the news of his father, Ahmed Sinai's heart-attack. His family reunites and becomes happy once again. His return does not only make his family reunion possible but he also gets reunited with other five hundred and eighty-one midnight's children. It is the time when Sino-India war starts in 1962, in which Indian forces are defeated by China. Saleem witnesses through the gift of telepathy that due to the Sino-India war, Chinese-Indians have to suffer a lot. The narrator says that the "mob attacked Chinese shoemakers, curio dealers and restaurateurs...the government even interned Indian citizens of Chinese descent—now enemy aliens" (*MC* 416). Thousands of Chinese-Indians from Kolkata, Darjeeling, Kalimpong, Jamshedpur, Mumbai and Northeast are arrested and send to the prison camps at Deoli in Rajasthan where they are kept for five years in terrible conditions and extreme surveillance. These people are accused of being spies and most of them are forcibly deported to China. Only some of them are allowed to return to their respective homes. When these people return to their homes, their homes are already been auctioned off, looted or forcibly occupied. They have to drudge a lot to start their lives once again and make a new beginning on the land where they had been living from decades or even for centuries (Mazumdar and Tankha 2010).

Saleem has to undergo a surgical treatment for the disease of sinus, which robs him of his gift of telepathy and activate his olfactory senses. With his hypersensitive nose, he becomes "capable of smelling sadness and joy, of sniffing out intelligence and stupidity" (*MC* 430). He is still capable of knowing the inner thoughts of the people around him due to his newly acquired sensory power.

Saleem and his family shift permanently to Pakistan at the end of the year 1962, where he "began to learn the secret aromas of the world, the heady but quick-fading perfume of new love" (*MC* 427). His father starts a new business and his family begins a new life. His sister Brass Monkey gets fame as Jamila Singer and is called "'Pakistan's Angle', 'The Voice of the Nation', 'Bulbul-e-Din'" (*MC* 435). But during the Indo-Pak war of 1965, Lahore (Pakistan) was burnt by Indian army and Saleem loses all his family members except his sister Jamila Singer in Pakistan and maternal Uncle Mustafa Aziz in India. In this war, Saleem also loses his memory. But his olfactory senses still enable him to be a proud young man. Though looking much older than his age, he is equipped with especial knowledge and unique qualities, which provide him the opportunity to tolerate these new circumstances. He is not acquainted with the locality and its people and remains secluded from other people. Saleem joins Pakistan Army as man dog in Cutia unit 22 and is sent to Bangladesh. The war of Bangladesh provides him with another opportunity to experience the alienation of people who are treated as aliens in their own country. He witnesses there the massacre of common people. Once again, the blood flows like mercurochrome in the lawns. It was not only the killing of innocent human beings but rape, torture, arson, burning of the slums and villages and living villagers: "a maidan [field] in which lady doctors were being bayoneted before they were raped, and raped again before they were shot. Above them and behind them, the cool white minaret of the mosque stared blindly down upon the scene" (*MC* 524-25). All this is done by the Muslims with the Muslims of other states.

After Indo-Pak war of 1965 and the triumph of India in Bangladesh in 1971, Indian Muslims confront discriminations in different socio-political spheres. Saleem's uncle Mustafa Aziz is a senior Civil Servant and number two in his Department but he was required of 'being a chamcha [henchman]' and "clearly the victim of anti-Muslim prejudice, in a contradictory but absolute loyalty to the government of the day" (*MC* 546). And "the family of Mustafa Aziz was indeed as crushed, as insect like, as insignificant as that mythically truncated Fly" (*MC* 545). On 16 December 1971 Saleem comes back to India with the help of one of his companion of midnight's children, Parvati, the witch through "the basket of invisibility" (*MC* 482). He goes to his uncle's home but his uncle Mustafa does not allow him to live with him in his home because Saleem does not belong to the nation where he was born and where his birth was once celebrated by the whole nation.

On 25 June 1975, Indira Gandhi imposes Emergency on India which results in the "suspension of civil rights, and censorship of the press, and armoured-units-on-special-alert, and arrest-of-subversive-elements" (*MC* 585). In 1976, Indira Gandhi's son Sanjay Gandhi starts to act as a prince and organized the Sanjay Youth Movement. Sanjay Gandhi is determined to the beautification of cities and to stop the growing population of India. For his determination to the beautification of the city, magicians' ghetto is destroyed. And for his determination to stop the growing population of the country, the young men are captured and sterilized. Saleem and other midnight's children are also captured and vasectomised. The Emergency is ended on 18 Jan. 1977.

Though Saleem is born in India and passed initial eleven years of his life in India, he leaves India in 1958, and lives for twelve or thirteen years in Pakistan where he lose all his family as well his memory, and later on spends few months of his life in East Pakistan (now Bangladesh). He returns to India in 1971. Saleem witnesses the prominent historical events of these three countries: India, Pakistan and Bangladesh. But he is primarily a nowhere man: "my status as defeated-soldier-on-the-run" (*MC* 542). He does not belong to any country, though he is always capable to be adjusted in any community and could confront any circumstances. Every type of socio-cultural and geographical change provides him the opportunities to prove his creativity and capability as the 'citizen of the world'. He and his family are always displaced by force, whether social or political, but never by their will: "In my family, we always go when we're pushed.... The boatman Tai drove my grandfather from Kashmir; Mercurochrome chased him out of Amritsar; the collapse of her life under the carpets led directly to my mother's departure from Agra; and many headed monsters sent my father to Bombay" (*MC* 118-19).

Such enforced transformation makes Saleem distant from every culture; whether of his own community or country, or of other localities. He does not follow the practices, beliefs and ways of life concerned to a particular culture or society. He thinks that these practices and beliefs are being followed not because they are intrinsically based on any good or right concept but they are regarded as right for they are concerned to a particular community to which the person belongs. And such practices make a man conservative on the level of humanity. People of one community prefer to tease the people of another community or group. Saleem and his family have to confront the similar circumstances. Ahmed Sinai's business is ruined when he is in Delhi and is demanded extortion money by the anti-Muslim group for the safety of his business in a communal crisis when India is about to achieve her independence: independence from every evil.

Though he is a stranger in the magicians' ghetto, he is welcomed there and finds himself attached to all the other strangers and identifies himself with them. Saleem is greeted as "Saleem Kismati, Lucky Saleem" (*MC* 541) in the magicians' ghetto because after his arrival in the ghetto, the magicians found more opportunities to getting money and new ideas for their magical tricks which make their talent more attractive: "Other artistes began to his new peaks of achievement—jugglers managed to keep one thousand and one ball in the air at a time, and a fakir's as-yet-untrained protégée strayed on to a bed of hot coals, only to stroll across it unconcerned, as though she had acquired her mentor's gift by osmosis" (*MC* 540-41).

Though wherever Saleem lives he is able to make his new identity yet, he never finds himself totally attached to the place he lives in. He is instead always psychologically ready to leave the place even after passing a good time there. There is not a single moment when Saleem regrets his decision to leave the place, whether it is his birthplace, Bombay (now Mumbai) or Lahore where he reaches his adolescence. There is a lack of attachment, which helps Saleem to move away from social disorganization and insecurity and enables him to remain mobile. He is never limited to a particular geographical region and remains emancipated from every limitation concerned to the geographical boundaries. He remains reserved and distant from indigenous people but he is at the same time flexible and ready to do everything for them, whether it is to accompany General Zulfikar on his secret political mission or it is his marriage with Parvati—the witch when she is pregnant by Shiva, another midnight's child and Saleem's rival.

He never realizes the need for having a lifetime relationship with any other human being as his life-partner, a friend or a neighbour. Saleem has never been acquainted with the locals but he is always appreciated by them because of his deep knowledge of human beings, which has been gained by him due to his gift of telepathy and olfactory senses. He is always surrounded by different cultures, e.g. he was born from Vanita (a Hindu) and William Methwold (a Christian), brought up in a Muslim family, got his education in a mission school and his friends are Hindu and Christian and he has to move to a Muslim country Pakistan with his family. And finally, he lives with the atheist magicians: "They were a people who denied the supernatural, they were artistes, and like all performers had an implicit faith in luck, good-luck-and-bad-luck" (*MC* 540). Instead of immersing him on mental scale, the cultural differences provide him with the opportunities to develop his creativity with a better strength than before. These cultural differences seem superfluous to Saleem. He lifts himself above to the sphere of worldwide chaos of cultural diversities and competing groups. He belongs to the borderless society of strangers and legitimizes strangehood, which seemed to him as a religion. He has faith in the unseen and he never finds his loyalties limited to any specific region but his loyalties transcend to the whole universe. Hence, he is emotionally moved with the same intensity when he comes to know the horrible experiences of Chinese Indians as he was moved with the horrible experiences of Indian Muslims.

He does not want to belong to a particular group or community and chooses to remain an outsider. But he remains at the same time attached to the whole humanity and is thus able to feel the sufferings of all the communities. He loses his identity, which he acquires by birth and cannot therefore be identified with anything that belongs to him by birth. Wherever he goes, he invents a unique identity for himself. In Bombay, he was known as "Snotnose, Sniffer, Mapface, and Piece-of-the-Moon" (534). When he joins Pakistan Army as man dog in Cutia unit 22, he is called Buddha because he had "learned the art of submission, and did only what was required of him" (488). He is treated as inferior because he does not follow the ways of life of the young people of his age. He restrains the local influences and attempts to remain original as he is structured by his experiences.

He is acquainted with the subtle and emotional aspect of transition. He learns new ways of thinking very easily because he can listen to the subconscious voices of the people, and can smell the intention of the people around him. Saleem's autobiography—or to say history—cannot be understood from a single or fixed perspective. His personality has the prism-like characteristics. Saleem is not a rootless traveller. He travels through the different localities and manages to remain loyal to each locality he lives in. His primary motive is the happiness of the mankind. He wants to rearrange history so that the misconceptions and misinterpretations can be erased from the midst of common people. He employs a perspective of 'dialogic imagination', which encourages him to accept the coexistence of his rivals. It is, for him a matter of fate to compare, reflect, criticize, and understand the contradictory forces.

In this novel, Rushdie presents the journey of a nation from a secular state to the state where communal card is used to get more and more political power, which in turn affects the life of every human being; whether it is of the simpleton or of powerful elite, of indigenous or a cosmopolitan. In his real life, Rushdie is struggling for his liberal ideals and freedom of expression and through his novels; he has raised his voice not only for a cosmopolitan but also for the whole humanity. Rushdie retells the tragedy of the minority, which usually occurs at the time of socio-political chaos in most of the nations. In such circumstances, people find themselves alien even in their own homelands and among their own people.

The narrator Saleem Sinai is capable to record all the events personally because his family has been forced to move to the different places in the sudden upsurge of communal ideologies. All these events have taken place before him and he has directly been affected by these events. The other source of his information is the experience of five hundred and eighty other midnight's children, who are expelled and who act as a gang which was spread all over the length and breadth of the country and whose headquarter were behind my eyebrows—'Midnight's Children's Conference' (*MC* 287). The novel *Midnight's Children* is tracing the betrayal of optimism that the common man have had after independence in the name of secularism and equal civil rights to all: "The disease of optimism, in those days, once again attained epidemic proportions" (*MC* 416). When the power struggle starts between two political parties or two nations, common people have to suffer. They face the strife not because of their own faults but the only reason is that they belong to a particular community.

Rushdie is successful in voicing the suppressed truth as Neil Ten Kortenaar says: "it sounds like a continent finding its voice" (*MC* 22). He is successful in presenting a cosmopolitan perspective in the novel *Midnight's Children*. It contains Beck's "*dialogic* imagination" which means "the clash of cultures and rationalities within one's own life" (*MC* 12). Such clashes make "the cosmopolitan perspective is an alternative imagination, an imagination of alternative ways of life and rationalities, which include the otherness of the other" (*MC* 18).

Note

1. I used the word "*Muhajir*" not from the text but as a metaphor to show the helpless condition of Indian Muslim immigrants in Pakistan. Though they were promised to get equal rights, yet they were deceived and treated as refugees.

Works Cited

Beck, Ulrich. *The Cosmopolitan Society and its Enemies*. Web. 13 Oct. 2012.

Hannerz, Ulf. "Cosmopolitans and Locals in World Culture." *Theory Culture Society.* Web. 12 Oct. 2012.

Hasan, Mushirul. "Adjustment and Accommodation: Indian Muslims after Independence". *Social Scientist,* Vol. 18 (1990): 48-65. Web. 08 June 2012.

Jani, Pranav. *Decentering Rushdie: Cosmopolitanism and the Indian Novel in English*. USA: Ohio State University, 2010.

Kortenaar, Neil Ten. "*Midnight's Children* and the Allegory of History". *Rushdie's Midnight's Children: A Book of Readers*. Ed. Meenakshi Mukherjee. Delhi: Pencraft International, 2003. 28-48.

Mazumdar, Jaideep and Ishan Tankha. "Shame: Wages of Loyalty." Web. 05 June 2012.

Niesen, Peter. *Bentham's Cosmopolitanism, Theory and Practice*. Web. 11 Oct. 2012.

Rushdie, Salman. *Midnight's Children*. London: Vintage Books, 2008.

6

The Dichotomous Nature of Decolonisation of India in Salman Rushdie's *Midnight's Children*

Sutanuka Ghosh Roy

What is history? Who writes it? Where does it start? Are these divine inspirations behind annals? When finally death comes how one should react to it? Is it possible to leave a trace of one's existence? Can a nation's history be represented by a single character? What is the exact nature of a nation? Ultimately what is the nature of history itself? History, after all, is not something to be read only. It is not possible for a person to be solely a history-reader. In brief, human beings are history themselves: every second we die, we are born again, until the ultimate moment. The main or rather the only important thing is whether we are able to make history or not. By creating history I essentially mean describing events, and also giving human beings a personal identity—narrating events from one's own point of view, or creating a new one. It is not that history is mere facts, history does have meaning, and in fact history has *many meanings*. In post-modern literature there are diverse opinions about history. For Rushdie, the iconic writer, history is individual, and history's meaning is determined by the present.

Salman Rushdie's novel, *Midnight's Children* published in 1981, is a modern epic, depicting India's decolonisation with the waning influence of British rule. In 1993, *Midnight's Children* was adjudged the 'Booker of Bookers', the best novel to have won the Booker prize in its first twenty-five years. The novel is divided into three books. The book begins with the story of

Sinai family and the readers are led with the events particularly up to India's Independence and partition. "Born at the stroke of midnight on August 15, 1947, at the precise moment of India's independence, the infant Saleem Sinai is celebrated in the press and welcomed by Prime Minister Nehru himself: "Dear Baby Saleem, 'My belated congratulations on the happy accident of your moment of birth! You are the newest bearer of that ancient face of India which is also eternally young. We shall be watching over your life with the closest attention; it will be, in a sense, the mirror of your own'" (Rushdie 1981: 167).

But this coincidence of birth has consequences, Saleem is not prepared for; his telepathic powers connects him with 1,000 other 'midnight's children'—all born in the initial hour of India's independence—are imbued with special powers. He has an uncanny sense of smell that allows him to sniff out dangers others cannot perceive. Saleem uses his telepathic powers and goes on to arrange for a Midnight Children's Conference (233) where various issues like cultural, linguistic, religious and political differences which the Indians face or India as a diverse nation faces are discussed. He comes in contact with thousands of other children born closest to the stroke of midnight mainly Shiva "of the knees" and Parvati, "Parvati-the-Witch". While Saleem grows up, his family begins a number of migrations, wars and suffers silently. Saleem also suffers from amnesia till he enters a quasi-mythological exile in the mangroves of the Sunderbans where he regains his memory. He reconnects with his childhood friends. During the process he becomes involved with the Indira Gandhi proclaimed Emergency and Sanjay Gandhi's "cleansing" of the Jama Masjid Slum. As a consequence he becomes a political prisoner. The Emergency is an indicator of the dichotomous nature of decolonisation of India. Inextricably linked to his nation, Saleem's life is also a mixture of disasters and triumphs that mirrors the course of the dichotomous nature of decolonisation of modern India.

Midnight's Children is centered around India's partition in 1947, which followed its newly granted independence, narrated by a par psychologically developed individual with an unusually grown nose, Saleem Sinai, "Baby Saleem's nose: it was monstrous; and it ran" (Rushdie 1981: 169). Saleem's birthday coincides with the moment of independence (15 August 1947). Exactly after thirty years, fearing his imminent death and the subsequent urgency of leaving a legacy of his very own existence in this world, he is compelled to tell his story to Padma his would be wife. We are taken back during World War I to the time when his grandparents Aadam Aziz and Naseem Ghani met and married, and then, slowly we begin to see Saleem closer and closer until we are back at the time of the narration.

Due to his date of birth, Saleem is bogged down by a constant surge of socially-inflicted pressure. He then discovers he has telepathic abilities and can read people's minds, he also discovers that this ability is also spread amongst other children of his generation: Telepathy, then: the inner monologues of all the so-called teeming millions, of masses and classes alike, jostled for space within my head (Rushdie 1981: 232).

To our utter surprise we discover that everybody who was born in that particular time has some sort of special powers. These are 'midnight's children':

> every one of whom was, through some freak of biology, or perhaps owing to some preternatural power of the moment, or just conceivably by sheer coincidence (although synchronicity on such a scale would stagger even C.G. Jung), endowed with features, talents or faculties which can only be described as miraculous. (Rushdie 1981: 271)

A boy from Kerala has the ability to step through mirrors and reemerge through any reflective surface, including the polished metal bodies of automobiles. A blue-eyed child from Kashmir can alter his or her sex by stepping into water. Still another, Parvati, is a true witch, with powers of conjuration and sorcery. To Shiva, Saleem's changeling brother, "the hour had given the gifts of war (of Rama, who could draw the undrawable bow; of Arjuna and Bhima; the ancient prowess of Kurus and Pandavas united, unstoppably, in him!)..." (Rushdie 1981: 277).

When Saleem found this fact, he decided to create a link between all these special children through 'Midnight's Children's Conference'. However, we are to remember that this is not the only story thread in this book: we also see a parallel development of the plot, namely Saleem's own family's difficulties and peregrinations to survive plagues, wars and his own mental issues (amnesia, cured in the Sunderbans jungle). Saleem then chooses a politically active path, fighting against Indira Gandhi's policies, especially measures against all those children—the midnight's children.

> Dark clouds were gathering in political skies as well: in Bihar, where corruption inflation, hunger illiteracy landlessness ruled the roost, Jaya-Prakash Narayan led a coalition of students and workers against the governing Indira Congress: in Gujarat, there were riots, railway trains were burned, and Morarji Desai went on a fast-unto-death to bring down the corrupt government of the Congress (under Chimanbhai Patel) in that drought-ridden state.... (Rushdie 1981: 575)

Subsequently, to Gandhi's political fall, the prisoners are set free. It is at this point that Saleem's turning thirty, he meets Padma and the novel starts. Exactly a year later, on his birthday, he marries Padma and predicts his death on the same day. In the end of his life, Saleem decides to turn his eyes to history. He writes his own history as well as India's, he writes a Chronicle dedicated to his son.

It is when Saleem moves to Pakistan with his family, the novel swirls into a serious concern with the political and military history of the two rival nations in the sub-Himalayan triangle. Under the surface of comedy, the tone darkens, it becomes Swiftian. There are passages of mordantly ironic satire juxtaposed against scenes of phantasmagoric horror. We are literally shocked by the story of the wife of Saleem's uncle Mustapha Aziz, who has been passed over forty-seven times for the headship of his department, is driven insane,

> By a life in which she has been required to begin 'being a chamcha' (to forty-seven separate and successive wives

> of number-ones whom she had previously alienated by her manner of colossal condescension when they had been wives of number-threes.... If Indira Gandhi had asked him to commit suicide, Mustapha Aziz would have ascribed it to anti-Muslim bigotry but also defended the statesmanship of the request, and naturally, performed the task without daring (or even wishing) to demur. (Rushdie 1981: 546)

Rushdie's story is an integral part of Indian Heritage (the readers feel as if not its personification itself), mingled with sunlight and darkness. Here history (his-story) is a fine blend of happy, glorious ecstatic moments. There is a sense of pride in being part of this wonderful mosaic.

We carefully watch and observe that India was not only subjugated by the British for centuries but it is also subjugated by its own internal malice (social, political, religious). Rushdie intentionally brings in the pickle metaphor. In the novel Indian history is compared with pickles. For pickles bring both pleasure, and a sore taste in the mouth. He writes in pickles too:

> What I hope to immortalize in pickles as well as words: that condition of the spirit in which the consequences of acceptance could not be denied, in which an overdose of reality gave birth to a miasmic longing for flight into the safety of dreams.... But the jungle, like all refuges, was entirely other—was both less and more—than he had expected. 'I am glad', my Padma says, 'I am happy you ran away'. But I insist: not I. He. He, the Buddha. Who, until the snake, would remain not-Saleem; who, in spite of running from, was still separated from his past; although he clutched, in his limpet fist, a certain silver spittoon? (Rushdie 1981: 503)

We the readers have to remember that the taste of pickles is not exactly sweet, at the same time it is not bad either, rather it has a complementary taste (like salt) which gives sense to the particular food we are eating. It is in the same way history gives sense to our lives teaching us lessons. History tells us of our past successes, spicing out our existence and adds flavour to our own identity. That is why Saleem chooses to write history and not fighting death.

Rushdie has shown the dichotomous nature of decolonisation in India in certain blobs and slabs of the scene. Here he writes of,

> [P]articularly at times when the state takes reality into its own hands, and sets about distorting it, altering the past to fit its present needs, then the making of the alternative realities of art, including the novel of memory becomes politicized.... Writers and politicians are natural rivals. Both groups try to make the world in their own images; they fight for the same territory. And the novel is one way of denying the official, politicians' version of truth. (Jain 218)

An analysis shows that *Midnight's Children* has depicted the 'State truth' about the war in Bangladesh. We have an epic in our hands. The obvious comparisons are to Gunter Grass in *The Tin Drum* and to Gabriel Garcia Marquez in *One Hundred Years of Solitude*. Rushdie takes a dig at both nations. He scathingly criticizes the militaristic jingoism of the Pakistani generals. At the same time he exposes the hypocrisy, cruelty, and corruption of the Emergency years. Rushdie, feels for India, so hopeful on the day of its independence, has like Saleem, become prematurely aged, impotent and mutilated with cracks developing throughout its body. Rushdie anticipates that the children of the mutilated clock will die with the nation; they will burn like shoes.

Meanwhile Shiva the destroyer, now a war hero, bestrides the land. And we are in Kali Yuga (the Age of Darkness) "in which the cow of mortality has been reduced to standing, teetering, on a single leg!" Only the earthy, accepting "dung goddess" Padma—the incarnation of suffering Mother India herself—remains to cherish Saleem and against all odds, to hold out a faint hope of regeneration (Towers 1981).

Midnight's Children depict the changes which came with colonialism in the native culture and consciousness and which then shaped the histories of these two nations—India and

Bangladesh. Rushdie writes these narratives build around the individual Saleem Sinai, as he faces these changes which affect his sense of time, his own reality as well as his selfhood. The crucial problem taken up in the novel is whether the common masses and India as a whole nation can face the surging tide over the forces of cultural and political imperialism of the British. The characters in this novel are the different aspects of the social and historical consciousness of the Indian people, delved out in figures drawn from the myths of their collective psyche as well as from their recent political history. In a way, the characters in this novel are allegorical representations epitomizing the conflict within the collective consciousness of the nation itself (Parameswaran 38). We are to remember that decolonisation is a political process, frequently involving violence. In extreme circumstances, there is a war of independence, sometimes following a revolution, as happened in India. More often, it has been noticed that there is a dynamic cycle where negotiations fail, minor disturbances ensue resulting in suppression by the police and military forces, escalating into more violent revolts that lead to further negotiations until independence is granted.

The British had to finally leave India. In rare cases, the actions of the native population are characterized by nonviolence, with the Indian independence movement led by Mohandas Karam Chand Gandhi being one of the most notable examples, in the entire world, and the violence comes as active suppression from the occupying forces or as political opposition from forces representing minority local communities who feel threatened by the prospect of independence. For example, there was a war of independence in French Indochina, while in some countries in French West Africa (excluding the Maghreb countries) decolonisation resulted from a combination of insurrection and negotiation. The process is only complete when the *de facto* government of the newly independent country is recognized as the *de jure* sovereign state by the community of nations. Despite these efforts though, the British Government continued to slowly lose their control of the Raj. The end of World War II allowed India, in addition to various other European colonies, to take advantage of the postwar chaos that existed in Europe during the mid-1940s. Gandhi, India's independence movement leader took the advantage in conducting a peaceful resistance to the British Empire's attempts to retake control of their "crown jewel". He became a symbol of both peace and opposition to British imperialism. Many Indian citizens began to view the British as the sole cause of India's violence leading to a new found sense of nationalism among the masses. With this new surge of Indian nationalism, Gandhi was eventually successful to garner the support needed to push back the British and create an independent India in 1947.

While pointing out the dichotomous nature of the decolonisation of India Rushdie is equally outraged by the English imposition on India as well as Indira Gandhi's 'Emergency' which did away with the liberal democracy in India. The dichotomy of decolonisation of India that we have discussed is not the only one which the actual writing challenges and dispels. A further closely related dichotomy of decolonisation of India, and one that is as pernicious as the one just looked at is between the "inner world" of the personal and the individual of the writer himself and the "outer world" of the public and the social, moving further "out words" from even there to the general and the universal. This again is a dichotomy that the intellectual temper of our times disfavours but which nevertheless too often seems to covertly make its way back into critical practice. As Rushdie puts it: "To conquer the English may be to complete the process of making ourselves free" (Rushdie 1981: 29).

It is not merely the freedom of Indian or Pakistani independence to which Rushdie refers, nor the process of "reverse-colonialism" in which British immigrants are the articulators of contemporary British cultural consciousness. As a writer enamoured of the experience of life as a member of minority groups, Rushdie mainly pursues artistic and political freedom, in both its social and cultural forms. He desperately attempts to break free from the Manichean binarism between the colonizers and colonized that is precisely at the centre of the colonial ideology. He uses India as a model, in its place offers multiplicity as the chief characteristic of post-independence cultures. We are to remember that the political nature of

Rushdie's use of the word "conquer" is tricky in nature. To conquer there must be a conquered, and hence a freedom won at the expense of another's loss. An upholding of this binarism, in its modified form, between colonisers and colonised is discernible in Rushdie's commentary on his own work and on the situation of the writer in the colonised world. The status of immigrant and a born Briton, however, makes it possible for Rushdie to plumb a multiplicity of commingled faiths, to write of and through a variety of literary sources and traditions, Eastern and Anglo-Western, and Rushdie further realizes that this sense of division and multiplicity ultimately defies any binarism. The readers comprehend that there is a corresponding ambivalence in Rushdie's post-independent India in which the language of the coloniser becomes not a tool for subjugation (in Ngugi Wa Thiong'o's treatise "Decolonizing the Mind" he shows how language is used as a tool for subjugating minds of the colonisers) but ironically one for an uneasy liberation. Rushdie explains:

> There is...an interesting North-South divide in Indian attitudes to English. In the North, in the so-called 'Hindi belt', where the capital, Delhi, is located, it is possible to think of Hindi as a future national language; but in South India, which is at present suffering from the attempts of central government to impose this national language on it, the resentment of Hindi is far greater than English. After spending quite some time in South India, I've become convinced that English is an essential language in India, not only because of its technical vocabularies and the international communication which it makes possible, but also simply to permit two Indians to talk to each other in a tongue which neither party hates. (Rushdie 1981: 17)

A book is not justified by the readers worldwide only by the author's political "worthiness" to write it, but by virtue of the quality of what is written. Rushdie's pluralistic narrative method in *Midnight's Children* expresses the desire for the reader to become aware of the multiple nature of life in India, as a result the readers above all more tolerant of difference: "For God's sake, open the universe a little more!" (Rushdie 1981: 6).

The stereoscopic vision that Rushdie presents in *Midnight's Children* answer the various questions that arise in the mind of the readers while reading the book: First of all everyone wants to find an answer to the enigmatic question—What is India? The readers ponder how well can it be represented in a post-modern world apart from it's the relationship of the coloniser and colonised? Rushdie shows that there is no one particular vision of post-independence India; in a view ironically similar to the colonial observations of other writers like Kipling and Forster, India cannot be judged by a single reading. India is an enigma itself. As Saleem puts it in *Midnight's Children*:

> There are many stories to tell, too many, such an excess of intertwined lives events miracles places rumours, so dense a commingling of the improbable and mundane! I have been a swallower of lives; and to know me, just one of me, you'll have to swallow the lot as well. Consumed multitudes are jostling and shoving inside of me.... (Rushdie 1981: 4)

Rushdie points out in *Imaginary Homelands* (1991) that India is a continent the size of Europe. It contains the world's largest "democracy" and is "home" to a sixth of the world's population, who nevertheless remain disunited by the lack of a common race, religion, or culture. The chief obstacle to a unified India is communalism, the religious hatred that is the expression of a basic, fundamental, and often bloody opposition between the Muslims and the Hindus.

In *Midnight's Children*, Rushdie offers a vision of a post-independence generation, the "midnight's children" of the novel's title born in the hour of midnight on the Indian day of independence (August 15th, 1947). They themselves are succeeded by a generation of Indian pragmatists. We find that Rushdie's vision of a generation of Indian pragmatists succeeding that of "midnight's children" is essentially optimistic, and by Rushdie's own candid admission, increasingly unlikely to be borne out in reality:

> My India has always been based on ideas of multiplicity, pluralism, hybridity: ideas to which the ideologies of the communalists are diametrically opposed. To my mind, the defining image of India is the crowd, and a crowd is by its nature superabundant, heterogeneous, many things at once. But the India of the communalists is none of these things. (Rushdie 1991: 14)

The presence of the British or what the common Indians call "Raj" is the unannounced shadow of the novel and Saleem and his alter-ego Shiva "of the knees" represent the nexus of ambivalence that belies the construction of a unitary identity of post-independent India.

In *Midnight's Children*, Rushdie uses the superabundant, polyglot, and heterogeneous India as a metaphor for the multiplicity of influences, styles, conversations, and ideas of India's contemporary culture. In an increasingly post-modern world the centre of India has shifted from the axis of London to a prolificacy of cultural centers. In today's India, national or literary identities no longer need be written or read in binary fashion. The basic notion of a centre and periphery defamed in terms of nationhood no longer holds in post-independent India. The literary debate which still continues concerning the dissolution of the British Empire and the subsequent literatures which have emerged from its fragmentation is still underdetermined in relation to the adherence to the binary paradigm of colonizer and colonized. The reluctance to abandon the centre-periphery debate in the context of post-independent Anglo-Indian fiction is essentially nostalgia for the Raj, and also for its basic semantic simplicity. We cannot deny that there is still a relationship between England and India at the same time we realize that it is no longer characterized in centre-periphery terms which encourage binary thinking. As Aadam Aziz comes to the realization about the intersection of Western and Eastern medicine in *Midnight's Children*:

> In the compartment the new Amina Sinai sat (in mint condition) with her feet on the green tin trunk which had been an inch too high to fit under the seat. With

> her sandals bearing down on the locked museum of her father's achievements she sped away into her new life, leaving Aadam Aziz behind to dedicate himself to an attempt to fuse the skills of Western and hakimi medicine, an attempt which would gradually wear him down, convincing him that the hegemony of superstition, mumbo-jumbo and all things magical would never be broken in India, because the hakims refused to co-operate; and as he aged and the world became less real he began to doubt his own beliefs, so that by the time he saw the God in whom he had never been able to believe or disbelieve he was probably expecting to do so. (Rushdie 1981: 85)

In *Midnight's Children*, Rushdie questions the authenticity by introducing the swapping of the children, from different castes, at birth. He does this intentionally to show the acts so as to reverse binary arguments, confuses forever the figures of good and evil with their opposites. Rushdie identifies the issue of re-appropriation as symptomatic of the English literature of cross-pollination. Rushdie puts it as: "What seems to me to be happening is that those people who were once colonized by the language are now rapidly remaking it, domesticating it, becoming more and more relaxed about the way they use it—assisted by the English language's enormous flexibility and size, they are carving out territories for themselves within its frontiers" (Rushdie 1991: 14).

The readers need to emphasize the direction that Rushdie indicates when he says "they are carving out territories for themselves within its frontiers"—there is no necessary implication of a writing back to the centre—emphatically not a writing back to an "authentic" source of a hieratic English literature "proper". On the other hand, the readers should well understand that, the suggestion is that of a consolidation within and a radiating out from the frontiers of an English language belonging to no one centre. As we read through the pages, we feel that Rushdie is engaged in the literary exercise of bringing the Third World into the First and thereby changing both worlds in the process, but in some ways he himself is caught in this position of dubiety. The metaphor of fragmentation and multiplicity is enhanced through Rushdie's use of magic realism in *Midnight's Children* which allows him, as Mujeebuddin Syed puts it, "freedom...to move between the Modernist/ postmodernist and folkloric traditions of India. Out of the dialects of this juxtaposition comes the peculiar, hybrid tale of India, incorporating a complex web of Hindu and Islamic (and even Christian) motifs, the philosophies of maya and karma and Sufism and interweaving private/personal and public/political histories of the Indian subcontinent" (97).

Rushdie employs a magic realism (through Saleem) in order to explore the multiplicity of representations of India. He employs this device to defy Western world's expectations of closure in a self-consuming narrative which is fraught with ruptures, and also with the double-codedness of the luminal. As Saleem says,

> Consumed multitudes are jostling and shoving inside me; and guided only by the memory of a large white bed sheet with a roughly circular hole some seven inches in diameter cut into the centre, clutching at the dream of that holey, mutilated square of linen, which is my talisman, my open-sesame, I must commence the business of remaking my life from the point at which it really began, some thirty-two years before anything as obvious, as present, as my clock-ridden, crime-stained birth. (Rushdie 1981: 9-10)

Midnight's Children offers a departure, then, from the binary configurations latent in the cultural analysis which is pioneered by works as Edward Said's *Orientalism.* In the same, Said uses a model of imperial hegemony essentially characterised by a Western intellectual tradition which first creates its own versions of Oriental cultures and subsequently imposes these on Oriental peoples in act of denigration. Said deftly points out a tautologous hegemony, in which the West justified its own domination of the Orient through a "fake" reading of Oriental culture, which it then sought to "civilize" by an act of cultural subjugation. However, as Anthony Cohen points out, "this kind of analysis of dominated cultures is open for debate "because it confuses the form of indigenous response with its substance" (Rushdie 1981: 3).

One has to remember, what Cohen seems to have in mind is that although the indigenous response might be perceived as a form of cultural retreat, in substance it was not. In *Midnight's Children* this is skillfully borne out in the opening section of the novel where the intrusive narrator comments briefly on the corrosive influence of Gandhi in India in 1919:

> Leaflet newspaper mosque and wall are crying: Hartal! Which is to say, literally speaking, a day of mourning, of stillness, of silence? But this is India in the heyday of the Mahatma, when even language obeys the instructions of Gandhiji, and the word has acquired, under his influence, new resonances...because Gandhi has decreed that the whole of India shall, on that day, come to a halt. To mourn, in peace, the continuing presence of the British. (Rushdie 1981: 37)

However, with India which became independent just three decades ago, historically what is conceived as an indigenous retreat in the face of the colonial legacy was turned around into an assertive stance by the late 1960s and the indigenous "badge" (what Cohen calls the "putative stigma of cultural inferiority") worn as a kind of valediction, which is nothing but an inverted symbol of superiority. Herein lays the dichotomous nature of decolonization of India. Rushdie does not, however, merely supplant the era of Indian independence within a wider, post-modern notion of universal pluralism. Rushdie knows very well that, the Indian continent already contains such pluralism: far from being subsumed by it, India itself is still subsuming. Pluralism itself is an Indian metaphor. Rushdie is stringently opposed to this subtle form of cultural amnesia in overcoming not so much a history of displacement, as one of the determination to exert control over destiny. He boldly asserts that India does not require a legitimating mode, but for Rushdie the annunciation of this sloughing off is the "chutnification of history" (Rushdie 1981: 459). It is the peculiar nature of Indian society that it marks a resistance to the binary configurations that dominate the essential Western thought. The novel clearly brings out the relationship between the colonizer and the colonized. This relationship is not expressed in terms of a static demarcation between imperial discourse and disempowered culture, but in terms of transformation. As Sara Suleri puts it:

> ...if colonial studies is to avoid a binarism that could cause it to atrophy in its own apprehension of difference, it needs to locate an idiom for alterity that can circumnavigate the more monolithic interpretations of cultural empowerment that tend to dominate current discourse. To study the rhetoric of the British Raj in both its colonial and postcolonial manifestation is therefore to attempt to break down the incipient schizophrenia of a critical discourse that seeks to represent domination and subordination as though the two were mutually exclusive terms. Rather than examine a binary rigidity between those terms—which is an inherently Eurocentric strategy—this critical field would be better served if it sought to break down the fixity of the dividing lines between domination and subordination, and if it further questioned the psychic disempowerment signified by colonial encounter. For to interpret the configurations of colonialism in the idiom of such ineluctable divisions is to deny the impact of narrative on a productive disordering of binary dichotomies. (Rushdie 1981: 4)

The decolonisation of India in 1947 resulted into its partition into two nations, India and Pakistan. Surprisingly, it was partitioned along religious lines. This partition granted independence to a supposedly Hindu India, and a Muslim Pakistan. It was further accompanied by large scale ethnic violence and mass migration on both the sides. Almost eighteen million people comprising of Hindus, Sikhs and Muslims became refugees forever. Almost one million people were killed in ethnic violence. Large number refugees migrated to the UK and the US. Women from both the sides were the worst sufferers. Thus technically the two nations became 'free', and this freedom was achieved at the cost of innocent lives.

For Rushdie, contemporary India is born with the magically empowered children of the novel's title on the day of Indian independence: August 15, 1947. The opposition asserted as between coloniser and colonised, which Suleri's discourse seeks to deconstruct and elaborate, has shifted from within India itself to the wider picture of India as a nation already arrived in the global scenario. Conceivably for the first time, as a cohesive national identity within the First World consciousness, this is newly articulate, and jostling with multicultural, multi-vocal identities. At the same time, Rushdie is claiming a place for his nation of origin firmly within the literature of the First World, and cautioning his readers of their own misconception of the processes of history and the aftermath of empire and imperial relations with the Indian East. His novel differs from the other Raj novels written by various authors, in so far as his vision of an Indian internationalism and multiculturalism embraces the politics of pluralism, whereas the Raj novels are more particular in the exploration of a British India.

Works Cited

Cohen, Anthony P. "Culture as Identity: An Anthropologist's View." *New Literary History,* 24:1 (1993): 1-15.

Jain, Jasbir, ed. *Creating Theory: Writers on Writing.* New Delhi: Pencraft International, 2000.

Mujeebuddin, Syed. "*Midnight's Children* and Its Indian Contexts." *Journal of Commonwealth Literature,* 19.2 (1994): 24-41.

Parameswaran, Uma. "Handcuffed to History: Salman Rushdie's Art." *Ariel*, 14.4 (1984): 34-45.

Rushdie, Salman. *Imaginary Homelands: Essays and Criticism.* London: Granta/Viking, 1991.

——. *Midnight's Children* (1981). London: Vintage Books, 2006.

Sara, Suleri. *The Rhetoric of English India.* Chicago: University of Chicago Press, 1992.

Towers, Robert. *On the Indian World Mountain.* Web. 25 Dec. 2013.

7

Interfacing Myth vs. History: A Postcolonial Study of Salman Rushdie's *Midnight's Children*

Ram Bhawan Yadav

The theoretical functioning of the myths in postcolonial English literature, in general, and Indian English novels, in particular, plays a vital role in the reformulation of natives' self and identity. Their implications in the literary texts are analytically interpreted/understood as revival (reformulation) of the Indian history, culture, myth and ethical revelation. The myth in the postcolonial context is termed as a revival of the self which has been degraded and degenerated by the colonial ideologies. So rewriting of mythological events from the *Ramayana,* the *Mahabharata,* the *Vedas,* the *Puranas* and others religious texts are used as a potent tool for the assertion of the self in postcolonial Indian English literature.

In Indian mythology, the concept of myths have conventionally been seen to be more significant and have more explanatory power than history, to some extent myth and history are correlated. Myths have been interpreted and understood as the oldest happenings in form of history of the nation which is believed to be true in the primitive culture. In modern India, it is believed to be the part and parcel of the existing Gandhian views as Ashis Nandy illustrates this: "Because they faithfully contain history, because they are contemporary and, unlike history, are amenable to intervention, myth is the essence of the culture, history being at best superfluous and at worst misleading" (1983: 59). Therefore, Indian writers tend to revive the primitive past of the nation by using in their writings myths, philosophies and literary and religious writings with contemporary national history. In this reference, the observation of T.N. Dhar is inevitable to mention: "Several indigenous forms of arts, literature theories of aesthetics, and various complex and highly refined philosophical systems, missed out on developing a well formulated Indian history and practice of history" (1999: 61). Indian writers in English blend myths with history in their literary works. Partha Chatterjee opines: "myth, history and the contemporary—all become part of the same chronological sequence; one is not distinguished for another; the passage from one to another, consequently is entirely unproblematic" (Chatterjee 123).

In Salman Rushdie's *Midnight's Children* (1981) (*MC*, henceforth), my attempt is to read and examine how Rushdie blends myths with history by using postcolonial theoretical approaches. Rushdie's strategy is to make this mythical implication literal and revive India's past to assert that Indians *too* have their glorious past on which their civilization is based. Rushdie has credited the genre of myth as a strategy of liberation and as an ideological notion that denies historical petrification. Rushdie also employs other generic forms besides myths, such as realism, the comic epic, even science fiction, but his aim is not so much to strive for wholeness, born out of pleasing commingling of genres as it is to portray the state of confusion and alienation that defines postcolonial societies and individuals. Rushdie seems to have conceived the issues of generic strategy in radical poststructuralist terms and relates the notion of liberation with the opposite resistance in postcolonial terms.

Rushdie's novel *MC* takes many issues/stories associated with mythical past of Indian history. The novel initiates its story with the connotation of autobiographical principle which celebrates Saleem's birth "I was born in the city of Bombay" (*MC* 9). But Rushdie subverts this mode of narration instantly by introducing fairy tale catch phrase: "once upon a time" (*MC* 9). So the very beginning of the novel acquires the tone from fairy tale. As Max Luthi says "Saleem continues this subversive process by immediately reverting to an increasing time bound narrative, preferring precise detail to vague collections—a direct contravening of the fairy tale convention" (*MC* 47-48). From the beginning, he exposes to be "handcuffed to history" (*MC* 35), i.e. official and narrator's own version too. In real sense, it is false beginning since Saleem's birth does not take place; it is not mentioned for other hundred and ten pages of the novel. The real beginning of the novel is Saleem's tale of his grandparents who are not his grandparents in real. Similarly, whom he first calls father and mother are not his real parents. So Saleem's narrative of his family has nothing, yet everything, to do with his lineage. Story of the novel is inquisitive and disrupted that indicates a kind of indelibility of history, i.e. biological history as well. Saleem has to initiate at some point if he has to "remake" his life in this narrative. As Edward Said has asserted:

> Beginnings have to be made for each project in such a way as to enable what follows from them. But the act of beginning, necessarily involves an act of delimitation by which something is cut out of great mass of material, separated from the mass, and made to stand for, as well as be a starting point, a beginning. (1983: 16)

In *Midnight's Children*, the meaning of this "cut out" is Saleem's natural lineage that is excised and displaced, suspended and kept hidden for years. This disconnection from the past stimulates the differences which he considers and lives as his own. This starting point is a choice wrought with ambiguity. This has been stated by Homi K. Bhabha as "commensurate with beginning, with speaking or writing in the first place" (1984: 93); this is a kind of ambiguity which can be solved "through the inception of an origin whereby history turns to a kind of myth" (1984: 93). Myth, then in the novel, is where Saleem initiates the beginning and where Rushdie directs this imaginative autobiographer to start.

Aadam Aziz is a hybrid of the first man of the Old Testament and his name starts from A – Z, which contains entire language, which in turn comprises the entire world. He is one of the significant phenomena in the self-created world of Saleem, the one who is legitimate and we are supposed to sallow and accept. He is in search for history and the same infatuated with it. That is why; he is seen to be very fond of every words of Wizened Shikara pilot, Tai: "smile, smile it is your history I am keeping in my mind" (*MC* 16), a history cherished by the memories of the old man or probably recalled in different mode and expressed simply because it is not similar to the conventional history. It adopts a different and difficult course toward the cacophony of discontinuous and interruptive discourse. Tai questions the idea of associating Christ's Crucifixion and Resurrection to the Middle East; on the contrary, he finds him as a balding ascetic in Kashmir, "beard down to his bald" (*MC* 16). Another instance is Jallianwala Bagh Massacre in 1919 where Aziz is saved phenomenally from death by a nose. As the narrator tells about it: "Brigadier Dyer's fifty men put down their machine-guns and go away. They have fired a total of a thousand six hundred and fifty rounds into the unarmed crowd. Of these, one thousand five hundred and sixteen have found their mark, killing and wounding some person" (*MC* 36).

This depiction, presented in the novel, is too precise that it fails to guess exact number of people wounded in the Massacre; the best estimates refer it to be, incidentally, greater than Saleem's body. It is also worth-mentioning that nobody indicates the number of cartridges used in carrying out the heinous act against the humanity. Even General Dyer later on acknowledges this. Karl De Schweintiz speaks about it "he gladly would have used them on the peaceful congregation, but he was unable to maneuver the unwieldy weapons used through the narrow alley way that led to compound" (*MC* 55).

Rushdie here seems to suggest that Saleem's account of history originates from a mythic revival and proceeds toward a mythic cycle. Saleem not only describes the archetypal myth related to nation's culture and history but personal myths too that are the part of other individuals: they penetrate his narrative history, influence and formulate him. He tells Padma that sometimes "legends make history, and become more useful than the facts" (*MC* 47). As the story advances, it becomes quite obvious that to narrate his story successfully, Saleem has to depend on myths, where the facts are discounted, mis-remembered altered, mocked deliberately. The episode of Amritsar massacre can be read as Saleem's subtext as against what Jerome J. McGann terms the colonial critic's "smug superiority" (1985: 1) who claims to understand history objectively with his notion of Eurocentric historiography where facts and figures are used. What Saleem does here is what has been stated by Nietzsche as the 'abuse of history'. So Rushdie/Saleem's writing can be seen as a subversive strategy to dismantle colonial history by highlighting numbers and figures by revisiting the mythic figures. Saleem's own historical self-reflexive facts presented in novel are itself questioned:

> Reading my work, I have discovered an error in chronology. The assassination of Mahatma Gandhi occurs, in these pages, on the wrong date. But I can't say, now, what the actual sequence of events might have been; in my India, Gandhi will continue to die at the wrong date. Does one error invalidate the entire fabric? Am I so far gone, in my desperate need for meaning, that I'm prepared to distort everything—to re-write the whole history of my time purely in order to place myself in a central role. (*MC* 166)

Saleem is re-writing the history of India by assigning himself the central role, but he does not assume himself as a protagonist who, in due course of the time, will alter history to expose himself in a central role. Saleem's sense of history essentially exposes him to be at the central of his story but does not show him as an actor who indulges in creating history simply by being himself. For example, the entire Sunderbans episode, the trauma of India Pakistan war which forces Saleem into "history less anonymity of rains-forests" (*MC* 360). In the Sunderbans, Saleem forgets history as he losses identity in the warring world. This situation also indicates towards the national consciousness of India and Pakistan, which in their endeavor to defeat each other, readily abuse history in Nietzschean term. Rushdie, by manipulating historical facts, places both nations without identities that exist in a dream-like world where only historical facts that churn from the propaganda machine are evaluated real: "In the first five days of the war voice of Pakistan announced the destruction of more aircraft than India has ever possessed; in eight days, All India Radio massacred the Pakistan Army down to, and considerably beyond, the last man" (*MC* 339). Rushdie's strategy to produce and create history in much of the novel is similar to the self-serving construction of the warring nations. The most of part of Saleem's formulation of history is not designed to serve, but to understand, himself. Timothy Brennan states that "*Midnight's Children* is a replaying of Hindu mythology: As author, Saleem, like Brahma (creator of universe) imagines the whole of Indian history, and contain it within him" (1989: 241). In the other words, Brahma who created this world and brought it into existence is incarnated as Saleem: "everything is in my head, down the last detail... everything and not just the few clues one stumble across" (*MC* 19). As he goes ahead to narrate his story he starts stumbling, forgetting, misremembering others, and eliding. It is seminal to find out the mistakes of Saleem which he never discovers and moreover that is equally significant when Saleem does discover his mistake, he refuses to acknowledge and correct them. After the episode of magical trip into the jungle, Saleem recalls how he/his companions were carried out on a tidal wave: "When they emerged from the jungle, it was October 1971. And I am bound to admit that there was no tidal wave recorded that month" (*MC* 368). But even the un-magical events of the contemporary politics are subjected to miss remembering which Saleem denies to improve: "And then it occurs to me that I have made another error—that the election of 1957 took place before, and not after, my tenth birthday; but although I have racked my brains, my memory refuses, stubbornly, to after the sequence of events. This is worring. I don't know what's gone wrong" (*MC* 222).

Here Saleem is simply telling memory's history while juxtaposing it with conventional history. In regards with memory Saleem says earlier that it "create its own reality, it's heterogeneous but usually coherent version of events; and no sane human being ever trust someone else's version more than his own" (*MC* 211). This is ironical strategy that Saleem employs to subvert the hard facts of conventional history; by strongly denying alternation in his written history, even some error is found, he indicates to the rigidity of history as text, the unchangeable nature of conventional history accelerated by the writing subjects who rival Saleem in their refusal to change their stories.

This self-examination provides Saleem reasons for pauses and reflections; he asks whether he is willing to "re-write the whole history of (his) times" (*MC* 166) and consequently, he concludes that he must do so because it is not only a history of his times but also a history for his times. It is associated with a history that exists as a creation of a present world but rather than a seemingly objective presentation of the past world. In the novel, Rushdie through the chutnification of history attempts to build a present world along with an acceptable past and a passable future, which is potentially hopeful. He expects that his pickled jars of history, "possess an authentic taste of truth and which are, despite everything, acts of love" (*MC* 461). It is now clear that it does not matter that his grandfather, his father and his mother were not really his grandfather, his father and his mother because, "the children of midnight were...the children of the *time*: fathered, you understand, by history. It can happen. Especially in a country which is itself a sort of dream" (*MC* 118). In this kind of country, a child such as Saleem is parented by everything that contains the state: old and new; British and India; Hinduism and Islam and Christianity; Imperialism and Marxism; rich and poor; myth and fact. Saleem's presentation of history is copious and its varsity is limited only by its teller that presents a number of parents, delineating his various heritages. Saleem narrates the family story of the Sinais, with whom he is related by the virtue of political setback and not by birth. Just after his birth he is endowed and blessed with three mothers and five fathers: Vanita, Amina, and Marry; and Winkie, Ahmed, Methwold, Nadir and Joseph.

Vanita is Saleem's biological mother, in her we see how India is being seduced by England. Methwold is sexually attracted to Vanita, whose apparently perfect hair is only an appearance, an illusion of superiority. Siva's natural mother Amina, who raises Saleem as her own, until it is known that he is not her own son, consequently leading Saleem to discover his actual lineage, appears to be a complicated case in herself. As the novel tells that she was born as Mumtaz, so it is through her history, that history of India unfolds, a history that is presented to the West, the legacy of Taj Mahal. The namesake of the dead wife of Shah Jehan, for whose memory the Taj was built, she is "the blackie whom [her mother] had never been able to love because of her skin of her South Indian fisherwoman" (*MC* 56). Thus, because of her black skin Mumtaz turns to be a burden to her family, which finds it difficult to marry her off, owing to both India and European prejudices favoring fair skin. But Rushdie in the novel manages to marry Mumtaz and it is subversive and hidden marriage to a man, Nadir Khan, whose political ideologies are absolutely antithetical to that of the dominant imperial power. Still, this marriage does not work and is never accomplished; the old, vainglorious India of Taj Mahal never unites with the new, politically conscious India of freedom fighters. Khan divorces Mumtaz, despite their love, and although he is father to Saleem no more than Ahmed, he is Saleem's dream father. Mumtaz even after her second marriage is unable to forget her first love. Even in her dreams she is visited by Nadir Khan and with whom she later arranges secret assignations. Even when Ahmed renames her Amina—a palindrome for "amina" the Greek word for the soul (the word 'amina' in Jungian psychology refers to the feminine presence within the male subject), she regains her identity and with it her love for Khan. And of course it is a love for a man whose name represents the lowest point, even as his ideals are reaching for a type of zenith. Mary and Joseph, the most important of various parents of Saleem, play a vital role in his telling of his story. It appears that Joseph's Marxist ideologies is at play in Mary's interchanging of Saleem with Shiva, "give the poor baby a life of privilege and condemning the rich born child to accordions and poverty" (*MC* 117). Mary's this action not only makes her one more mother to Saleem in a nurse-made role, but also provides poor Saleem a mother in form of Amina and a family lineage in form of the Sinais. Mary can be compared with the Biblical Mary who provides life to a man who has no single mother, consequently making him a child among children born to history.

Though Saleem is born with a number of parents, yet they are by no means the last of those who figure among his mothers and fathers. Later even Nadir Khan achieves father status, so too Schaapsteker, Zulfikar, Picture Singh and his uncle Hanif, who along with his wife Pia, become parents to Saleem when the discovery of his blood-type proves that he is not child of Amina and Ahmed. With his multiple parentage it becomes clear that Saleem really does not have only one parents at all, which again places him not in a family but a political situation, as a child of history. Rushdie further elaborates:

> I thought that as Saleem is a character who claims all his life to be connected to history, to be controlling history, to be somehow responsible for history, he could not be allowed to get away with that all his life without being dragged out of the comfort of his family. He has to be un-housed, he has to lose the cocoon around him, and he has to be thrown into the middle of all his history that he claims to be influencing. (Rushdie 1985: 10)

Saleem find himself in this middle of history which is entrapped between families, countries, cultures and types of history where he attempts to discover regeneration. This process places the writing of self as a central and at the same time de-centres the same writing self. Apart from telling his own story as a central character, he also disintegrates himself by recounting the stories of families not his own, not his story even though they are contained within him. As they act within him, as he remembers tales and re-tales them for Padma and the reader, he starts to perceive the fissures in his own skin, the cracks that tell the story of the fragmentary existence of his de-centred self.

Thus, it is evident from the above discussion that Rushdie has strategically used Saleem to re-write myth and history, to present a plurality of familial and cultural histories, both willfully and unconsciously, in order to mock and dismantle oppressive colonial history of British imperialism. The mistakes made by Saleem intend to question Indian sensibility, both in mythic and modern context. The historical facts presented in novel are precise but often inaccurate according to the conventional history of India. At one place in the novel, Saleem claims that concrete tetra pods were applied to reclaim land scheme in Bombay, in fact there are quite a number of tetra pods along Marine Drive but they are used in protecting sea wall that is barring the Arabian Sea from reclaiming land. Elsewhere, in the novel, he laments that there is no officially assigned day to worship *Mumbadevi,* the deity from whose name the city derives its identity—Bombay. But on the contrary, there is a day set aside for this goddess. Saleem writes how Ganesh sits at the feet of Valmik who dictates the *Ramayana* to him but in reality Ganesh is known to have transcribed the *Mahabharata* while sitting at the feet of Vyasa. So it is obvious that Rushdie/Saleem is not just questioning the British version of Indian history, but the very given-ness of history, the inaccurate selectivity and assumed legitimacy of facts and myths. In doing so, he is freeing the facts from their rigidity (an act of subversion and challenge) by accepting that "reality is built on your own prejudices, gullibility, and ignorance, as well as knowledge and analysis" (Rushdie 1981: 100). It may appear that Saleem must be wrong in order to write, but it should be kept in mind that to re-tale, Saleem has first to bring into this world that comes from his head. So to understand him, according to him, we must swallow a world. In this way, *MC* proves itself to be, as Rushdie says the Indian readers usually see the novel, mythical, historical and political. Rushdie's this story owes a lot to the oral narrative tradition of India that helps the narrator in formulating the format of storytelling. In oral tradition of storytelling, the storyteller lets their story make an associational jump, as Rushdie says: "it goes in spirals and loops...every so often reiterating something that has happened earlier to remind you and frequently digressing you into something that the storyteller appears just to have thought of" (1985: 7). Owing to the human fallibility of the storyteller and the frailty of memory, Saleem's story encounters many uncertainties and discontinuities. The certainty appears only when Saleem makes a telepathic connection with other children of midnight, but this certainty also does not last long, as it is destroyed by his entire family. Having devoid of any possibility of certainty, he can only continue by way of re-telling, by re-telling his history. What fears Saleem most is absurdity, an evitable outcome of an overly ordered world, a singularity that denies the possibility of other possibilities.

So, Saleem's very storytelling process of rupture and discontinuity becomes a political act, for as Rushdie says that "when your version differs from official version, when remembering becomes a political act" (Rushdie in *Novelists* 251). In one of his articles, "Outside the Whale", Rushdie castigates those who are too passive to be disturbed by the unceasing storm of history and politics. He further says that we are all "radioactive with history and politics" (*MC* 137). He suggests that time has come to debunk that old lie of objective reality. This debunking strategy then becomes an active tool of resistance against that which so indelibly imprints itself on our consciousness as true. But throughout *MC*, Saleem puts himself as a subject on the top of such an imprint, preferring his self-admittedly perfect memory to a given history that pretends to be subjectless. In this way, Saleem goes from being a subject of colonialism to a subject who, through acknowledging the given colonial history, overrides it with a sense of self-presence, a response that Rudolf Bader calls *Vergangenheitsbewaltigung*, i.e. an overcoming of one's past that enables a coming to terms with self (*MC* 78).

In the light of discussion, *MC* can be seen as misremembering. It is taking the facts and rejecting them. It is taking history, history normally taken for granted, and rejecting it from gotten sea of truth. It is looking at a tale as a tale. It is inspiring the reader to follow this lead, to accept its validity, to swallow this tale. The paper attempted to interrogate the Eurocentric version of history to assert Indian history, myths, and politics in its own cultural and historical forms, which has been devalued or manipulated by colonial ideologies. In *MC*, Saleem, the narrator of the novel narrates the story of his life (reminding him as postcolonial subject hood) viewing through a lens which has been adulterated by a former colonial presence. This makes him to realize that whatever he sees is neither irrevocably true nor potently false. It repudiates the traditional history of

India which is written by the British, is slated with Eurocentric preoccupations.

Works Cited

Bhabha, Homi K. "Representation and Colonial Text: A Critical Exploration of Some Forms of Mimeticism." *A Theory of Reading*. Ed. Frank Glover-Smith. Brighton: Harvester, 1984: 93-122.

Brennan, Timothy. *Myths of Nation: Salman Rushdie and the Third World (India)*. Dissertation Columbia University, 1987. Ann Arbor: UMI, 1989.

Chatterjee, Partha. "History and the Nationalization of the Hinduism." *Social Research*, 59(1): 111-49.

De Schweintiz Jr, Karl. *The Rise and Fall of British India: Imperialism as Inequality.* London and New York: Methuen, 1983.

Dhar, T.N. *History and Fiction Interface in Indian English Novel.* New Delhi: Prestige Books, 1999.

McGann, Jerome J. *The Beauty of Inflections: Literary Imaginations in Historical Method and Theory*. Oxford: Clarendon Press, 1985.

Nandy, Ashis. *The Intimate Enemy: Loss and Recovery of the Self under Colonialism*. New Delhi: OUP, 1983.

Rushdie, Salman. *Midnight's Children*. 1981. London: Vintage, 1995.

———. "'ERRATA' Unreliable Narrator in *Midnights' Children.*" *A Sense of Place*. Ed. Britta Olinder. Goteburg: Gutenburg University of Commonwealth Studies, 1981. 45-62.

———. "*Midnights' Children* and *Shame*". Lecture/Interview. *Kunapipi* 7.1 (1985): 1-19.

———. "Outside the Wale", *Granta*, 11(1984): 123-38.

———. Interview. *Novelists in Interview*. Ed. John Haffendon. London & New York: Methuen, 1985. 231-61.

Said, Edward. *The World, the Text and the Critic*. Cambridge: Harvard University Press, 1983.

Parameswaran, Uma. "Handcuffed to History: Salman Rushdie's Art." *Ariel*, 14.4 (1984): 34-45.

8

Salman Rushdie's *Midnight's Children*: A Kaleidoscopic View

T. Sasikanth Reddy

Rushdie's narrative technique is marvellous. He is the master of narration at present time. The charm of his themes consists in their narrative qualities. His novels demonstrate the unique narrative which lures the reader ever onward into the pandemonium of the text. His narrative technique is used for the factual rendering in historical setting. His manner is unbiased as with strict objectivity he renders the personal experiences and situations. Rushdie's narrator constructs his own reality, which is dependent upon the events of the outside world but it is interpreted privately, because everybody interprets it through its own mood and way. He gives the heightened picture of reality through a realization of true self and thus rejects the partial realities. However, while doing so, he renders this reality with a touch of fantasy.

Rushdie's novels are complex, many layered with episodic causality, bearing strong influence of post-modernist novels as well as principles of the Indian art forms. His exalted diction, elevated word usage and felicitous word phrases leave strong impinge on the readers. We see the use of daring literary innovations and disorderliness, such the unconventional word play. Rushdie's technique of novel writing deserves the highest place in Indo-Anglian literature. About his technique, Rushdie told in an interview:

> For instance there is a technique that Dickens used a kind of background or setting for his works which is

> completely naturalistic background, he imposes totally surrealistic image. What I tried to do though not to quite in the Dickensian way was to make sure that the background, the bedrock of the book was eight—that like Bombay, the cities were recognizably correct so that fantasy could be rooted in that kind of reality. (Dharkar 351)

Rushdie is a master manufacturer of felicitous phrases. He gives them aromatic ingredients. They are diffused all over his works. His oeuvre is resplendent with them. In the novel *Midnight's Children,* Saleem Sinai's seminal description of himself gives a glance of that: "Child of an unknown union, I have had more mothers than most mothers have children, giving birth to parents has been one of my stranger talents—a room of revise fertility, beg and the control of contraception, and even of the widow herself" (Rushdie 242).

Although *Midnight's Children* deals with the theme of history, it also makes strong political comments. In addition to the historic political context, the novel refers to the recent social, moral and cultural issues of the Indian subcontinent. This novel actually explores a parallel between the story of Saleem Sinai, the protagonist, and the contemporary history of Indian subcontinent. It begins with the birth of Saleem Sinai that coincides with the birth of India as an independent nation in the midnight of 15 August 1947. Saleem Sinai, the narrator and the protagonist of the novel, has been 'mysteriously handcuffed to history' and his 'destinies indissolubly chained' to the destiny of India. Rushdie's allusions to history in *Midnight's Children* affect a Surrealistic atmosphere through a weaving of characters, plot and the events. In other words, he creates magic realism by combining facts and fiction fantasy and realism quite naturally. He so meticulously chooses the dates of the events around the characters that they appear to be part of contemporary history themselves.

Salman Rushdie uses the device of one of the oldest narrative techniques, i.e. of the first person narrator recounting his life story to a sympathetic listener. He pours long narratives at one go in breathless haste in large paragraphs without any full stops. Padma named after the lotus goddess pulls him up when he falters. Rushdie openly expresses his contempt for linear narration. The novel *Midnight's Children* does not have a continuous forward narration rather it is complex and interrelated, based on structure repetitions and episodic casualties, which is in fact one of the strong points of the novel, as it is the perfect hitching of the content to the form. Rushdie omits the linear narration as Saleem says:

> But have is Padma at my elbow, bullying me back into the world of linear narrative, the universe of what-happened-next. At this rate, Padma complains, you'll be two hundred years old before you manage to fell about your birth. She is affecting non-chalance but does not fool me. I know how that she is despite all her protestations, hooked. No doubt about it: my story has her by the throat...fighting down the proper privet of the successful storyteller, I attempt to educate her.... Padma-pressures of what happened next and remembering the finite quantity of time at my disposal, I leap forwards. (Rushdie 38)

Padma prefers the option always open to audiences and deceits him when the narrative tale as up on the traditional independent power of the storyteller to do what he likes with a dependent and slotted audience "she is captivated, helpless as a mongoose frozen to immobility by the swaying, blinkers eyes of a hooded snake, parlay said yeast by love" (121). The narrator is deprived of a narration and loses its meaning he pursues of which he has given at the novel's inaction as his main impetus:

> How to dispense with Padma? How give up her ignorance and superstition, necessary counter weights to my miracle-laden omniscience? How to do without her paradoxical earthiness of spirit, which keepers-kept? My feet on the ground? I have become, it seems to me, the apex of an isosceles triangle, supported equally by twin deities, the wild god of memory and lotus goddess of the present...but must I now become reconciled

> to the narrow one-diversionary of a straight line? (Rushdie 39)

The presence of Padma is essential for Saleem's narration of the story. Her continuous absence has disastrous consequences for Saleem's confidence and control of his material of the past,

> But today, I feel confused, Padma has not returned and in her absence my certainties are falling apart. Even my nose has been playing tricks on me—by day, as I stroll between the pickle vats tended by our army of strong, hairy armed, formidably competent women, I have found myself to distinguish lamer-odors form lime.... Re-reading my work, I have discovered an error in chronology. The assassination of Mahatma Gandhi occurs, in these pages, on the wrong date: But I cannot say, now, what the actual sequence of events might have been, in Indira Gandhi will continue to die at the wrong time. (Rushdie 140)

We have been attributed to Saleem's fallible memory but this is in fact a device of the novelist to keep the reader alert and the same time it also hints at the unrelishieity of the writer, as well as of history geography. As we see in the date of Gandhi's death or General Sam Manekshaw's acceptance of the surrender of Pakistani army at the end of Bangladesh war. The narrator says:

> Does one error invalidate the entire fabric? Am I so far gone, in my desperate need for meaning that I'm prepared to restart everything—to re-write the whole history of my times purely in order to place myself in a central role? Today, in my confusion, I can't judge. I'll have to leave it to others. For me there can be no going back, I must finish what I've started, even it, initially what I finish turns out not to be what I began.... (Rushdie 240)

At the very beginning Rushdie maintains a continuous effort at synchronizing nation and domestic life, so that the odyssey of his grandfather's and parents become the odyssey of the nation from the year 1915 up to about the year 1977. The convergence of the national and the domestic life is underscored repeatedly in the novel. Saleem subsumes most matter of public record within himself so the inheritable subjectivity of any chronicling process if incarnated in his appropriation of responsibility for major events within the historical brands of his narrative. The narrator links himself with the contemporary events. He says: "In this way I became directly responsible for triggering off violence which ended with the partition of the state of Bombay, as a result of which the city became the capital of Maharashtra ...about Indo-Pak war of 1965" (Rushdie 342). He expresses:

> Let me state this quite unequivocally, it is my first conviction that the hidden purpose of the Indo-Pak war of 1965 was nothing more not less than the crimination of my benighted family from the face of the earth. In order to understand the recent history of our times, it is only necessary to examine the bobbing-pattern of that war with an analytical, unprejudiced eye. (Rushdie 245)

Saleem's character represents the consciousness of the country experiencing its life and the time. At the same time, Saleem works as Rushdie's alter-ego can also an allegorical representation of Indian independence. Saleem like Rushdie, (born two months before) is born on the exact hour of the Indian independence, representing Rushdie's own observation in comic vein or in fantastic modes at the political state of the country. Rushdie with his English father, Indian mother, mission schooling and cared by a catholic 'ayah' give symbols to link the autobiography of an individual to the history of a nation.

Saleem represents the history of India as an album; a family album he is at the center draws correspondences between national event and his personal life. His reference of self is dissolved in fantasy, forging connections in order to confer meaning on chaos. He is aware that he is bound by his egotistical frame of reference so that his interpretation of history is always to some degree based upon his imagination, he still cannot do anything else but trust his own memory. This Rushdie calls: "Memory truth, because memory has its own special kind. It selects, eliminates, alters, exaggerates, minimizes, glorifies and verifies also; but in the end it creates its own reality" (Rushdie 340).

This vast narrative spanning over sixty-three years of India's history, also including some glimpses of Pakistan and Bangladesh, achieves its compactness through some special devices. The use of repetitive imagery and summary of previous happenings revive the reader's memory. He deliberately uses the same language to highlight the great differences for instance, Saleem himself is born at Dr. Narlikar's Nursing Home, "at the precise instant of India's arrival at Independence" (Rushdie 340). While his son Aadam Sinai, is born in a 'night shadowed slum' of emergency. The narrator thinks of himself as preserving both vegetables and events. He says:

> Every pickle-jar (you will forgive me if I become florid for a moment) contains, therefore the most exalted of possibilities: the feasibility of the classification of history; the grandiose of the pickling of time, I however have pickled chapter. Tonight, by serving the lid finally on a jar bearing the legend special formula 'No. 30 Abracadabra' I reach the end of my long-winded autobiography, inwards, and pickles, I have immutable in both methods. We must live, I'm afraid with the shadows of imperfection. (Rushdie 138)

He makes clear the sense of his narrative: "At Braganza pickles, I supervise the production of Mary's legendary recipes; but these are also my special blends, in which, thanks to the powers of my drained nasal passages, I am able to include memories dreams...ideas" (Rushdie 244). The events are intermingled in the story of Saleem as vegetable acquires the Special flavor of the spices in which they are pickle. The events of different time echo each other this idea is suggested again and again that people and events are leaking in to other events. The novelist is very good at descriptions; his hero can smell even emotions and so one finds even emotions, and so one finds even inanimate things impregnated with emotions and smelling of them.

Another important part of Rushdie's narrative technique is his building up a sense of suspense. He casually mentions a person before that person is appeared in actuality. The identity of Mrs. Braganza is not revealed until the end of the story when we find that she is no one else but Saleem's own nurse Mary Pereira whose chutneys he remembers. Thus, Indira Gandhi is portrayed quite early in the novel as widow when Saleem is approaching at his tenth birthday. Later by incidents we move to know that widow is no one else but, i.e. Indira Gandhi. On the technique of novel Ron Shepherd states:

> *Midnight's Children,* differs from earlier fiction in that most of the usual ground rules associated with the older from of diction are broken: the narrative fluctuates uncertainly between first and third person; ordinary notions of fictional realism are subverted, natural law becomes unnatural or supernatural even though the novel is not in any straightforward sense religious or metaphysical, the novel is full of cryptic clues, archaic utterances and seem always on the point of offering some important explanation, of arriving at some goal or conclusion but what this conclusion is one cannot be sure. It is a novel of signs and gestures and sleight of hand narrated with a passion for narrating other than for clarifying meaning. (Ron 33)

We frequently see the narrator's shift into dream and nightmare, which sees him as a narrator both in the first person and the third person, which mars the credibility of the character as a separate entity. In the narrative, the reader is shuffled between the past, present and future, which is a deliberate attempt by the novelist to present the variety and multitudinous of the country and her people. The interplay of the private and public lives in the novel imparts a unity to the novel, where fact and fantasy reinforce each other in order to give a heightened picture of reality. Rushdie sets the outline for the plot structure of the novel. For instance, the passage narrating Brass Monkey's fight with reimburse draws parallels between situations those are widely a part in time and space. The blood on Evie Bums face is a symbol of the blood caused by the rioters in Bombay.

Rushdie's *Midnight's Children* is an ironic commentary on the major political events that took place between 1947 and 1978. Like a historian, Rushdie records major historical events and like an artist he reaches history. We get the story of the narrator as well as of the Indian subcontinent. Rushdie is dexterous in employing the technique of irony in the description of the post-independence India.

> I remain, today half convinced than in that time of accelerated events and diseased hours the past of India rose up to confound her present, the new born, secular state was being given an awesome reminder of its fabulous antiquity, in which democracy and votes for women were irrelevant so that people were seized by atavistic, longings, and forgetting the new myth of freedom reverted to their old ways, their old regionalist loyalties and prejudices, and the body politic began to crack. (Cuto 20)

Rushdie makes a good use of rhetoric language. To make his language more effective Rushdie employs certain linguistic devices, which make the novel more appealing and powerful. The city-riots in Amritsar is quite geographic, "Amritsar dung was fresh and (worse) redundant. Nor was it all bovine. It issued from the rumps of the horses between the shifts of the city's many tongas, ikkas and ghorries, and mules and men and dogs attended nature's calls, mingling in a brotherhood of sheet" (Rushdie 238).

This juxtaposition of mules, men and dogs in one brotherhood of shit is suggestive of the author's disgust with the city. Same description we find in the city of Karachi. Through each juxtaposition, Rushdie ventilates his disgust with the cities in India as well as those in Pakistan. We also see the influence of Bombay film industry in the novel. Rushdie adopts the structure of Bombay film industry in broad perspective, which provides him perfect model for the novel. Thus, novel is very close to Hindi film. Rushdie adopts its many clichés in the novel such as, sudden recognitions, identity confusion, etc. to present his complex theme of the history of the Indian subcontinent. The exchange of two bodies born in Dr. Narlikar's nursing home by the nurse Mary Pereira is very interims to the scene of Hindi films. The novel is also a sort of comic epic genre, a form which is a fusion of Homeric, mythic and tragic connotation.

The story of the novel spreads through six decades and almost three generations of India's pre- and post-independence history. It is an epic in the sense that it tries to describe or contain "an India whose stories are too innumerable to be contained" (Rushdie 320).

Rushdie's use of refreshing language, felicitous phrases and literary allusions are other factor for the immense popularity of *Midnight's Children.* The rich exploitation of sound and meaning in language will for a long time is Rushdie's greatest contribution to the diversification of the Indian novel in English. His basic concern in the novel is to bring in India, not only as a grand theme but also through the medium. For this purpose, Hindi, Urdu or Hindustani words and phrases picked from their colloquial usages. This synthesis of the English and Hindi is abundant in the novel.

It begins with the opening pages of the novel, where Saleem tells us that he has been called by various names in his family such "piece of the Moon" for which the actual Hindi and an English word come together forming a phrase as a name, such as Picture Singh still further, traditional name such as 'Padma' and 'Ganesha' are used and their etymological and mythical aspects are also referred to. Rushdie coins the phrase as "what its name", "to begin at beginning", "cursing curses at dogs", "dreaming dream", which sparkle the narrative shedding off its monotonous coloring of a cliche. Maria Cuto's statement seems correct: "*Midnight's Children* evokes this lost center in language that conveys the ineffable and inescapable Indianness of the novelist" (Cuto 21).

Rushdie inserts North Indian vernacular language habits into flawless English intoned sentence makes the double usage of the same word for fluent effect as "chhi, chii", Padma covers her ears: "My God, such a ditty-filthy man I never knew!"... (Rushdie 118). Rushdie inserts crisp, befitting vernacular words! Phrases, into flawless English sentences, viz: "...and now Tai Bibi leaning out of a window shouts, 'Hey, bhanchued! Little sister-sleeper, where you running? What's true is true...!'" (Rushdie 122). We can take another example such as: "...the Nawab had invited all of these to his daughter's hennaing ceremony" (Rushdie 463). Rushdie offers vernacular idiom through transliteration as, "...donkey from somewhere!" (Rushdie 77). Further, he also says: "...mad man from somewhere" (Rushdie 79).

At the end the image of narrator is cracking up. In his rumple life now he is in imminent danger of disintegration as we can see from the voice of Saleem: "My hopeless, universed body...began to crack.... Parched, it yielded at last to the effects of a lifetime's battering...because it is the privilege of and the curse of midnight's children to be both masters and victims of their times..." (Rushdie 70).

Rushdie presents history through the metaphor of chutnification, which gives way to his narrative. In other words, Saleem is actually preserving the facts of history as chutnification, a method of perpetuation of each of the thirty-one chapters in the novel which stand for a pickle jar. Saleem suggesting the future leaves the last jar empty. Thus, the novel ends literally against closure.

Works Cited

Cuto, Maria. "*Midnight's Children* and Parents: The Search for Indo-British Identity". *Encounter.* Feb. 1982.

Dharkar, Rani. "An Interview with Salman Rushdie". *New Quest,* No. 42 Nov-Dec. 1983. 351-58.

Ron, Shepherd. "*Midnight's Children* as Fantasy: The Novels of Salman Rushdie". *Perspectives on the Fiction of Salman Rushdie.* M.D. Fletcher, Ed. Netherlands: Rodopi Editions, 1994. 74-89.

Rushdie, Salman. *Midnight's Children.* London: Arrow Books, 1981.

———. *Shame.* Calcutta: Rupa Books, 1983.

9

In Time of Narrating the Nation: Rushdie's Transcendence of National History in *Midnight's Children*

Asis De

It is a general tendency of the readers of Salman Rushdie's *Midnight's Children* (1981) to see the narrative as a national allegory recreating an imaginative form to modern India and its history. In its 'Introduction' of the 2006 edition, Rushdie's statement is quite noteworthy: "In the West people tended to read *Midnight's Children* as a fantasy, while in India people thought of it as pretty realistic, almost a history book" (*MC* xv). In time of theorizing the notion of the nation with reference to Indian political history of the twentieth century, *Midnight's Children* always remains a preferred choice of the critics of Indian Anglophone fiction. In Rushdie's own words, "the book has been criticized in India for its allegedly despairing tone...[but] the story is told in a manner designed to echo...the Indian talent for non-stop self-regeneration" (*Imaginary* 16). For the sake of my argument in this paper, I would like to start from his phrase "non-stop self-regeneration", which clearly belies any rigid idea of historiography and simultaneously opens space for critical debate favouring Rushdie's intention to transcend the fixity of a nation in a strict sense of geo-political sovereignty. Benedict Anderson's notion of the nation as 'an imagined community' adds to Rushdie's concept of 'non-stop self-regeneration' on the common ground of imagination. In Rushdie's case, imagining a political community from the moment of its birth or political autonomy, re-describing its history in an alternative way through the eyes of a fictional character (the narrator-protagonist of the narrative) does not limit the scope for positive regeneration, but helps finding new angles to enter the reality of a nation. To me, Martine H. Dutheil's critical assessment seems to be quite correct as he points out that in *Midnight's Children* Rushdie tests the "power of fiction to capture—and invent—a new reality" (10).

A writer is usually affected by the historical milieu in which s/he lives and the periods of an earlier time with which s/he associates his/her identity. In the book *Nation and Narration* (1990), Homi K. Bhabha puts his observation: "Nations, like narratives, lose their origins in the myths of time and only fully realize their horizons in the mind's eye" (1). In framing a narrative, a novelist can use 'history' both consciously and unconsciously, as s/he perceives it in his/her 'mind's eye'. Sometimes the novelists use authentic materials from the history of a nation-state, while sometimes they create 'imaginary homelands'. Historical reality may be used as an integral part of the narrative in terms of time and space but should be transmuted in the process of creative expression into wider dimensions of universality and timelessness. The intermingling of the historical and the fictional is the most challenging part of the job of a novelist dealing consciously with politico-historical events. For Rushdie, the freedom movement of India was not merely a struggle for political autonomy but a culture in itself, an all-pervasive experience that became a part of the life of all the sensitive and enlightened Indians at that time. By employing several symbols, images, metaphors and tropes, Rushdie's narrator-protagonist has marvelously invented a 'being' of the nation in *Midnight's Children* and associated that 'being' with his own life as both of them share a similarity in question of the time of their birth: "at the precise instant of *India's arrival* at independence, *I tumbled forth* into the world" (*MC* 3; my emphasis). In *Midnight's Children*, Rushdie's protagonist-narrator Saleem Sinai could well be seen as an allegorical figure, who is 'metaphorically' related to the modern nation of India, as the "metaphor of birth is part of the larger metaphor of the nation as a person" (Kortenaar 2004: 34). Norbert Schurer emphatically points out the historical significance of the 'moment' of Saleem's birth: "It is most significant, however, that Saleem finally spills the beans about the exact moment he is born: the stroke of midnight on August 15, 1947, the moment of India's independence" (22). Some more words of the narrator-protagonist in the very opening paragraph—"I had been mysteriously handcuffed to history, my destinies indissolubly chained to those of my country" (*MC* 3), signal to the readers that actual politico-historical events would remain significant throughout the narrative.

As a whole, *Midnight's Children* hinges on the exact time of Indian independence in 1947 as the narrative covers a time span of thirty years before Independence and symmetrically ends thirty years after it. The narrator-protagonist recounts the social and politico-historical events leading to Independence and Partition and beyond. According to Catherine Cundy, "one of the chief achievements of *Midnight's Children* is the way in which it serves as a testament to the importance of memory in the recreation of history and the constitution of the individual's identity" (32). The narrator reflects over the experiences of three generations of Sinai family and covers the entire Indian subcontinent and its history. Though the narrative begins chronologically in 1915—the year Saleem's grandfather Aadam Aziz returns from Europe to India (coincidentally this is the year Gandhi returned to India from South Africa), Rushdie liberates his readers from the monotony of chronology, tyranny of cause and effect and adherence to objective reality. He blends history and fiction and allows elements of fantasy to encroach upon the recorded facts of history. This departure from a conventionally realistic narrative style is a key aspect of Rushdie's work, which is often described as magic realism. This label conveys Rushdie's use of fantastical occurrences as an essential part of his fictional world. The magic realist author is not limited by the same restrictions that govern the objective reality of everyday world, and is, therefore, able to explore the world fully through his imagination. At one point of the narrative, for instance, Saleem becomes transformed into a sniffer dog used in the Bangladeshi war of Independence. Such touch of fantasy allows Rushdie to create a fictional world, through which the narrator comments on the political realities of modern India. In *Realism and Power: Postmodern British Fiction*, Alison Lee argues that instead of being linear and whole, "history is discontinuous and fragmented" (48). The historical events in the novel come to us being refracted through the narrator-protagonist Saleem, who is the biological child of the departing English colonizer Methwold and a low-class Hindu lady named Vanita and who is later raised by the Indian Muslim couple Ahmed and Amina, thus becoming a symbol of East-West cultural hybridity. I do not agree with David W. Price when he finds Saleem to be "a critical historian" (126). Saleem only provides his own version of history and his own ideas of nation as he records these at a very turbulent phase of his life. *Midnight's Children*, as Fletcher notes, "Provides a commentary on Indian political history...by linking domestic events in the life of the narrator, Saleem Sinai, and his family to the public events of Indian history" (10).

To elaborate upon my point, I would like to make a graphic summarization of the major politico-historical events described in the narrative:

Novel	Individual	National
Book One	Background	1919 - Jallianwala Bagh Massacre
Book Two	Birth and Grouping in India and Pakistan	1947 - Independence 1956 - Language Riots 1958 - Coup in Pakistan
Book Three	Adulthood, Amnesia and After	1965 - Indo-Pak War 1971 - Birth of Bangladesh 1975 - Declaration of Emergency 1977 - Lifting of Emergency

All these major historical events find expression through Saleem in such a way that Andrew Teverson in his book *Salman Rushdie* finds the novel to be close enough to a historical novel:

> *Midnight's Children* is a novel that is preoccupied at the level of ideas by history and historicity, by the ways in which history is recorded, by the techniques with which a period is conjured and contained (or not contained), and by the ways in which the individual 'historiographer' understands (or misunderstands) his relationship with his material. In all these respects

> *Midnight's Children* seems to conform to the broad definition of the historical novel. (126)

The first historical event in the novel is Jallianwala Bagh massacre of 1919. This incident takes a whole page for its delineation. The involvement of Aadam Aziz is so deep that his body becomes metaphorical of the site of massacre. Next event is the rise and fall of Sheikh Abdullah which is very much functional as it helps in the progress of the coalescence of nation and self. Amina marries Ahmed Sinai in June 1946 after the failure of her first marriage with Nadir Khan, the impotent idealist and a believer of liberal Communism. Earl Mountbatten held a press conference and announced the partition of India on 4th June, 1947. On the same date, Amina and Ahmed Sinai left for Bombay just after the midnight of August 13, 1947. Pakistan came into being on August 14, 1947. Vanita and William Methwold bring Saleem into existence while Amina and Ahmed bring Shiva. Saleem is born at the exact moment of India's Independence. Saleem grows up in Sinai family while Shiva in the slums. Saleem has to carry the 'historical burden' of his birth and invests his life and narrative in describing the zeitgeist of both his childhood and adulthood.

At nearly the end of Book One when the narrator-protagonist reflects—"the children of midnight were also the children of *the time*: fathered, you understand, by history" (*MC* 159), the reader takes the sense of 'the time' to be synonymous with 'history'. Again, in the very penultimate paragraph of Book One as Saleem narrates the incident of the news-correspondent's interviewing his mother just a few days after Saleem's birth and the photographer's gifting of a cheque of hundred rupees, he uses the idea of 'history' in a rather different sense: "I shall, however, merely thank them for celebrating my arrival, and forgive them for their lack of a genuine historical sense" (*MC* 161). Actually, a true sense of history does not confine one to facts or any particular event, but insists on a proper appraisal of the continuity of time—from the past through the present and to a rather unknown future. When Saleem re-reads his work, discovers "an error in chronology" (*MC* 229) and asks himself—"Am I so far gone, in my desperate need for meaning, that I'm prepared to distort everything—to re-write the whole history of my times purely in order to place myself in a central role?" (*MC* 230), it becomes evident that his role is certainly not that of "a critical historian" as David Price finds him, but that of a storyteller who plays a nicely balanced game "at the mind's divisions between fantasy and reality" (*MC* 231).

Next important event is the assassination of Mahatma Gandhi, which takes a rather short space in the narrative but delineated quite starkly. Language riots of 1956 have been dealt in with effectively tragic pathos. States were recognized on linguistic base: 'Language divided us' (*MC* 186). The Language riots make the evolution of the nation sanctified and renewed only by the rituals of blood. Then the narrator-protagonist links the death of Aadam Aziz with the death of Jawaharlal Nehru. Saleem migrates to Pakistan with his mother and witnesses the imposition of Martial Law on 7th Oct. 1958. Relations between India and Pakistan and also between India and China worsen. India becomes aggressive in the Indo-China war of 1962.

Saleem returns to India in 1962, and takes an attempt to convene the eponymous children intending to discover the meaning of their shared miraculous destiny. In several ways that convention, identified as the Midnight's Children Conference in the narrative, reflects the religious, linguistic, cultural and political diversities of a single nation. In 1963, Saleem goes back to Pakistan and documents Indo-Pak war of 1965. At this time, he loses the majority of his family in an air raid. For more than five years (1965-70), he remains a citizen of Pakistan (*MC* 340). He suffers from an amnesia and is enrolled in CUTIA (Canine Unit for Tracking and Intelligence Activities), Unit 22 of the Pakistani army (*MC* 337).

On March 25, 1971, Sheikh Mujibur Rahman proclaimed the state of Bangladesh. The Pakistani army perpetrated inhuman cruelty. At this time Saleem is suddenly re-endowed with his memory in the jungle of the Sundarbans. He returns to human settlements in Bangladesh and discovers some old acquaintances from Bombay. Then Saleem enters India illegally and reaches to Delhi. He tries to trace the remnants of his biological family but fails, and afterwards takes up residence in a slum area where street performers live. This section of the narrative comes closer to the then Bombay Talkie material. On 12th June 1975, Allahabad High Court finds Indira Gandhi to be guilty of "malpractices during the election campaign of 1971" (*MC* 582). At the midnight of June 25, 1975, Indira Gandhi imposes Emergency. Saleem questions in vain the aphorism: "Indira is India and India is Indira...but might she not have read her own father's letter to a midnight's child, in which her own sloganized centrality was denied, in which the role of mirror-of-the-nation was bestowed upon me?" (*MC* 597). It seems that Rushdie wants to see this historical imposition of Emergency by Mrs. Gandhi as a personal lust for power bordering on godhood. As Saleem reflects: "...we, the magical children of midnight, were hated...by the Widow, who was not only Prime Minister of India but also aspired to be Devi...a multi-limbed divinity with a centre-parting and schizophrenic hair" (*MC* 612). The reference to Emergency imposed by 'the Widow', the 'Prime Minister of India' and the ironical 'a multi-limbed divinity with...schizophrenic hair' certainly allude to Indira Gandhi, but it does not imply that Saleem is simply a 'critical historian' who is chronicling the details of the political and historical reality of his nation. Rather, it seems wiser to me to see Saleem as an everyman figure, who is very much conscious of the political scenario of his nation and enjoys certain liberty of expressing opinion about it. He is just any conscious citizen of the nation who has the habit of commenting upon his nation's present and future and even making caricature of the politico-historical figure of his dislike.

In 1976, Sanjay Gandhi rose to power and carved out two of his projects with ruthless action: clearance of Delhi slums and mass vasectomy: "They are doing nasbandi—sterilization is being performed" (*MC* 600). For a time Saleem is incarcerated with other midnight's children. His optimism is at stake and he takes these events as signals of the end of the potency of the 'midnight's children': "Here you are in world without faces or names; here people have no memories, families or past; here is for *now*, for nothing except right now" (*MC* 634). In a way, I agree with Neil Kortenaar's particular observation: "*Midnight's Children* offers a self-conscious fictional alternative to the lies that form the myth of the ruling Nehru-Indira Gandhi-Sanjay Gandhi dynasty" (1995: 54). The last historical event is the election of 1977, when Janata Party defeats Indira Gandhi's Congress: "Urine drinkers have come to power. The Janata Party ...did not seem to me...to represent a new dawn" (*MC* 616). The novel ends with a prophecy by Saleem. It warns of a bleak future: "It is the privilege and the curse of Midnight's children to be both masters and victims of their time...and to be unable to live or die in peace" (*MC* 647).

The narrative framework of *Midnight's Children* consists of a tale—comprising Saleem's own life story, which he recounts orally to his would-be wife Padma. And the India of *Midnight's Children* is a world, which is thoroughly pervaded by miracles—so thoroughly, indeed, that "the miraculous comes to appear routine" (McHale 77). This novel has been compared time and again in its scope and execution to works such as Laurence Sterne's *Tristram Shandy* or Gunter Grass's *The Tin Drum*. It presents, very much alike, an encyclopedic exploration of an entire society through the story of a single person. The 'midnight's children' in the novel are, very much the reality of a still-young nation paralleling and "mirroring public history in their private histories" (*ibid.* 95). In Rushdie's strategic employment of magic realism the use of Indian mythology is remarkable: Shiva is seen to represent violence and destruction in India (in Hindu mythology, Lord Shiva is seen as the power of destruction). Rushdie uses "autobiography as history, story-telling elements, synthesistic fusion of time and events, a quality of mythic sweep that dislodges history from chronometric time in order to abstract its essential meaning" (Parameswaran 5). *Midnight's Children* challenges the usefulness of something definitively Eastern or Western: in the narrative, Shiva is seen to use American slang in his speech. Rushdie's ability to cross cultural and imaginative boundaries can be read as a way of emphasizing the diversities and pluralistic nature of Indian society.

I find Sabrina Hassumani's assessment to be fairly acceptable, when she comments: "Rushdie's best fiction is always self-conscious and aware of its limitations: *Midnight's Children*, for example, does not attempt to pass itself off as 'the' story of the subcontinent; rather, the re-telling of its history is presented as one flawed version among many" (22). Behind the apparent adoption of the frame of Indian national history of the twentieth century, Rushdie virtually makes a clever denial of its objectivity by relying more on the tricky memory of Saleem and by using the narrative mode of magic realism. Saleem's individual understanding of Indian national history is very much a personalized version, and therefore, should be seen as far removed from the 'official' objective history of the nation.

Note

The abbreviation used for the novel, *Midnight's Children*, in the course of discussion is—*MC*.

Works Cited

Ahmad, Aijaz. *In Theory: Classes Nations Literatures*. 1992. New Delhi: Oxford, 2010.

Bhabha, Homi K., ed. *Nation and Narration* (1990). London and New York: Routledge, 2000.

Cundy, Catherine. *Salman Rushdie*. Manchester: Manchester University Press, 1996.

Dutheil, Martine H. *Origin and Originality in Rushdie's Fiction*. Bern: Peter Lang, 1999.

Fletcher, M.D., ed. *Reading Rushdie: Perspectives on the Fiction of Salman Rushdie*. Cross/Cultures 16. Amsterdam: Rodopi, 1994.

Hassumani, Sabrina. *Salman Rushdie: A Postmodern Reading of His Major Works*. Fairleigh: Dickinson University Press, 2002.

Kortenaar, Neil Ten. "'*Midnight's Children*' and the Allegory of History." *ARIEL: A Review of International English Literature*, 26:2 (April 1995): 41-62.

———. *Self, Nation, Text in Salman Rushdie's Midnight's Children*. Quebec: McGill Queen's University Press, 2004.

Lee, Alison. *Realism and Power: Postmodern British Fiction*. London and New York: Routledge, 1990.

McHale, Brian. *Postmodernist Fiction.* New York and London: Methuen, 1987.

Parameswaran, Uma. *The Perforated Sheet.* New Delhi, Chennai and Hyderabad: Affiliated East-West Press, 1988.

Price, David Walter. *History Made, History Imagined: Contemporary Literature, Poiesis, and the Past.* Champaign/Chicago: University of Illinois Press, 1999.

Rushdie, Salman. *Midnight's Children* (1981). London: Vintage Books, 2013.

———. *Imaginary Homelands: Essays and Criticism 1981-1991.* London: Vintage Books, 2010.

Schurer, Norbert. *Salman Rushdie's Midnight's Children: A Reader's Guide.* London and New York: Continuum, 2011.

Teverson, Andrew. *Salman Rushdie.* New Delhi: Viva Books, 2010.

Section–C

Treatment of Imagined Temporalities, Cosmopolitanism and Narrative Strategies: Recent Perspectives

10

Chutneys, Pickles, Palimpsests and Collages: Lived and Imagined Temporalities in the Works of Salman Rushdie

Bini B.S.

For Salman Rushdie, history denotes a medley of complex life-worlds of polysemic experiences in which the private and the public spheres merge into each other. The plurality and unfinalizability of time and strategies of narrating it in his works propose a mode of analysis enriched with an ironic perspective of history. The image that Rushdie frequently uses for history, a story with juggled incidents or disunited episodes, suggests a subversive-narrative possibility and alternative dimensions of temporality. In his novels, individual stories leak into the stories of societies, nations and the world. When history gets personified in dictators who claim to have regulated the course of events, Rushdie supplements history with a political subtext and deftly weaves his powerful critique into the folds of narration. History as a discipline or knowledge, Rushdie knows, is an epistemic-narrative trope that is not free from the effects of power.

Foucault's criticism of the conventional historiography in *Archaeology of Knowledge* (1969), "the great silent, motionless bases that traditional history has covered with a thick layer of events" (Foucault 4) is similar to Rushdie's dismissal of the monolithic view of history. Foucault argues for a plural view of history that accommodates "several pasts, several forms of connexion, and several hierarchies of importance, several networks of determination, and several teleologies" (Foucault 5). History in Rushdie's works takes the form of a polyphonic narrative which is dappled with hues of hilarity, violence, shame, pain and caustic satire. Experiences and events become uncertain phenomena that are better interpreted not in concrete terms of history in the conventional mode, but through the subtleties of allegory, metaphors and anachronism. Rushdie philosophizes about history as time and takes it to a metaphysical plane while he discusses several temporalities in *Midnight's Children* (1981) in terms of *kaala* and *yugas*. Each *yuga* has characteristics (*guna*) of its own and a cyclical pattern of recurrence.

The metaphors that Rushdie uses to indicate time and the lives of individuals intervening into and changed by events make history darkly poetic and grotesque. History can sometimes be a subjective lived experience and a medley of fragmented and discontinuous memories of incidents, places and people—real and imaginary.

A Critique of Historiography and Seeking Alternatives through Fictional Narration

Rushdie explicitly states his mistrust of traditional mode of narration and official versions of history. His novels exemplify the ways in which postmodernism problematizes history and fiction. History in his novels is disjointed, provisional, plural and subjective. He is aware of the power of imagination that synthesizes and transforms the historical raw material into works of fiction. Imagination unshackles the mind of the creative genius from the basic and rudimentary facts of history. Rushdie transforms nations, people and incidents into fantasies through narratives strategies of surrealism and magic realism. According to Rushdie fantasy is "a method of producing intensified images of reality" and also one of the functions of fiction is to "find techniques for making actuality more intense, so that you experience it more intensely in the writing than you do outside writing" (qtd. in Hoffenden 1985: 246).

For Rushdie, a historical fact is an indisputable sacrosanct truth; he transforms history by allowing fact and fiction to imbricate and seep into one another. For him history and fiction have no border lines since the former, in the process of understanding, recording and narrating can be like the latter. In his view, both history and fiction can be lived forward and written in retrospect. Rushdie feels that fictional form gives scope for "the miraculous and the mundane to co-exist at the same level, in which the sacred and the profane can be simultaneously explored" (*Imaginary* 376). He defends the liberty to let one's imagination run riot and make history *fabulous* in a fictional narrative. History is not only made by recorded events, but also made up and narrated. So like a story of life and the anecdotes within it, history can consist of or be concocted with recorded, remembered, imagined, exaggerated, underestimated and distorted elements. In *Imaginary Homelands*, Rushdie justifies his blatant use of fabulation: "I genuinely believed that my overt use of fabulation would make it clear to any reader that I was not attempting to falsify history, but to allow fiction to take off from history" (*Imaginary* 408).

History for Rushdie is a story indeed, but it is not narrated with a scheme of beginning, middle and ending. The techniques to cross the borderlines of time such as flashback and visions of future are used by Rushdie. The resulting narrative is fragmented and digressive. The metaphor of juggling in *Haroun and the Sea of Stories* (1990) indicates the narrative technique in some of his novels: "I always thought that storytelling is like juggling. You keep a lot of different tales in the air and juggle them up and down; if you are good you don't drop any" (Rushdie 1990: 108-09).

The nonlinear mode of storytelling alluded by the metaphor of juggling implies the random selection and projection of multiple story lines. It is a technique which Rushdie uses in his novels for which he is indebted to the oral tradition and epics of India.

> 'The Ocean of the Streams of Story', which is a literal translation of the title of the work *Kathasaritsagara* in Sanskrit, combines all the stories in the universe and is in a state of constant flux and turbulence. We are told that "because the stories were held there in fluid

> form, they retained the ability to change, to become new versions of themselves, to join up with other stories. (Rushdie 1990: 72)

The ocean is never still but ever alive. A character in *Grimus* (1975) expresses his predilection for stories which are "like life, slightly frayed at the edges, full of loose ends and lives juxtaposed by accident" over the ones which are "neat, tight and organized in some grand design" (Rushdie 1975: 141).

Through the metaphors of 'chutnification' and 'pickling', Rushdie not only emphasizes the haphazard selection of events but also their lack of chronological ordering in *Midnight's Children*. The narrative that meanders through the labyrinths of events, with numerous digressions, breaks and ruptures, gives several dimensions to the concept of history in this novel. Rushdie overlooks the notion of continuity in and logical coherence of narration. There are curious parallels between the autobiography of the protagonist and the history of the nation. Rushdie is aware that history is partly formed in and by the people. In *Midnight's Children*, Rushdie describes how history forms the lives of people through the narration of the experiences of Saleem Sinai who is handcuffed to history. The technique of allegory is made use of by Rushdie in his novels to deal with various periods of history. Rushdie analyses each age in its contemporariness. In his novel *Shame* (1983), he makes it very clear that "time cannot be homogenized as easily as milk" (Rushdie 1983: 13). The narrative voice of *Shame* asks: "...is history to be considered the property of the participant solely? In what courts are such claims staked, what boundary commissions map out the territories? Can only the dead speak?" (Rushdie 1983: 28).

Rushdie suggests in his novels that history is a matter of temporal perception and it is invented and put together by people, in the same way as a person is invented by his circumstances. This concept of history has parallels with the process of fictional creation in that it is similar to how a character is invented in the novel. In the *Enchantress of Florence* (2008), the available records of Mughal history are used to create the fantasy of

Akbar's India and the Rajput wife, Jodha turns out to be a fragment of Akbar's imagination. Rushdie thus claims that what we find in 'authentic' historical records may be mere fantasy. People and incidents are created or altered to suit the purpose and politics of the ruler. The travelers and seafarers in this work explore such realms of fantasy that can never be mapped in reality. By asserting the fact that historical writing that is considered 'real' and so 'reliable' is concocted and manipulated, Rushdie vindicates the right to turn history into fantasy using imagination.

The narrative technique used by Rushdie has similarities to the epic and *Puranic* modes of narration. The story moves backwards and forwards. The middle of the story often is suggestive of beginnings and endings. Flashbacks and visions of the future invade the present that Saleem inhabits in *Midnight's Children.* Saleem Sinai's historical accounts subvert, through many critical counter narratives, British imperialist history and the official versions of history generated by the Indian politicians. The realization of Saleem that India is entering the *kaliyuga* or the dark ages which precedes an absolute destruction shows a historical sense entangled with the concept of time in Hindu mythology. Saleem indicates the cyclic nature of temporality in the context of Indian history:

> I remain, today, half-convinced that in that time of accelerated events and diseased hours the past of India rose up to confound her present; the new-born, secular state was being given an awesome reminder of its fabulous antiquity, in which democracy and votes for women were irrelevant...so that people were seized with atavistic longings, and forgetting the new myth of freedom reverted to their old ways, their old regionalist loyalties and prejudices. (*Midnight's* 294)

In the novels of Rushdie, there is an inclination towards the present; the personae inhabit the terrains of the present that are haunted by the chimeras of the past, both actual and imagined. Future confronts the fictional personae with uncertainty. The boundaries between memory and real experiences, dreams and visions are blurred. This kind of switching over from past to present and future and from memory to the experienced and to the imagined in a random manner creates a chaotic experience of time in the works of Rushdie.

Rushdie challenges the official versions of truth and the concept of authenticity while dealing with historical raw material. He is aware of that plane of history which is kept silent and invisible. History is a social as well as personal experience in fiction. Each society has its own notions of time and history. Through creative writing, the socially constructed time is often subverted or reconstructed in other guises. In Rushdie's works, history is a curious and muddled blend of memory, perception, experience, imagination and vision. Memory is understood as a power to transform. Memory is not reliable as it uses the freedom of selection and elimination; it can highlight and play down the events of history. Time has a personal dimension when it is being interpreted by the individual through his experiences and in a wider sense, we find in his novels how historical experience becomes a mass fantasy and a collective fiction. In *Imaginary Homelands*, Rushdie opines: "History is always ambiguous. Facts are hard to establish and capable of being given many meanings.... The reading of Saleem's unreliable narration might be...a useful analogy for the way in which we all, everyday, attempt to read the world" (Rushdie 1990: 25).

For Rushdie, imagination is a means of challenging the fixity of conventional historiography. Imagination, according to Rushdie is "the process by which we make pictures of the world" (*Imaginary* 143). Imagination helps one to write "books that draw new and better maps of reality and make new languages with which we can understand the world" (Rushdie 1990: 100). Rushdie does not try to suggest that imagination is infallible. Rushdie's conceptualization of imagination as the agent of synthesis and transformation, which is capable of liberating us from the crude facts of history, shows a possibility of treating history in fiction. About *Midnight's Children,* he comments in *Imaginary Homelands*, "I tried to make it as imaginatively true as I could, but imaginative truth is simultaneously honourable and suspect" (Rushdie 1990: 10). Rushdie differentiates between invention and imagination: When the first provides only 'make-believe', the second offers "reliable accounts of the horrific metamorphosed reality of our age" (Rushdie 1990: 204). He does not deny that "imagination can falsify, demean, ridicule, caricature and wound as effectively as it can clarify, intensify and unveil" (Rushdie 1990: 143).

Rushdie feels that salvaging of the past in the present is subject to the vagaries of reminiscence and foregrounds memory as an integral feature of the depiction of the times past. In *Imaginary Homelands*, he observes that a narrative about the past is a process of "remaking the past to suit our present purposes, using memory as our tool" (Rushdie 1990: 24). The intentional errors in memory indicate the unreliable nature of memory. The mixing up of historic pasts and the modern age in the works of Rushdie through memory and visions not only helps to cross the borderlines of time; the technique of anachronism used in the works of Rushdie serves also as a tool for satire and fantasy. Incidents like the Jallianwala Bagh tragedy and the assassination of Gandhi are given with wrong time references in *Midnight's Children*. The purpose is to suggest the unreliable nature of memory and also to remind the readers ironically that in India, Gandhiji always dies at the wrong time; his death has to be inevitably untimely. It shows the dubious nature of historiography and the unreliability of the writer.

Tai the boatman in *Midnight's Children*, who sets history in motion, remembers the arrival of Christ to the Kashmir valley. His description of a fat, bearded, polite, bald and gluttonous Christ chatting fluently in Hindi both fascinates and intrigues Aadam Aziz. Tai claims that on the cushions of his shikara, Jahangir himself has reclined. Aadam's boyish mind travels to different lands and meets strange people, as Tai spellbinds him with the narration of his eccentric visions which are not restricted by the boundaries of time and the insistence on accuracy. Rushdie also uses the technique of fictionalizing real events. In *Midnight's Children*, the killing of Homi Catrack, a film magnate and lover of Lila Sabarmati, by the cuckolded Colonel Sabarmati is the famous Nanavati case. He discusses the Bombay riots in the same manner in *The Moor's Last Sigh* (1995).

Making Sense of History through Metaphors and Symbols

The symbolic references to historiography, such as pickling in *Midnight's Children*, weaving of shawls in *Shame* and the art of painting on the huge canvas and creating a scattered collage of eras and events in *The Moor's Last Sigh,* metaphorically suggest various possibilities of recording history. Like pickle, history is preserved in memory to spice up the meal of the present; the memories and thoughts are conserved for future use. But they get transformed into something else.

The concepts in the works of Rushdie, such as the reconstruction of history and the understanding of the past in the present, are expressed using the metaphors 'chutnification' and 'pickling'. In the 'chutnification' of history many discourses come together in the historical narrative, giving it an indeterminable quality. 'Pickling' is a process of preserving the past to be tasted in the present and future. Each chapter in *Midnight's Children* falls into a pickle jar, the last one being left empty for preserving the future. The novel metaphorically ends with a note against closure. The processes of chutnification and pickling imply preservation and distortion at the same time. It is from the compulsions and traumas of the present that the narrators of the novels of Rushdie take off to the past and the future. The present in the novels of Rushdie is a puzzle for those who live in it. The attempts to escape it by retreating into memory or by imagining the future commonly appear in his novels. The characters wander through the pathways of time, exploring the world from its contemporariness to the antiquity and the imagined futures.

The fragmented vision through a perforated sheet suggests the possibility of understanding history as a plethora of disorderly events. In *Midnight's Children*, Aadam's vision of his future bride is fragmented, so is the historian's perspective of India as a newly independent nation. When these fragments are put together in a narrative grid, shape and beauty are assigned to history. The understanding of an age through fragmented events does not give any clue about the wholeness of experience; or one gets a sense that wholeness is illusory. It is something that is aspired for, but never possibly achieved. Rushdie suggests that this notion of wholeness is a contrived one, whether it is in the case of an individual, history or nations. The narrative voice of *Shame* describes the vision of Pakistan: "I am forced to reflect that world in fragments of broken mirrors.... I must reconcile myself to the inevitability of the missing bits" (*Midnight's* 69).

Rani Harappa in *Shame* weaves the scenes of her husband's cruelty and the consequences of his autocracy into shawls. The multicoloured strands of memory and imagination reconstruct the hitherto de-visualized tales of Iskander Harappa's misdeeds. The shawls that are never worn and kept locked in an iron box represent the unexpressed protest of the oppressed. Rani Harappa's shawls focus mainly on what is excluded from history. For each of the celebrated virtue of the tyrant Iskander, the shawls offer an alternate view. In the shawls of Rani Harappa, Rushdie combines historical and literary motifs. The shawls represent the act of accusation and condemnation of the narrowness of Pakistani society. This is emblematized through Sufia Zinobia who blushes at the shames of her nation and like a saint endures its shamelessness.

Rushdie deems it necessary to portray shame, a very real emotion, by allegory. It is at 'a slight angle to reality'. Rushdie overtly attaches Pakistan, 'a miracle that went wrong' and Sufiya Zinobia, 'the wrong miracle'. In essence, Sufiya Zinobia characterizes an entire nation. She blushes at Pakistan's shame created from violence, corruption, and the forced displacement of people. Her character represents certain incidents of history as shameful phenomena that consequently end in violence. Rushdie makes Sufiya Zinobia's shame literally unleash a beast from within, suggesting that shame manifests itself through violence.

Through the metaphor of the palimpsest, Rushdie illustrates a process of historiography that thrives on systematic elimination and strategic inclusion. The image of the palimpsest in *Grimus* analyzes the possibilities of multi-dimensional perspectives. Virgil Jones, the historian asks:

> Is it not a conceptual possibility that here, in our midst, permeating all of us and all that surrounds us

> is a completely other world...? In a word, another dimension...if you conceal that conceptual possibility, you must also concede that there may well be more than one. In fact, infinity of dimensions might exist, as palimpsests, upon and within and around our own. (Rushdie 1975: 52-53)

In *Shame,* the narrator observes that to build Pakistan, it was necessary to cover up India's history. A palimpsest always obscures what lies beneath. The idea of the palimpsest provides the key to understanding the narrative layers in *The Moor's Last Sigh* also. The literal palimpsest as depicted by Aurora's painting and the metaphoric palimpsest as a layering or re-creation allude to prospects of recording history. The city of Bombay as well as the country is referred to as palimpsests:

> ...under world beneath the Over world, black market beneath white, when the whole life was like this, when an invisible reality moved phantom wise beneath a visible fiction, subverting all its meanings.... How could we have lived authentic lives? How could we have failed to be grotesque? (184-85)

In *The Moor's Last Sigh*, historiography becomes an art that gives enough scope for the imagination and whims of the historian. In this novel, Rushdie initiates a historiography of the downtrodden masses in India that results in the problematisation of historiography. History in its diverse aspects—events, memories, majority outlooks, minority views, subjective and objective perceptions, experiences, political incidents, individual responses—all come in the montage of Rushdie's fiction. In historiography, the preference for the plural over the singular is represented through the paintings of Aurora. The "torrential reality of India" (45) awakens her imagination. Figures from Indian history consort with hybrids of her imagination. Vasco da Gama is present as an ancestor-spectator.

Aurora's paintings suggest, indirectly, Rushdie's techniques of representation as a writer and hence offer some strategies for reading his works. Like Aurora's paintings that form a jumble of contemporary vistas juxtaposed in symbolic or mythical scenes,

Rushdie's novels are an assortment of realism and imaginative fantasy. He offers glimpses of antiquity and contemporary social critique. The creative liberty involved in interpreting the present against the foil of obscure pasts is permissible in making use of the historical material in fictional writing. Like painting, fiction is an art. The artist's freedom can be asserted through the reinterpretation of memory, available records of history and lived or narrated experience.

The paintings of Aurora in *The Moor's Last Sigh* have a similar symbolic significance of the embroidered shawls of Rani Harappa in *Shame*. Aurora's obsession with "the mythic romantic mode in which history, family and politics and fantasy jostle each other" (203) is comparable to Rushdie's way of making use of history as a material for fiction. Aurora's paintings assume the status of allegories and like mirrors reflect the countenances and many moods of the nation. The nation and its jerky ride in, across and along 'time', called mythology or history can be mapped on the expanses of fiction.

History is often associated with pictorial aspects in the work of Rushdie. The collage of contemporary events in the paintings of Aurora, is created through the cleverly manipulated depictions of scenes from myth and romance. Like painting, history becomes an art which is open to be interpreted by the observer. Umeed Merchant in *Ground Beneath Her Feet* (1999) captures the disastrous incidents using a high resolution camera, an act symbolizing the recording of a violent and disquieting present. The recorded things give an impression of being exact replicas of reality; but the photographer can select the angle, focus on what he chooses to include and leave out what he wants to exclude. Umeed knows that a photograph is a moral decision taken in a split second and a photographer occupies some space between voyeur and witness. The photographs taken by Umeed scream out the drama of the world. The sick, the dying, the rich, the greedy, the ecstatic, the killed, the children, the adults, the good and the bad populate the photographic world.

The motif of quest is used in the works of Rushdie as a symbolic exploration of the unmapped terrains of temporality.

The traveller, instead of finding an answer to his queries, is confronted with more and more questions unfolding before him. In his novels, the endlessness and inconclusiveness of history as knowledge is revealed through the various quests through the landscapes strewn with events and memories. Moreover, these homeless journeys suggest the permanent exile of the modern man. The state of the immigrant and the predicament of exodus are treated as a contemporary reality and are symbols of the process of history itself.

The parallels between history and the rootless, routeless wanderings can be traced in the works of Rushdie. *Midnight's Children* is an odyssey of sorts. The unchartered journeys of Saleem Sinai become wanderings which commence and continue without any order or method. The bits and pieces of incidents that are cut, torn and ripped at random from diverse periods of history are arranged in a muddled collage. Saleem's unique power to enter the minds of others enables him to understand history from various perspectives and he lives through different levels of experience. In his meandering accounts, Saleem challenges William Methwold's desire to preserve the vestiges of Europe and the black widow's attempts to freeze history as a monument unto herself through continuous questioning and inquiry. The quests of Saleem Sinai and the Moor, the protagonists in *Midnight's Children* and *The Moor's Last Sigh* respectively, are characterized by aimlessness. An individual's escape from historical junctures that threaten one's life is a recurring motif in the novels of Rushdie. The aspect of fleeing from threats with a bundle of fear and hatred is portrayed in *Midnight's Children* and *Shame*. Bloody violence is a major theme in these novels. Violence creates shame and the pack of shame is heavy on the heads of those who flee for refuge. Rushdie's own life has a similar phase in which he had to escape his persecutors after declaring of the *fatwa*. His plight as a political exile is captured poignantly in the Memoir, *Joseph Anton* (2012). Rushdie use third person narrative to suggest that in the contemporary times of subtle dominations, threats against creativity and freedom of expression dogs everyone.

The works of Rushdie show the ambivalence of alienation and belonging. This dual consciousness of the migrant has a major role in moulding Rushdie's historical vision. As an expatriate writer, Rushdie belongs to the nation without directly participating in its life and inhabits alien lands without belonging to them. In his works, we find a deliberate interweaving of Indian life and its mythological parallels. He thus provides a colourful inter-text of myth and fantasy to the history of the nation.

Rushdie's use of language in the novels shows translatedness because his English has purposely absorbed the styles and vocabulary of the local dialects of Indian languages. Rushdie adopts varying tones, sober to light-hearted and has an inclination to use hyperbolic tropes of narration. He is highly inventive in the use of language. The tone is deceptively casual and there is a touch of irony and a profusion of satire in his writings. Rushdie uses a casual style even while discussing very serious issues. This tone is often misleadingly informal. Rushdie's approach is not a simple literary experimentation in which stylistic devices are given more importance than character and plot. Rushdie blurs the distinctions between the tragic and the comic, the horrible and the ridiculous and the serious and the trivial. His satire is made vigorous by an intense understanding of character and society and is imbued with a strong loathing for the social ills.

History and Social Critique

Rushdie's fiction presents a fragmented genealogy of historical events with an intrinsic critique of the present. The critique unravels the complex associations between history as knowledge, the play of power and the human subject. Rushdie give us dark and horrifying pictures of our todays. But his purpose is to make us realise the necessity of immediate action to save our future that is threatened to be lost and destroyed in the turbulence of the present. The novel, *Fury* (2001) is about the unrest and instability of the present in the globalized world inhabited by people with confused memories and absolutely no sense of the past. *Shalimar the Clown* (2005) depicts a paradise that has turned into hell and this transformation is traced through history by juxtaposing the memories and perspectives of many characters. The violence and communalism in the Kashmir valley has many origins and unpredictable consequences. One has to pay back history with one's own life; no one is excluded, the unfaithful wife, the wronged husband who becomes a terrorist and the American Ambassador, a living martyr of the holocaust. *Shalimar the Clown* translates the local occurrences into global history.

Rushdie's message is not one of utter pessimism, but a warning to humanity seeking refuge in false optimism about the progressing present world. A person living in the present should treasure the dreams and convert them to actions and learn from one's memories. Rushdie says, "I am a writer. I do not accept my condition. I will strive to change it; but I inhabit it. I am trying to learn from it.... Our lives teach us who we are" (*Imaginary* 414).

Rushdie see politics as history in action which often turns to farce and tragedy, or both at once. His political world is ruthlessly Orwellian, replete with betrayals and violence. For him politics is always inconsequential, opportunistic, self-serving and demagogic. It never leaves ample scope for effective resistance to oppression. From a pedestal well above the quagmire of politics, he proclaims his condemnation of all ideological positions. The Right and the Left alike are criticized for their unprincipled power politics. No one is free from Rushdie's nonconformist censure: Indira Gandhi and the dynastic politics of congress, Pakistan's great generals, communist parties, religious fanatics, naxalites, dictators, capitalism, empire and so on.

Rushdie insists that the restrictive frameworks and the confining norms of fiction need not affect a writer. The social critique in his work and the sense of history should not be directed or regulated by the censorship lobbies. Art has the power to interpret and highlight the suppressed dimensions of human experience. When these dimensions are set free, literature and art becomes a common arena for people to meet and communicate. A great work of art is a bridge built between people and different ages. According to Rushdie:

> Literature is an interim report from the consciousness of the artist and so it can never be 'finished' or 'perfect'.

> Literature is made at the frontier between the self and the world, and in the act of creation that frontier softens, becomes permeable, allows the world to flow into the artist and the artist to flow into the world. (*Imaginary* 427)

In the opinion of Rushdie, a novel is "part social enquiry, part fantasy, part confessional. It crosses the frontiers of knowledge as well as topographical boundaries" (*Imaginary* 58). Rushdie asserts for fiction an imaginative variety of truth where freedom rules in place of institutional control. Fiction can ignore the commonplace facts and still appeal to the world of imagination to maintain that it corresponds to the true or authentic depiction of human experience in and across time. *The Satanic Verses* (1988) asserts that no limits can be set to the imaginative variety of truth. One may reinterpret the life of the Prophet and his messages. All is possible in fiction.

Rushdie's idea of imagination is ambivalent. The significant exclamation of Gabriel in *The Satanic Verses* "If I was God, I'd cut the imagination right out of people" (122) suggest a curious reversal of priorities. Rushdie does not want the imaginative truth to claim the supreme authority of reality that masquerade as absolute and objective. In *Imaginary Homelands*, Rushdie expresses his view about the need to define the limits for imaginative freedom. Freedom of imagination, if overemphasized might represent a secular fundamentalism, and it is likely that it would "lead to excesses, abuses and oppression as the canons of religious faith" (418). Of all the art forms, literature can still be the most free because "the interior spaces of the imagination is a theatre that can never be closed down" (426). This does not mean that Rushdie considers literature a privileged category. According to him "the only privilege literature deserves—and this privilege it requires in order to exist—is the privilege of being the arena of discourse, the place where the struggle of languages can be acted out" (427).

As a writer, Rushdie follows the technique of gathering the threads and motifs of life, experience and memory and weaving them into a fictional narrative. Patchworks of events, emotions of all colours and a mélange of perspectives merge on the very fabric of history. His novels contain a chaotic hotchpotch of myths, cacophonous voices, jostling personalities and events. The multi-dimensionality of narratives makes his novels a huge canvas designed to display the collage comprising historical incidents and bits of memory. It is not necessary to tell apart lived experiences and a life lived in imagination. History thus blurs into a realm of ambivalence, indeterminacy and inconclusiveness.

Works Cited

Adam, Ian and Helen Tiffin, eds. *Past the Last Post: Theorizing Post-Colonialism and Postmodernism*. New York: Harvester, 1991.

Afzal Khan, Fawzia. *Cultural Imperialism and the Indian English Novel: Genre and Ideology in the Novels of R.K. Narayan, Anita Desai, Kamala Markandaya and Salman Rushdie*. Pennsylvania: Pennsylvania State University Press, 1993.

Ahmed, Aijaz. *In Theory: Classes, Nations, Literatures*. London: Verso, 1992.

Aloysius, G. *Nationalism without a Nation in India*. New Delhi: OUP, 1997.

Birch, D. "Postmodernist Chutneys." *Textual Practice*, 5.1 (1991): 1-7.

Chaudhuri, Una. "Imaginative Maps: A Conversation with Rushdie." *Turnstile*, 2.1 (1990): 36-47.

Dharker, Rani. "An Interview with Salman Rushdie." *New Quest*, 42 (1983): 351-60.

Foucault, Michel. *The Archaeology of Knowledge* (1969). London: Routledge Classics, 2002.

Grant, Damian. *Salman Rushdie*. Plymouth: Northcote House, 1999.

Guha, Ranjit. *Dominance without Hegemony: History and Power in Colonial India*. Delhi: OUP, 1998.

Hoffenden, John, ed. *Novelists in Interview*. London: Methuen, 1985.

Parameswaran, Uma. *The Perforated Sheet: Essays on Salman Rushdie's Art*. New Delhi: Affiliated, 1988.

Rushdie, Salman. *Grimus*. London: Victor Gollancz, 1975.

———. *Midnight's Children*. London: Jonathan Cape, 1981.

———. *Shame*. London: Jonathan Cape, 1983.

———. *The Jaguar Smile: A Nicaraguan Journey*. London: Pan Books, 1987.

———. *The Satanic Verses*. London: Viking, 1988.

———. *Haroun and the Sea of Stories*. London: Penguin, 1990.

———. *Imaginary Homelands: Essays and Criticism 1981-1991*. London: Granta, 1991.

———. *East West*. London: Jonathan Cape, 1994.

———. *The Moor's Last Sigh*. London: Jonathan Cape, 1995.

———. *The Ground Beneath Her Feet*. London: Jonathan Cape, 1999.

———. *Fury*. London: Jonathan Cape, 2001.

———. *Step Across This Line*. London: Jonathan Cape, 2002.

———. *Shalimar the Clown*. London: Jonathan Cape, 2005.

———. *The Enchantress of Florence*. London, Viking, 2008.

———. *Joseph Anton: A Memoir*. London: Jonathan Cape, 2012.

Weatherby, William J. *Salman Rushdie Sentenced to Death*. New York: Carroll & Graf, 1990.

Young, Robert. *Colonial Desire, Hybridity in Theory, Culture and Race*. London: Routledge, 1995.

11

Nation and Non-narration: Multiplicity, Hybridity and Heterogeneity in Salman Rushdie's *The Moor's Last Sigh*

Manjeet Kumar Kashyap

I

The paper proposes to examine nation and non-narration to understand multiplicity, hybridity and heterogeneity in Salman Rushdie's *The Moor's Last Sigh*. The fiction of Rushdie is related to modern Indian historiography and the Indian nation. Therefore, it is necessary to provide contextual knowledge for understanding his fiction. Rushdie does not depict the history, and narrates the nation in conceptualisation of its glorious past; instead, he contests and radically re-interprets the meta-narratives of history and nation. The idea of nation and narration in his fiction is created through multiplicity, hybridity and heterogeneity. He conceives even the very concept of 'home' as "a scattered, damaged, various concepts in our present travails" (Brydon 6). Such views refer to shift away from homogeneous nation-states based on the ideology of assimilation to a much more similar and dissimilar definition of nation as a construct of multiplicity and heterogeneity of the subject.

Non-narration is an involvement into traditional and accepted mode of narrative and tends to diminish or ignore the function of coherence and reliable narrative structure for producing a crisis of understanding. The mode of non-narrative is important in postmodern texts because it attempts to "resist narrative, reinvent the structures of narration, and/or perform theoretical evaluations of systems of narration within the created world of their own design" (Harryman 1). The function of non-narrative is to undermine and subvert the "discourses related to cognitive and narratological theories of authorship, periodization, the master narrative of late capitalism, the gendered subject and formal innovation, and the role of literary narrative in politically marginal communities" (1-2). The term addresses innovative postmodernist strategies that reshape, redistribute, undermine, and radically break rules of storytelling in order to disrupt the irregular power relations, the complex relationships between private experience and larger social forces, the limits of knowledge, the psychological and social functioning, and the cooperative construction of meaning. Harryman considers non-narrative as "a strategy of intervention" (2). Describing the nature and function of non-narrative, Lyn Hejinian and Barrett Watten write: "Narrative was suspect—it was the horizon of official meaning and interpretation, the real prison house to which we have been confined by history. An open field of meaning offered a way out of the confinements of narrative and closure, and non-narrative writing strategies became vehicles of choice" (Harryman 2).

The link between the novel and the "narration" of nation is very old. Timothy Brennan writes, "Nations, then, are imaginary constructs that depend for their existence on an apparatus of cultural fictions in which imaginative literature plays a decisive role" (49). The novel is not the only such imaginative vehicle, but it plays significant roles in the rise of nation-states. The growth of novel has coincided across cultural contexts. The fiction of Rushdie cannot be read without references to history and context. The "manner of its presentation," Brennan argues, accounts for the novel's centrality, "objectifying the 'one, yet many' of national life, and...mimicking the structure of the nation, a clearly bordered jumble of languages and styles" (49). In this context, Homi Bhabha also writes:

> Nations, like narratives, lose their origins in the myths of time and only fully realize their horizons in the mind's eye. Such an image of the nation—or narration—might seem impossibly romantic and excessively metaphorical,

> but it is from those traditions of political thought and literary language that the nation emerges as a powerful historical idea in the west. An idea whose cultural compulsion lies in the impossible unity of the nation as a symbolic force. (1)

The fiction of Salman Rushdie is concerned with displacement of the cultural location and national identities through "hybridity" and multiplicity. In his fiction, the representation of India and its social, cultural, religious, metaphysical, familial, historical, political and geographical aspects are not just a theme but a point of debate, speculation, reflection and contestation. These aspects are significant in Rushdie and Indian fiction in English since the publication of *Midnight's Children*. On surface, the protagonist, Salim, tells his story to Padma as they both work together in a pickle factory. But the narrative strategy is not simple which attempts to represent alternative realities of the "birth-of-a-nation", memory and document, myth and history through the juxtaposition of the private and the public, and the historical and the biographical. The novel attempts to narrate the history of Indian nation and Pakistan but the very attempt is put under suspicion from the beginning. In a way, it punctures the idea of providing realistic representation. The narrative in the novel takes the form of non-narration by adopting the mode of fairy tale and oral narrative in the representation of the historical records. The novel opens in the form of fairy tale:

> ...Once upon a time. No, that won't do, there's no getting away from the date: I was born in Doctor Narlikar's Nursing Home on August 15th, 1947. And the time? The time matters, too. Well then: at night. No, it's important to be more.... On the stroke of midnight, as a matter of fact. Clock-hands joined palms in respectful greeting as I came. Oh, spell it out, spell it out: at the precise instant of India's arrival at independence, I tumbled forth into the world. (Rushdie 1)

The narrative technique in the novel reduces the national events to personal happening of individuals; for instance, the independence of the nation with his birth, India's first nuclear explosion with the return of Shiva's warlike arrival, etc. The macro-scale of history is always related back to the micro-scale of the individual. One of the most important aspects of non-narration in the novel is unreliable narrative. The factual errors are introduced into the narrative, the relationship between history and personal experiences are brought into the question. At one point it says that it finds an error in chronology and has given wrong date of the assassination of Mahatma Gandhi, the father of the nation. The question of heterogeneity and multiplicity are introduced in form of providing alternative version of history and reality. As the narrator says, "[T]here are so many stories to tell, too many, such an excess of intertwined lives events miracles places rumours, so dense a commingling of the improbable and the mundane!" (Rushdie, 1981: 9). The novel also exploits a range of literary and cultural resources from allegory, satire, and surrealism to Hindi cinema, Hindu mythology—the Ramayana and the Mahabharata—the speeches of Jawaharlal Nehru, newspaper accounts of actual incidents science fiction, political slogans, and advertising jingles. Saleem comes to believe that by crafting his own narrative, he can control events in his life as well as have an effect on the life of the nation.

The publication of *Midnight's Children* in 1981 opens a new dimension in Indian writing in English in terms of adopting postmodern playfulness, the turn to history, the experiment with language and the like. The technique of non-narration in the form of magic-realism, metafiction, unreliability, multiplicity and heterogeneity continues in all the successive fiction of Rushdie. The anarchic structure of *The Satanic Verses* swaps Saladin Chamcha's purgatorial quest through diabolic London with Gibreel Farishta's religious paranoia and glorious visions. Rushdie's novels are concerned with the migrants' relationship with their homeland. The rootlessness, in *The Ground Beneath Her Feet,* is viewed as antisocial because it disorients from home, family, clan, race, and nation. The narrator, Rai, finds himself and the Muslims marginalized in Bombay. They also face different types of problems—prejudices, threat during travelling, space in school bus, racial discrimination, etc.—in the migrated country. The novel depicts the contemporary situations in postcolonial, globalized and multicultural contexts.

The novels account the interaction of personal and national, the traumas underlying postcolonial Indian identities, the lasting influence of British culture, and the inaccessibility of a purely Indian past which leads to a third zone emerging after the contact among the local, the national and the global. The cultural encounters in *The Ground Beneath Her Feet* are represented by the celebrity culture projected by remix of narratives and Bollywood's glamour, suspense, romance, etc. In this way, it becomes a zone of hybridity and cultural dislocation and its drawbacks. *Fury* depicts the cultural differences of competing immigrant and native voices. The protagonist encounters Italian immigrants and transplanted black southerners mixing in racial and linguistic ways that break his connection to both places. *Shalimar the Clown* shifts the focus to the recent political events in Kashmir which have influenced the lives and transnational mobility of people.

Rushdie revisits the geographical location of *Midnight's Children* in his *The Moor's Last Sigh*. *The Moor's Last Sigh* tells the complicated story of four generations of a Christian-Jewish family involved in the spice trade in India. The novel is in a way leave-taking from the issues of Indian subcontinent. It is narrated by Moor, the son of the double dealing spice merchant Abraham Zogoiby, a Spanish Jew who is presumably the illegitimate descendant of the Arab sultan Abu Abdullah of Andalusia (known as Boabdil), and the Catholic matriarch-cum-artist Aurora da Gama, a descendant of the renowned Portuguese explorer, Vasco da Gama. Like Scheherazade, Moor protracts his own life by spinning the yarn of the Zogoiby da Gama saga from within an Alhambra-like citadel in Benengeli, Spain. Here he is held captive by Vasco Miranda, who is a decidedly second-rate artist and Aurora's spurned lover. It is for Vasco Miranda that Moor writes the story of his family's life, from his premature birth and high-speed ageing, through his family's business feuds, to his fatal visit to Benengeli to recuperate his mother's painting, also called *The Moor's Last Sigh*, which Vasco has stolen by way of revenge.

The novel starts with the story of a spice trader, Moraes Zogoiby who is popularly called 'Moor' who takes care for his ancestral spice trade business with full of enthusiasm at Cochin. Albeit under pressure of lots of troubles, he feels himself capable how to carry out the risky task of spice trade well, such as "the menace of emerald smugglers, the mechanisation of business rivals, the growing nervousness of the British colony in fort Cochin, the cash demands of the staff and of the plantation workers in the spice Mountain, the tales of communists trouble making and Congresswallah politics" (9). It is "a last sigh", in Moor's words, "for a lost world, a tear for its passing". The Moor's narrative shows not only what the nation has become but what it has promised at the birth: reflecting such as A.K. Mehrotra argues that "a historical generosity of spirit", a free India was supposed to be "above religion...above class...above hatred...above vengeance...above tribe...above language...above ignorance...above stupidity" (316). India seems as if it were a model example of that very modern observable fact, an "imagined community" whereby people at a large scale come together to make up that political and cultural body known as the nation.

The nation such as Sudipta Kaviraj argues "India is not an object of discovery but of invention" in the nationalist imagination. The Indian nation-state is a recent construct in consequence of historical accidents and political transformations that took place over the nineteenth and twentieth centuries. The Moor's family is observed to be stuck in the freedom fight under the leaderships of Annie Besant and Bal Gangadhar Tilak for the implementation of an independent Indian Parliament for the splendid future of the country. Rushdie describes,

> In 1916 Francisco Da Gama joined the Home Rule campaign of Annie Besant and Bal Gangadhar Tilak, hitching his star to the demand for an independent Indian parliament which would determine the country's future. When Mrs. Besant asked him to found a Home Rule League in Cochin and he had the nerve to invite dock-labours, tea-pickers, bazaar coolies and his own workers to join as well as local bourgeoisie. (19)

The discourse of the construction of the nation India is not timeless, one and same for everyone. Bhabha rightly says, "The nation's 'coming into being' as a system of cultural signification, as the representation of social *life* rather than the discipline of social *polity,* emphasizes this instability of knowledge" (Bhabha 1-2). The question of belonging underpins the notions of location not only in terms of one's relationship to a particular community, time or place, but also one's openness towards communities outside as a "citizen of the world". In the novel, the narrator tells the history of a Christian-Jewish family in India in order to shows a transition from cultural purism to cultural pluralism. There are no more insider/outsider issues, us/them sentiments, or "freaks" to exclude, which prevent individuals from interacting with each other.

The Moor's Last Sigh concerns with the way in which "a national definition has to struggle to incorporate the individual". It does so by inventing historical and ethnic categories in their attempts to create cultural cohesion. The history of nation-building made the novel the paradigmatic site for "imagining" the national foundations. A marked preoccupation with history and an urge to re-visit and critically re-examine the past has been at the crucial concern of the novel. The identity of the narrator Moor is allocated and imposed from outside, where memories are systematically suppressed in the pre-colonial past, and the urge to revisit the past becomes indispensable for the processes of reconciliation and identity reconstruction. By the time Moor tells his story to the narrator-in-exile, he is "alone now, motherless...appear[ing] to lose his metaphorical role as a unifier of opposites, a standard bearer of pluralism, ceasing to stand as a symbol—however approximate—of the new nation" (Rushdie 66). Thus, Moor is polarized between his story and History, wherein his long-awaited vision of family (i.e. national) unity stands in bleak contrast to the rupture body politic of the Zogoiby family. The greater the layers of deceit underlying his family's history, therefore, the lesser the Moor's inclination to piece together the fractured narrative of his past. Moor is caught within the paradox of exile: he living with the illusions of the past is to live with "folly" of imagination and to step out from the past is possible only through imagination, which is a creative act that can liberate him from the shackles of his story and History. The root of Moor's family is typically mixed Indian heritage. On one side, the depiction of Indian nationalism as an escalating/ethnocentric movement, with a "Hindu preference for the eternal stability of caste" and "natural residents" (299) is emphasized by the Moor's parallel universe of the darker side of Spain's modern history, where "folk had been plunged into deep morning" (387) over Franco's death. The formation of ethnic and cultural identity is entangled in the "large and liminal image of the nation" which escalates in Bhabha's words, "a particular ambivalence that haunts the idea of the nation, the language of those who write of it and the lives of those who live it. It is an ambivalence that emerges from a growing awareness that... the cultural temporality of the nation inscribes a much more transitional social reality" (1).

The idea of nation in *The Moor's Last Sigh* can be aligned with the position adopted by Fanon in his essay "On National Culture", in which he insists that the "nation is not only the condition of culture" but "a necessity", since "the re-establishment of the nation" will not only "give life to national culture" but "make such a culture open to other cultures" (197). The novel, in its study of nation through narratives, attempts to change the conceptual object itself. What Bhabha says in theory, Rushdie does in the novel. In order to offer a comprehensible illustration I would quote them. Bhabha says: "If the problematic 'closure' of textuality questions the 'totalization' of national culture, then its positive value lies in displaying the wide dissemination through which we construct the field of meanings and symbols associated with national life" (3).

Moraes comes to see the New Bombay (and all India by extension) as a simulacral city succumbing to an invisible, greed-driven entrepreneurial class and mammon-minded intellectual élite. He questions "the 'totalization' of national culture" and shows multiple lying of tales upon tales, in the form of palimpsest that constitutes India:

> The city itself, perhaps the whole country, was a palimpsest, Under World Beneath over World, black market beneath white; when the whole of life was like this, when an *invisible reality* moved phantom wise

> beneath *a visible fiction, subverting all its meanings...* how could any of us have escaped that deadly layering? How trapped as we were in the hundred percent fakery of the real...could we have penetrated to the full, sensual truth of the lost mother below? How could we have lived authentic lives? How could we have failed to be grotesque? (Rushdie 184; emphases added)

This palimpsest engagement which characterizes historical and cultural inheritance, provide a critique of post-independence state practice then moves into classic postcolonial resistance territory with the blatant strategy of, what Bill Ashcroft call, "abrogation and appropriation" (39).

The Moor, "expelled from his story, [and tumbling] towards history" (Rushdie 2), is caught within the paradox of his own exilic condition. By approaching his story from the perspective of an outsider, he is able to see the "polished and fantasticated" (11) nature of his family's history. On the one side, the Moor endeavors to "make light" of the darker side of his own history, and on the other, by "making light of the dark", he becomes responsible for bringing to light to "darker" elements. In this way, Moor's thoughts are embedded in two different domains. At this position, Bhabha says, "What emerges as an effect of such 'incomplete signification' is a turning of boundaries and limits into the *in-between* spaces through which the meanings of cultural and political authority are negotiated" (Bhabha 4)? The idea of hybridity, in-betweenness and doubleness is illustrated in the novel in the following words: "...the doubleness in Grandfather Camoens...his willingness to permit the coexistence within himself of conflicting impulses...that hate-the-sin-and-love-the-sinner sweetness, that historical generosity of spirit, which is one of the wonders of India" (32).

Hybridity appears in many guises, including what the mythical land whose loss the original Moor sighed for. The title of the novel (which is also the title of series of Aurora's paintings) is based on the legend that Arab Andalusia's last sultan, the weak and quixotic Boabdil. In one of his interviews, Rushdie says that it embodies a "composite culture" thrived with "Christians and Jews and Muslims living side by side for hundreds of years". As his namesake cried for Andalusia, our Moor and his creator both mourn the loss of a tolerant, multicultural India whose demise Rushdie dates at the rise of the Hindu right in the 1990s. Elsewhere, the same ideal becomes Moor's vision of love, "the blending of spirits, as mélange, as the triumph of the impure, mongrel, conjoining best over what there is in us of the solitary, the isolated, the austere, the dogmatic, the pure; of love as democracy, as the victory of the no-man-is-an-island, two's-company any over the clean, mean, partheiding Ones" (289).

For Rushdie, an art embrace divergent tradition and elements that function outside the law. "I am a bastard child of history", he happily declares in an essay in *Imaginary Homelands* (394). Throughout the novel, he explicitly connects the bastard with the work of feces art. Thus Moor: "*Bastard*: I like the sound of the word. *Baas,* a smell, a stinky-poo. *Turd*, no translation required. Ergo, *Bastard,* a smelly shit, like, for example, me" (104). An indirect etymological connection supports Moor's privileging of the bastard. Moor describes Vasco Miranda's parody *pietà* as having "stigmatised hands", reminding us of the link between stigma and stigmata and thus equating chosen people and outcasts (415). Moor is both; so, of course, was Jesus, the world's most famous bastard. With the gloss of Rushdie's bilingual pseudo-derivation, the single epithet neatly encapsulates linguistic mongrelization, both in itself and as a figure for racial and religious miscegenation, along with illegitimacy: in other words, the three elements essential to literary expression.

In the face of intractable religious fanaticism and political extremism, Rushdie intimates, such abstract notions as hybridity, plurality, multiculturalism, and liminal subjectivity may potentially be vacated of their historical significance and resistive value. The rich examples of hybridity in the novel are depicted through the contact of the Eastern and the Western traditions in India. Rushdie shows that the European tradition such as Christmas takes on a new meaning in an Indian context, and simultaneously it is brought closer to its original meaning:

> Christmas, that Northern invention, that tale of snow and stockings, of merry fires and reindeer, Latin carols and *O Tannenbaum*, of evergreen trees and Sante Klaas with his little piccanniny 'helpers,' is restored by tropical heat to something like its origins, for whatever else the Infant Jesus may or may not have been, he was a hot-weather babe; however poor his manger, it wasn't *cold*; and if Wise Men came...they came, let's not forget it, from the East. (62)

The story of Granada's downfall provides the background for the failure of India's pluralism. In fact, this story is woven into the narrative of *The Moor's Last Sigh* to represent modern India and for the ruptures of cultures not only in India but in the modern world. The significance of the Granadan theme is considered as Rushdie's engagement with the competing discourses of fundamentalism and pluralism in India's national and cultural history. The novel also conjures the history of Arab-Spain as a viable multicultural model that the author wished for post-independence India. Rushdie's postmodern superimposition of many countries' history and India's national narrative in *The Moor's Last Sigh* is both nostalgia for exotic and lost Golden Age and a postcolonial hybridity as an empowering subject position. Removed from its Moorish setting and grafted onto India's national history, Boabdil's legend not only indexes the imbrications of various historical and national narratives, but it also helps re-think the relationship between modern memory and the past, politics and representation, in the articulation of a contemporary hybrid subjectivity. Rushdie's appropriation of Boabdil's notorious story in *The Moor's Last Sigh* reveals suggestive allusions to the pitfalls of seeing medieval Arab-Spain as the possible locus of a recoverable multicultural utopia. A(a)dam's history, recounted in novel, is a synopsis of part of the story of *Midnight's Children*:

> It seems he was originally the illegitimate child of a Bombay hooligan and an itinerant magician from Shadipur U.P., and had been unofficially adopted, for a time, by a Bombay man who was missing believed-dead, haying mysteriously disappeared fourteen years ago, not

> long after his allegedly brutal treatment by government agents during the 1974-77 Emergency. (342)

Rushdie's treatment of the myth of hybridity as the opposite version of the myth of authenticity is manifest in Aurora's Moor paintings. Superimposing public commentary with personal experience, Aurora's paintings are divided into three phases. The first phase (1957-77), which she painted between Moraes's birth and Indira Gandhi's electoral defeat, is defined by their colourful, optimistic variations upon the Boabdil story. The second phase (1977-81), established her as India's uncontested artistic voice, but marked by a sense of loss and despair. The third and final phase (1981-87), presents "'the dark Moors', those pictures of exile and terror", in which the Arab King becomes for the first and last time her primary subject matter (Rushdie 218). Aurora's final Moor paintings begin to exhibit a postmodern sense of disintegration and fragmentation:

> Aurora had apparently decided that the ideas of impurity, cultural admixture and mélange which had been, for most of her creative life, the closest things she had found to a notion of the Good, were in fact capable of distortion, and contained a potential for darkness as well as for light.... This "black Moor"... became a haunted figure, fluttered about by phantoms of his past which tormented him though he cowered and bid them be gone. Then slowly he grew phantomlike himself...was robbed of his lozenges and jewels and the last vestiges of his glory; obliged to become a soldier in some petty warlord's army...reduced to mercenary status where once he had been a king, he rapidly became a composite being as pitiful and anonymous as those amongst whom he moved. Garbage piled up, and buried him. (303)

In addition, Vasco's Indo-European hybrid art soon develops into profit-oriented, self-serving exoticism. His Western-style artistic career, described as a "spiced-up rehash of the European surrealists...for which the owners of public buildings would pay truly surrealist sums" (148), shows the extent to which the so-called hybridity art can be compromised by a consumer-based cultural market. As Moraes explains, had it not been for the "huge foreign-currency fortune" that Vasco amassed while promoting his career in cities like New York and Lisbon, he would not have been able to build his Alhambra-like "hilltop folly" in Benengeli (253).

To conclude, the fiction of Rushdie deconstructs simplistic construction of nation, culture and identity based on tradition, geographical origin, and cultural location. Thus, it challenges the very categories on which the national identities are forged. Rushdie's narrative de-narrates the nation by not making distinction between fantasy and realism. The nation is neither romanticized nor sentimentalized, but it is nevertheless acknowledged as a palimpsest construction in the imagination. In this way, the narrative of the novel embodies the trends of non-narration, that is, it does not follow a linear, realistic and progressive structure of narrative. The breaks in narrative open multiplicity and heterogeneity leading innumerable interpretations of the novel. In consequence, what Saleem Sinai calls "the chutnification of history" in *Midnight's Children* has now become Aurora's "junkyard collage" in *The Moor's Last Sigh* (315). It also asserts Stuart Hall's sense of the postcolonial relation with the past as "always-already 'after the break'". The novel evinces Hall's awareness of that relationship as "always constructed through memory, fantasy, narrative and myth" (226). Rushdie's own art is the best example of the cultural hybridity he celebrates. For Rushdie, all culture, and especially Indian, is palimpsest in nature.

Works Cited

Ashcroft, Bill et al. *The Empire Writes Back*. London and New York: Routledge, 1989.

Bhabha, Homi K. "Introduction: Narrating the Nation." In *Nation and Narration*. Ed. Homi K. Bhabha. London: Routledge, 1990. 1-7.

Brennan, Timothy. "The National Longing for Form." *Nation and Narration*. Ed. Homi K. Bhabha. London: Routledge, 1990. 44-70.

Brydon, Diana. "Canadian Writers Negotiating Home Within Global Imaginaries." DRAFT: Literature For Our Time ACLALS Conference August 2007. Web. 26 July 2014.

Fanon, Frantz. *The Wretched of the Earth*. Trans. C. Farrington. Harmondsworth: Penguin, 1967.

Hall, Stuart. "Cultural Identity and Diaspora." *Identity: Community, Culture, Difference*. Ed. Jonathan Rutherford. London: Lawrence and Wishart, 1990. 222-37.

Harryman, Carla. "Introduction: Non/Narrative." *Journal of Narrative Theory* 41.1 (Spring 2011): 1-11.

Rushdie, Salman. *Midnight's Children*. London: Jonathan Cape, 1981.

———. *The Satanic Verses*. London: Vintage, 1988.

———. *Imaginary Homelands*. New York: Penguin Books, 1991.

———. *The Moor's Last Sigh*. London: Jonathan Cape, 1995.

———. *The Ground Beneath Her Feet*. London: Vintage, 1999.

———. *Fury*. London: Vintage, 2001.

Mehrotra, Arvind Krishna. *An Illustrated History of Indian Literature in English*. New Delhi: Permanent Black, 2003.

12

Globalization and Cosmopolitanism: Major Themes in the Works of Salman Rushdie

Hetal K. Kachhia

Introduction

Ahmed Salman Rushdie is a British-Indian postcolonial writer. The reason behind the aspects of globalization and cosmopolitanism in his writing is his birth and acquaintance with the cosmopolitan city like Bombay and his long stay in Britain. His journey from Bombay to Britain and *Grimus* (1975) to *Joseph Anton* (2013) provided him with a lot of experiences and acquaintance with many issues that he has depicted in his works. It becomes quite necessary, at this moment, to discuss briefly relevant issues in his novels. Published in 1975, his first novel *Grimus,* with the story of Grimus and Flapping Eagle, was not a great success, but still the elements of 'migration' and 'isolation' that are related to diasporic sensibility, could be found, which, in fact, was presenting his own migration and isolation from his own country. *Midnight's Children* (1981) not only won him the Booker Prize for the year 1981, but also universal recognition, which also presented themes from hybridity to migration and isolation to cosmopolitanism, which are the part of cosmopolitan culture in a globalized world. In his third novel *Shame* (1983), Rushdie depicted the political scenario of Pakistan, but made it of global importance by stating, "My view is that I am not writing only about Pakistan" (*Shame* 29), again makes it of global value. His most controversial work, *Satanic Verses* (1988) was accused by Muslims for blasphemy, has also to do with the themes of migration and cosmopolitanism. *Haroun and the Sea of Stories* (1990), a work of fantasy which focuses on the journey of Haroun to Land of G, Valley of K and Kahani also denotes the theme of migration. *The Moor's Last Sigh* (1995) has also to deal with the cosmopolitan cultures of the cities like Bombay and Cochin. *The Ground Beneath Her Feet* (1999) was declared by Toni Morrison as 'a global novel' as it presents both Western and Eastern culture with the multilingualism of its characters and has context from Greek mythology, European philosophy, and reference of contemporaries like Milan Kundera and great personalities of music. *Fury* (2001), in presenting 'fury' of every man in this world, becomes globally important, through the character of Malik Solanka that emphasizes on the themes like migration and cosmopolitanism. *Shalimar the Clown* (2005) also follows the same themes of migration and cosmopolitanism in presenting from California and Los Angeles of U.S.A. to Kashmir and Shalimar of India and characters from different cultures. *The Enchantress of Florence* (2008) also moves between continents and moves from the court of Akbar to Renaissance of Florence. His last fictional work *Luka and the Fire of Life* (2010) which is considered to be a sequel to *Haroun and the Sea of Stories* (1990) presents the journey of Luka towards the Fire of Life, having inspired from video games, which again stresses on the element of migration.

Globalization and Cosmopolitanism in Salman Rushdie's Works

As defined on Wikipedia, "'Globalization' is a common term for processes of international integration arising from increasing human activity an interchange of worldviews, products, ideas, and other aspects of culture." As Bruce Robbins puts it in the "Comparative Cosmopolitanisms", "the word 'cosmopolitan' immediately evokes the image of a privileged person: someone who can claim to be a 'citizen of the world' by virtue of independent means, expensive tastes, and globe-trotting life-style" (248). Thus, both 'globalization' and 'cosmopolitanism' focuses on the world as a whole rather than on a particular locality or group within it. Both the concepts emphasize on being at home with diversity. As Salman Rushdie writes in *Imaginary Homelands* (1991), "Indian writers in this islands, like others who have migrated into the north from the south, are capable of writing from a kind of double perspective: because they, we, are at one and the same time insiders and outsiders in this society" (*Imaginary* 19). In this sense, Salman Rushdie seems to be very much at home in characterizing the diversities of the universe.

Rushdie has presented characters with wide diversity in community, language, professions, cultures, ethnicity, class and other aspects of life that makes his novels more 'global' and 'cosmopolitan': Aadam Aziz, Naseem Ghani, Alia, Mumtaz-Amina, Emerald, Mustapha, Hanif, Nadir, Major Zulfikar, Ahmed Sinai are Muslims, majority of them are from India, William Methwold, an English man, and Mary Pareira are Christians, Vanita is a Hindu in *Midnight's Children* (1981); Iskander, Raza Hyder, Arjumand Ironpants, Sufiya Zinobiya are Muslims from Pakistan in *Shame* (1983); Gibreel Farishta, Saladin Chamcha—Indian Muslims and Allie Cone—an English lady in *The Satanic Verses* (1988); Malik Solanka—an Indian Muslim in *Fury* (2001); Shalimar—a Muslim and, Boonyi—Kashmiri Pandit girl are Indians and, Maximilian—a Jew brought up in France, educated in Paris and a USA ambassador in India in *Shalimar the Clown* (2005); Ormus Cama—a Bombay born Parsee in *The Ground Beneath Her Feet* (1999); Niccolo Machiavelli and Argalia-Florentines in *The Enchantress of Florence* (2008), who are people presenting variety in their nationality and ethnicity. Different professionals have been depicted by Rushdie using his skills of accurate characterization such as Aadam Aziz—a doctor, Major Zulfikar—an officer in Pakistani army, Ahmed Sinai—a merchant, Mary Pareira—a midwife/nurse, Brass monkey/Jamila—singer, Mustapha—a civil servant, Nadir Khan—Personal Assistant to Mian Abdullah, Hanif—a film director, Pia—an actress, Picture Singh—a snake charmer, Wee Willie Winkie—a singer/entertainer, Commander Sabarmati—a high ranked official in Indian Navy, Dr. Narlikar—a doctor and a businessman, Farooq, Shaheed and Ayooba—Pakistani soldiers, Mian Abdullah—a post-partition politician, Tai—a boatman, Ramram Seth—a prophet in *Midnight's Children* (1981); Rashid—a storyteller, Mr. Butt—a driver, Snooty Butto —a politician, General Kitab—the commander in Guppee Army, Blabbermouth—a woman knight, Mali—a gardener in *Haroun and the Sea of Stories* (1990); Malik Solanka—a dollmaker in *Fury*; different politicians in *Shame* (1983); Shalimar—a chauffeur and Maximilian Ophuls—USA ambassador to India in *Shalimar the Clown* (2005); Ormus Cama—a lyricist in *The Ground Beneath Her Feet* (1999); Aurora—a famous national artist and tutor, Moor's father—a clerk in family spice business in *The Moor's Last Sigh* (1995).

According to Bruce Robbins in his "Introduction Part I: Actually Existing Cosmopolitanism", "Cosmopolitanism are now plural and particular" (2), and rather than investing in a singular, transcendental, understanding of cosmopolitan, Rushdie has interest in cosmopolitanisms in plural as he deals with nations, emigrants, cities, diaspora, etc. His novels, in a way, reflect Rushdie's own position being a Muslim Indian staying in Britain and his own sensibility on this issue. Timothy Brennan, in *Salman Rushdie and the Third World: Myths of Nation* (1989), has noted "class resentment and a resistance to being represented by a cosmopolitan intellectual were crucial components of the protests" (145). Salman Rushdie after presenting the loss and pain of dislocation and migration in *Imaginary Homelands* focuses on the advantages of crossing the boundaries of nation. He says, "While the Indian writer who writes from outside India is obliged to deal in broken mirror, some of whose fragments have been irretrievably lost [...] broken mirror may actually be as valuable as the one which is supposedly unflawed" (9-21). Rushdie is anxious over the crisis in Bombay's Cosmopolitan and secular identity while depicting cosmopolitan. Rushdie who has acquaintance with three different countries: India—where he born, Pakistan—where his family lives and England—where he migrated, instead of believing in 'rootlessness' believes in 'multiple rooting'.

Rushdie has presented in his novels a wide variety of places from small villages of Kashmir—Pachigam and Shalimar to big metropolitan cities like Bombay, Cochin, New York, Los Angeles; from ancient India of Mughal time and Florence of Renaissance to fantastic world of Land of G, Valley of K, Alifbay, Kahani along with the global account of America, Britain etc. To give it a more global touch, Rushdie has depicted real, and modified historical events such as the Independence of India, the Jallianwalla Bagh massacre, two world wars, the scenario and the tension between Hindu-Muslim during partition, wars for Kashmir, imposition of the State of Emergency in India by Indira Gandhi, conflict with Pakistan on the issue of independent Bangladeshi state, etc. as in *Midnight's Children*; an account of Bugatti automobile company, the existence of Jihad and the condition of Kashmiris, terrorism, imperialistic attitude of foreigners in India, etc. in *Shalimar the Clown* (2005); scenario of Pakistan after the partition and its rulers, politics, gender issues, the Bangladesh issue as depicted in *Shame* (1983); reign of Akbar, Renaissance of Florence, gender discrimination, etc. as in *The Enchantress of Florence* (2008); an account of the assassination of American President John F. Kennedy, the Watergate scandal, the classical rock songs for which he gives credit to John Linnon or the Kinks, etc. in *The Ground Beneath Her Feet* (1999). Even Rushdie has given account of historical figures in his works either by direct mention or by drawing fictional characters from these great personalities like the Widow/Indira Gandhi, 1st Millennium historians al-Waqidi and al-Tabari, Benazir Bhutto—former Prime Minister of Pakistan, Zulfikar Bhutto, Raza Hyder, Ayatollah Khomeini, famous figures from history of Rock music, Indian emperors, Ottoman assassins, Vasco da Gama, Moorish king of Granada, etc. to make his works more universal.

His works seems to be globalized not only in a way that it presents rich combination of the references from Greek mythology, European philosophy and context of contemporaries to the history of the rock 'n' roll music and Indian film industry, etc., but is full of multiple genres: comedy, satire, history, fantasy, mythology, etc. Rushdie gives a global description of the Aadam in *The Moor's Last Sigh* (1995) saying, "his elephantine ears are akin to 'star TV satellite dishes', his call to unity is a mere front for developing citizens in the interest of 'optimis[ing] manpower utilization'" (341). He is, as Rushdie terms him, 'the battering RAM' (342).

If we look at the terms 'globalization' and 'cosmopolitanism' as the intermingling of different cultures and its different aspects and phenomena into one another, we can say that the works of Salman Rushdie compose a global and intermingled fictional world by including the element of 'intertextuality', from his own works to the different allusions from others' works, which makes the recurrences of characters and places possible from one text to another. The characters like William Methwold and Homi Catrack from *Midnight's Children* (1981); S.S. Sisodia from *The Satanic Verses* (1988); Aurora Zogoiby from *The Moor's Last Sigh* (1995) and the settings of Malabar Hill, Bombay; Warden Road and Everest Villas, etc. reappear in *The Ground Beneath Her Feet* (1999). In the *Luka and the Fire of Life* (2010), Luka is shown as the younger son of Rashid and the younger brother of Haroun from the *Haroun and the Sea of Stories* (1990). Aadam, from the *Midnight's Children* (1981) reappears in *The Moor's Last Sigh* (1995). The classical mythology, European philosophy and the contemporaries like Milan Kundera have also been alluded in his works. According to Sherif Hetata, in *Fragmentation, Dollarization and God,* "To maintain the global economy and the global culture, unification must exist at the top among the few.... People must remain divided, confused, fragmented" (283), which is very much true for the works of Salman Rushdie in depicting fragmentation, confusion and division in both characters and narration.

Hybridity

The term 'hybridity' has been most recently associated with Homi Bhabha, who explained the term in his work as the interdependence of colonizer and colonized. According to Homi Bhabha, 'hybridity' subverts the narratives of colonial powers and dominant cultures. The series of inclusions and exclusions on which a dominant culture is premised are deconstructed by the very entry of the formerly-excluded subjects into the mainstream discourse. The dominant culture is contaminated by the linguistic and racial differences of the native self. Hybridity can have at least three meanings—In terms of biology, ethnicity and culture. Kraidy perceived hybridity as a cultural effect of globalization who defined it as the culture logic of globalization as it entails that traces of other cultures exist in every culture, thus offering foreign media and marketers transcultural wedges for forging affective links between their commodities and local communities (2005: 148). According to Shankar, "the emphasis on hybridity results from the fact that postcolonial theory has characterized postcolonial societies as hybrid societies, and many of the signature themes of postcolonial criticism and theory have emerged directly out of this characterization of the postcolonial condition" (2004: 83). Salman Rushdie's works also possess the examples of hybridity which operates at different levels. In *Shalimar the Clown* (2005), the hybridity is presented through the birth of India, who is an illegitimate child of Maximilian Ophuls, an American ambassador and Boonyi, a Kashmiri girl, who is the outcome of two different cultures. In *Enchantress of Florence* (2008), European visitor tells Mughal Akbar to be his long lost relative, born of an exiled Indian princess and an Italian from Florence. In *Midnight's Children* (1981), it is presented through Saleem Sinai, who is a biological child of Vanita, an Indian and William Methwold, an Englishman. This hybridity is further emphasized and enhanced when Shiv—the biological child of Ahmed and Amina and Saleem Sinai—of Vanita and William Methwold, after being exchanged by Mary Pareira, grow up in the culture other than their own.

Hybridity can also be found in the narrative technique as his fictional works are the rich combination of different genres including realism, fantasy, history, satire, comedy, tragedy, etc. that is responsible for making 'Cosmopolitanism of Genres'. At another level hybridity can be found in identity, i.e. characters with confusing multiple identities. Saleem, Shiv, Mumtaz/Amina, Gibreel Farishta, Saladin Chamcha, Shalimar, etc. can be put into this category. This hybridity operates at the level of language as well, using which Rushdie discovers new words like '*chutnification*'. This hybridity is visible in intermingling of Indian storytelling technique and Western novel writing, presenting factual account and fictional one, or rather creating semi-fictional account by the combination of real and unreal, by making allusions from 'great' works to a very much new creation. This hybridity is visible in the narration in using fragmentation, flashback, beyond imagination aspects and the very much new approach to the depiction of the existing history.

Migration

Migration is a displacement or disruption that affects both a person's language and thus, identity. Sanga (2001: 117) focuses on the idea of hyphen as in Indo-Anglian or Anglo-Indian and not only its role in complicating the emigrant's identity, but also its power to create an interstitial space, a space—between, which is uniquely migrant's and constitutes something entirely new and unspoiled. According to Susheila Nasta, in *Home Truths: Fictions of the South Asian Diaspora in Britain* (2001), "Rushdie's self-conscious construction of the migrant as metaphor—his formulation of 'migrant aesthetic has been taken up in recent years as a kind of manifesto by critics keen to 'fetishize Rushdie as the contemporary postcolonial writer par excellence'" (137). Salman Rushdie, in his essay *Imaginary Homelands* focuses on the experiences of a migrant by saying that "a migrant's eye view of the world [...] written from the very experience of uprooting, disjuncture and metamorphosis (slow or rapid, painful or pleasurable) that is the migrant condition" (393-414). *Satanic Verses* presents two migrants Saladin Chamcha and Gibreel Farishta who move from Bombay —India to London—England. Falling from an exploding plane the identities of both of them gets changed: Farishta becomes archangel Gibreel; Chamcha becomes devil. Through Gibreel's increasing scrizophrenic fantasies and dreams, the geographical and temporal locations of the novel shift between the historical founding of Islam in the seventh-century Arabia desert and the pilgrimage across the subcontinent to Mecca led by butterfly-clad Ayesha in the twentieth century.

Rushdie gives positive outlook regarding immigration in both his essay *Imaginary Homelands* and in his fiction. Aijaz Ahmad, a critic, who examined *Shame* (1983), in his *In Theory: Classes, Nations Literatures* (2008), argues that Rushdie "submerges the class question and speaks of migrancy as an ontological condition" (13). Ravathy Krishnaswami argues that Rushdie's mythology of migrancy, by privileging a de-territorialized postcolonial consciousness free from the pain of multiple dislocation, minimizes differences of class, gender, race and nation to suggest that the migrant transcends such political collectivities (139). Whereas Michael Gorra in *After Empire: Scott, Naipaul, Rushdie* (1997) says, "the writer's conceptualization of migrancy remains unavailable to ordinary people and is best suited for those most able to live with a sense of uncertainty and improvisation—for the gifted and the well-off, those for whom shuttling between London and Bombay is the literal not the figurative truth" (172). Salman Rushdie believes that among the great struggles of man—good/evil, reason/unreason, etc.—there is also this mighty conflict between 'the fantasy of home' and 'the fantasy of away', the 'dream of roots' and 'the mirage of journey'. His each and every novel contains the theme of migration. *Grimus* focuses on the journey and migration of Flapping Eagle, a young Indian, after his sister Bird Dog's disappearance and his exile from Axona, who wanders earth for 777 years 7 months and 7 days in quest of his sister and visits Calf Island. Sense of alienation and isolation which are the outcomes of migrancy and being an outsider, his objective and efforts are to get adjusted with the new atmosphere and society has been focused by Rushdie.

In *Midnight's Children* the theme of journey has been quoted over and again. In beginning of the novel Aadam Aziz is mentioned to be back from Germany, after five years of study, his visit to Kashmir and his stay at Agra. Journey, in its broader sense, concentrates on the journey from Mumtaz Aziz to Amina Sinai—which is a journey for the acquisition of original identity, which is also applicable in the case of Saleem Sinai, Shiv and Brass Monkey/Jamila Singer. Saleem's parents—Ahmed Sinai and

Amina Sinai—are shown to be departing from Agra for Delhi. Hanif migrated to Bombay to make his dream of becoming a film director come true. Amina, Saleem and Brass Monkey migrated to Pakistan from India. They moved to Karachi then. The sense of alienation and isolation with diasporic sensibilities and a sense of loss are visible after Saleem's departure to Pakistan with the case of his loss of his identity. His sense of alienation and isolation compels him to return to India.

Fury presents the migration of a Cambridge educated millionaire from India, Malik Solanka, who leaves his family and leaves for America in frustration and fury. It is also about the journey from Cambridge-educated Malik Solanka to a doll maker. *Haroun and the Sea of Stories* (1990) presents the journey of a child-Haroun Khalifa to the Land of G, Valley of K, the Dull Lake and Kahani with his father, Rashid. *Luka and the Fire of Life* (2010) presents the journey of twelve-year-old Luka, younger brother of Haroun towards the Fire of Life, for which he has to pass through the River of Time, in search of Fire of Life to keep his father from falling into a deep sleep. In *Shalimar the Clown* (2005), Maximilian Ophuls is a migrant to India who is an American ambassador, who was brought up in France. Shalimar—an Indian Muslim from Pachigam, Kashmir —is presented as an emigrant who leaves India after having been betrayed by Boonyi, takes training from insurgent groups in Afghanistan and the Philippines, leaves for USA and eventually comes back to India after the completion of his goal of taking revenge. In its broader sense another kind of migration, which is mental or intellectual journey, has also been presented in which, Shalimar, from a good, kind and affectionate person becomes a member of Jihad and assassinates Maximilian Ophuls by becoming his chauffeur. In *The Enchantress of Florence* (2008), there is a mention of a European visitor, who, having finished his journey comes to the court of Akbar. Timothy Brennan called *The Satanic Verses* "the most ambitious novel yet published to deal with the immigrant experience in Britain" that captures the immigrants' dream-like disorientation and their process of "union-by-hybridization" (quoted in Netton 45). Rushdie said about *The Satanic Verses* (1988) that it was not about

Islam, "but about migration, metamorphosis, divided selves, love, death, London and Bombay (*Ibid.* 78). The very beginning presents them as migrants who are victims trapped in a hijacked plane in a flight from India to Britain. In the majority of his novels, different characters leave their native place for fulfilling their goal and to find new identity, but in that very effort they remain failures as for them the border seems to have become 'the only reliable consistent home' and they 'can never settle fully on either side' (Sanga 2001: 17).

Depiction of 'nation' and 'metropolitan'

To compose globalized fiction, Rushdie has depicted in his works other countries along with India. As India has always been associated with the concept of multiplicity and plurality and diversity, it becomes prime focus of Rushdie. Rushdie, in "The Riddle of Midnight" mentions: "I come from Bombay, and from a Muslim family, too. 'My' India has always been based on the ideas of multiplicity, pluralism, hybridity: ideas to which the ideologies of the communalists are diametrically opposed. To my mind, the defining image of India is the crowd and a crowd is by its very nature superabundant, heterogeneous, many things at once" (32). This diversity of India and cosmopolitanism of Bombay have been recurrent themes in his novels. Saleem refers to *India*, in *Midnight's Children* as a "nation which had previously never existed [that] was about to win its freedom, catapulting us into a world which, although it had five thousand years of history, although it had invented the game of chess and traded with Middle Kingdom Egypt, was nevertheless quite imaginary; into a mythical land, a country which would never exist except by the effort of a phenomenal will....except in a dream we all agree to dream" (124).

In *The Moor's Last Sigh*, his approach to the city—Bombay becomes rather negative, having been affected by the *fatwa* on him due to *The Satanic Verses*. For him, Bombay, his once most favourite city, becomes a city seeped low into darkness and despair. He mentions its dual nature, the squalor in slums, the underworld and the failed secularism. Besides, his works focus on the failure of nation-forming process of India and

Pakistan. The effect of globalization has been presented as "the corruption of money and the corruption of power, united in super-corruption that no opponent could withstand". In *Imaginary Homelands* (1992), Salman Rushdie says, "It may be that writers in my position, exile or emigrants or expatriates, are haunted by some sense of loss, some urge to reclaim, to look back, even at the risk of being mutated into pillars of salt. But if we do look back, we must do so in the knowledge—which gives rise to profound uncertainties—that our physical alienation from India almost inevitably means that we will not be capable of reclaiming precisely the thing that was lost; that we will, in short, create fictions, not actual cities or villages, but invisible ones, imaginary homeland, 'Indias' of the mind." Thus, he talks about 'fantasized Indo-nostalgia' in presenting real India—India that was and India that is—with the India of his dream and fantasy and composing works by keeping in mind both at the same time. In one of his interviews with Charlie Rose, Rushdie asserts,

> I don't think there was ever a moment when I thought [India] would split...it just does exist. It just is there, does exist, and it ain't gonna break up.... Anti-Partition, un-partition, by which I don't really mean political unity. The oldest object I possess, given to me when I was born, is a block of silver on which is engraved the map of 'undivided India', 'the real India'.

Thus, national borders mean little for Rushdie who believes in 'undivided India' and 'the real India'—which means India without any kind of rivalry with the nation that belonged to India in pre-Independence era, India with 'a sense of acceptance' for all kinds of diversities. As being regardless of the national boundaries, Rushdie, in his works, depicts not only India with its rich diversities, but also, the countries around the world such as Britain and USA. Being fond of Bombay, he mentions the cosmopolitan aspects of Bombay in the majority of his works. Not only Bombay, but metropolitan cities like Cochin, New York, and Los Angeles, California, Mexico, etc. are part of his intellectual property.

Salman Rushdie, in his works, presents 'globalization' and 'cosmopolitanism' by focusing on globalized issues, globalized themes—migration, diaspora, hybridity, etc., cosmopolitan culture around the world, globalized events, different places around the world, various characters with different temperament, and globalized genres in combining them and making a 'hotchpotch' of characters from different cultures, various genres and nations, settings around the world by combining factual with fantastic, by presenting the realities, molding them according to the necessity of narrative and to take the readers away from the realities that are mentioned by him only, to the fantastic world on the wings of imagination, by fragmentation: presenting distant and nearer past, depicting it with the present. He makes his works globally accepted and appealing in presenting 'cosmopolitanism of genres': history, comedy, tragedy, myth, realism, satire, magic-realism and 'fantasized Indo-nostalgia' etc. symbolically to present the cosmopolitan culture and to make it of global importance in presenting the sensibilities of the emigrants—their journey from 'rootlessness' to 'multiple rooting' from the perspective of one [Salman Rushdie] who is one among them. In this sense, the works of Salman Rushdie becomes a treasure of globalized and cosmopolitan culture.

Works Cited

Agnes, G. *Postmodern Nations in Salman Rushdie's Fiction*. 2009. Web. 20 Sept. 2012.

Ahmad, Aijaz. *In Theory: Classes, Nations Literatures*. London: Verso, 1992. Print.

Berlatsky, E.L. *The Real, The True and The Told: Postmodern Historical Narrative and the Ethics of Representation*. Web. 30 Sept. 2012.

Bhabha, Homi K. *Location of Culture*. London and New York: Routledge, 1994. Print.

Brennen, Timothy. *Salman Rushdie and the Third World: Myths of Nation*. London: Macmillan, 1989. Print.

Brians, P. *The Irrelevance of Postcolonialism to South Asian Literature*. Web. 30 Sept. 2012. Print.

Calhoun, C. *Cosmopolitanism and Nationalism*. 2008. Web. 30 Sept. 2012.

Gorra, Michael. *After Empire: Scott, Naipaul, Rushdie*. Chicago: University of Chicago Press, 1997. Print.

Herbert, C.V. *Representations of Migrant and Nation in Selected Works of Rohinton Mistry and Salman Rushdie*. 2006. Web. 23 Sept. 2012.

Jani, P. *Decentering Rushdie: Cosmopolitanism and the Indian Novel in English*. 2010. Web. 30 Sept. 2012.

Kraidy, Marwan M. "Hybridity in Cultural Globalization." Web. 13 Aug. 2014.

Lahiri, S. *Local vs. Cosmopolitan: A Comparison of the Home and the World and Midnight's Children*. Web. 30 Sept. 2012.

Lipod, E.M. *The Delicacy of Equivalence. Reproduction or Transfer? A Cognitive Angle on Metaphors in Salman Rushdie's Satanic Verses*. 2008. Web. 13 Aug. 2014.

Miller, C.C. *Salman Rushdie's 'Stereoscopic Vision:' Postcolonial Environments in Midnight's Children*. Web. 23 Sept. 2012.

Nasta, Susheila. *Home Truths: Fictions of the South Asian Diaspora in Britain*. New York: Palgrave, 2002. Print.

Needham, A.D. *Salman Rushdie and the Third World: Myths of the Nation*. Web. 30 Sept. 2012.

Netton, Ian Richard. *Text and Trauma: An East-West Primer*. Richmond, UK: Routledge, 1996.

Pirbhai, M. *The Paradox of Globalization as an Untotalizable Totality in Salman Rushdie's The Ground Beneath Her Feet*. Web. 30 Sept. 2012.

Robbins, Bruce. "Comparative Cosmopolitanisms." Web. 12 July, 2014.

———. "Introduction Part I: Actually Existing Cosmopolitanism." Web. 12 July, 2014.

Rushdie, Salman. *Midnight's Children*. London: Vintage Books, 1981. Print.

———. *Satanic Verses*. New York: Viking, 1988. Print.

———. *Imaginary Homelands: Essays and Criticism 1981-1991*. New York: Granta Books, 1991.

———. *Grimus*. London: Vintage Books, 1996. Print.

———. *Fury*. London: Jonathan Cape, 2001. Print.

———. *Shalimar the Clown*. New Delhi: Random House Group. 2005.

———. *Luka and the Fire of Life*. London: Jonathan Kape, 2010.

———. "The Riddle of Midnight." Web. 16 Dec. 2014.

Sanga, Jaina. *Salman Rushdie's Postcolonial Methapors—Migration, Translation, Hybridity, Blasphemy, and Globalisation*. Connecticut: Greenwood, 2001.

Shankar, S. "Midnight's Orphans: or a Postcolonialism worth Its Name." *Cultural Critique*. Vol. 56. No. 1 (2004): 64-95. Print.

13

Salman Rushdie's *Shame*: A Study of Narrative Strategies

Nesha Sabar and *Pramod Kumar Das*

A narrative is an organised form of language that communicates the intentions of the narrator in an ordered manner. It takes different modes to facilitate a narrator to convey the message successfully, as Gerald Genette discusses in his *Narrative Discourse: An Essay in Method* (1983) such as order, duration, frequency, mood and voice. It also can be considered as conjunctions of story and discourse. While a story just is a sequence of events, a narrative recounts those events, perhaps leaving some occurrences out because they are from some perspective insignificant, and perhaps emphasizing others. In a series of events, a car crash takes a split second. The narrative account, however, might be almost entirely about the crash itself and the few seconds leading up to it. Narratives thus shape history (the series of events, the story of what happened).

Moreover, a narrative is the organisation of language into a structure which conveys the order of events in a connected manner within a given time and space. Critics and theorists have attempted to define a narrative from their own theoretical positions. Such attempts are still on as the horizon of narrative art keeps on expanding. Gerald Prince, for example, defines narrative as the recounting of one or more real or fictitious events communicated by one, two or several narrators to one, two or several listeners. Following Prince it may be assumed that narrative is a form of recounting of an event or an occurrence, and the process involves a teller and a listener. A narrative is certainly about something and the process is complete when a narrator and a narratee are involved. Fiction is considered as the most articulated form of narrative art. As fiction is both a self-consuming art (fiction) and represents fact (representation) it always seems its own narrative horizon.

A narrative, to use a layman's point of view, is basically a story, whether in prose or poetry, which involves incidents and characters, and what the characters say and do. A narrative is usually told by a narrator, whether in the first, second or third person. However, narratology or the study of narrative, treats narrative not in the traditional way, as a fictional representation of life, but as a systematic formal construction. Structural narratologists try to analyse the way in which a narrative discourse fashions 'story' into an organised structure of a literary 'plot'. Novelists use various narrative strategies to arrest their reader's attention and its importance cannot be waved aside. Mark Currie opines: "Narrative is central to the representation of identity, in personal memory, and self-representation or in collective identity of groups such as regions, nations, race and gender. Narrative is inescapable as language in general, or as cause and effect, as a mode of thinking and being" (Currie 1998: 5). There might even be difficult levels of narration, in the sense that there might be narration of a story and also narration in a story. Lockwood in *Wuthering Heights* narrates the story of Health Cliff and Catherine, but he is also a character in it. The postmodern novel displays flexibility of narrative manipulation and multiplicity of interpretations which are central to postmodernist thought.

When we think of narrative, we usually think of it as an art, however modest it is. We think of it as novels or sagas or folk tales or, at least, as anecdotes. We speak of a gift for telling stories. But as true as that narrative can be an art and that art thrives on narrative, narrative is also something we all engage in, artists and non-artists alike. We make narratives many times a day, every day of our lives. And we start doing so almost from the moment we begin putting words together. As soon as we follow a subject with a verb, there is a good chance we are engaged in narrative discourse. "I fell down", the child cries and in the process, tells her mother a little narrative. It is worth quoting Roland Barthes's landmark essay on narrative (1966) at length:

> The narratives of the world are numberless. Narrative is first and foremost of a prodigious variety of genre, themselves distributed amongst different substances as though any material were fit to receive man's stories. Able to be carried by articulated language, spoken or written, fixed or moving images, gesture, and the ordered mixture of all these substances; narrative is present in myth, legend, fable, tale, novella, epic, history, tragedy, drama, comedy, mime, painting, (think of Carpaccio's Saint Ursula), stained-glass windows, cinemas, comics, news items, conversation. Moreover, under this almost infinite diversity of forms narrative is present in every age, in every place, in every society, it begins with the history of mankind and there nowhere is nor have been a people without narrative. All classes, all human groups, have their narratives, enjoyment of which is very often shared by men with different, even opposing, cultural backgrounds. Caring nothing for the division between good and bad literature, narrative is international, trans-historical, trans-cultural and it is simply there like life itself. (Porter Abbott 4)

Narrative is the representation of an event or series of events. Event is the key word here, though some people prefer the word 'action', without an event of an action, you may have a 'description', an argument, a lyric, some combination of these or something else altogether, but you won't have a narrative, 'My dog has fleas' is a description of my dog but it is not a narrative because nothing happens. My dog was 'bitten by a flea' is a narrative. It tells of an event. The event is a very small one, 'the bite of a flea' but that is enough to make it a narrative.

The Methods of Narrative Strategy

The methods involved in telling a story are the procedures used by a writer of stories or accounts. Narrative technique is a general term (like device, or resources of language) that asks us to discuss the procedures used in telling of a story. When a writer wishes to tell a story, he uses a number of narrative techniques to impart the story to readers. He may choose to draw upon a wide variety of these techniques to accomplish his goal. Examples of the techniques we might use are: point of view, manipulation of time, dialogue, or interior monologue, etc.

Narrative refers to the succession of events, real or fictional, that are the subjects of this discussion, and to their several relations; in this sense means the study of a totality of actions and situations taken in them, without regard to the medium, linguistic or otherwise, through which knowledge of that totality comes to us.

The prime point of our discussion here is the narrative strategies in Rushdie's *Shame*.

Narrative Strategies in Salman Rushdie's *Shame*

One way to understand *Shame* (1983) is through the lens of Rushdie's narrator's postcolonial narrative devices. Rushdie has used many narrative techniques as mimicry, fairy tale, meta-fiction, magical-realism, history and intertextuality, etc. Mimicry is also a representation of what has been presented and a repetition of something itself repetitious. Mimicry tips the hand of its non-originality and implies the non-originality of that which it mimics. These specific descriptions of mimicry help explain numerous examples of mimicry in *Shame*. In the words of David W. Hart, "Rushdie's mimicry is clearly related to parody and satire. Parody, with its ironic trans-contextualization and inversion, is repetition with a difference, one text is set against another with the intent of mocking it or making it ridiculous" (7). In *Shame* what we notice is the colonial mimicry of three Shakil sisters who give away party to the foreigners in the cantonment after the death of their father. "Rushdie subverts this narrative of colonial mimicry when he has the sisters orientalized the 'Western' entertainment through inherently Anglo and upper-class stereotypes" (9). He also mimics the political figures of Pakistan such as Benazir

Bhutto as is the Virgin iron pant; and Zia-ul-Haq, who wants to throw Pakistan back into the middle ages, is General Raza Hyder, who ends up fleeing for his life, only to be destroyed, in an ending similar to Greek tragedy. In the novel, Rushdie caricatured the real figure as mimicry, e.g. Muhammad Zia-ul-Haq as Raza Hyder and Zulfikar Ali Bhutto as Iskander Harappa. In this way, he has mimicked the political figures of Pakistan. Rushdie's first person narrative leaves the reader to decide what is relevant within *Shame* by proposing magic and fiction alongside 'realism'. When addressing Rushdie's method of composing ideas in *Shame*, he makes it obvious to the reader that he is the first person narrator. Readers are bluntly allotted this information as Rushdie commonly uses asides and personal anecdotes, even inserting his own parents and sister.

Rushdie has incorporated various narrative devices in *Shame* to make it more amusing and inviting to readers especially the mode of fairy tale which usually begins with any kind of story as Rushdie begins with "Once upon a time" which is a visible act of fairy tale. Ashlima says "in traditional fairy tales the moral typically centre on the presentation of existing values and the maintenance of social stability" (4). But the novel itself is a satirical depiction of political figures in Pakistani; if we take it as fairy tale it complicates the story of actual values system of the characters in the novel.

Intertextuality

Intertextuality literally means the shaping of texts' meanings by other texts, or the study of the way in which the text of one poem or prose may relate to the text of another poem or prose. It can also be defined on the relationship between texts. The term intertextuality has itself been borrowed and transformed many times since it was coined by poststructuralist Julia Kristeva in 1966. As a critic William Irvin says, the term has come to have almost as many meanings as users, from those faithful to Kristeva's original vision to those who simply use it as a stylish way of talking about allusion and influence. If authorial voice and narrative voice are important notions in analyzing the issue of commitment, intertextuality is similarly significant for the analysis of the textual narrative. "The intertextuality of Rushdie's writing is very astounding. It is perhaps the single most striking element in all of his fiction, and it is also a notion which the texts themselves play with" (Kuortti 16). According to Allen Thiher, intertextuality is simply a *de facto* recognition that we live in a world constituted by multiple kinds of discourse that interfere and obliterate each other as well as complete and complement each other (191). It can be noted that intertextuality is a postmodern concept. Here Allen Thiher examines the changes that have taken place with the turning of modernism since 1945 towards something which is often called postmodernism. David W. Hart describes:

> Intertextuality in *Shame* is closely connected with the concept of a palimpsest which Rushdie describes in the novel as a Pakistani condition. *Shame* serves as a good illustration of the idea that postmodern intertextuality is a formal manifestation of both a desire to close the gap between past and present for the reader as well as the desire to rewrite the past in a new context. It directly confronts the past of literature and of historiography. (16)

It suggests Rushdie to have rewritten Pakistani political history and which has cost him much to be in Pakistan for his ridiculous intertextual narratives. Now he has become an exilic writer, writing about his own country while residing in foreign country and thus, those who read his novel especially the westerners would feel dismal and somber. As David Hart puts it "Western readers who are not familiar with an exilic migrant life may indeed feel overwhelmed by the referential excess in the novel. To those readers, Rushdie is saying, 'welcome to my world'. In addition, the text is also filled with western references that may be unknown to some eastern audiences" (17).

Shame is a typical intertexualized novel as the plot construction is concerned. Here it is essential to take note of the distinction made between 'traditional' and 'postmodern' notions of text. 'Text' traditionally is understood as the wording of anything written or printed, the very 'words' and 'sentences' as originally written. In poststructuralist arguments against this definition of text, 'originality' is the key word; and subsequently writing is the work of the text which asserts that the very words of a text are not the original words of the text, that are by definition, quotations, parasitical or parenthetical comments, parodying, self-parodying the text and making use of pastiche and clichés.

History

History is nothing but an interpretation of the historical events which implies a synopsis of data of dates, names, battles, coups, political happenings, religious and traditional paraphernalia, social situations, cultural phenomena, and other details relating to events. History brings about an understanding of the past and its relation to the present. Rushdie configures history in his own way. *Shame* is a mixture of politics, history, satire, fantasy and allegory. It is a novel of fictional distortions. It offers a fanciful jumbling of historical items. The novel covers up an underlying theme of shame: while shamelessness pervades it unobtrusively. The politics, religious and cultural events contribute to the entirety of historical events form the backdrop of the novel. The novel covers the history of Pakistan over a period of thirty-six years—from 1947 to 1983, from the birth of Pakistan to the present, the year of the publication of the novel. Rushdie fictionalizes the factual events collected from history. He tactfully portrays the shameful activities like obscenity, permissiveness, debauchery, untruthfulness, ill-treatment of women or gender bias, smuggling, and lack of patriotism as a guide to contemporary Pakistan.

Essentially, history is another system of representation. It makes use of narrative and rhetorical strategies to generate certain kinds of knowledge and images. Facticity and authenticity are effects of narratives about events and facts rather than immanent features of the facts themselves. Hence, the form of representation of those facts and events are crucial because, they influence the way an audience receives the images: do we believe in what is being represented on screen or on paper? Rushdie's fiction is thus fragments of historical identity.

One could understand *Shame* by analyzing the history. The very meaning of history is always the history of power, where the weak have no real say, but just to accept it. As Pinkie Aurangzeb contemplates the way Iskander conducts himself:

> History is natural selection. Mutant versions of the past struggle for dominance; new species of fact arise, and old, saurian truth go to the wall, blindfolded and smoking last cigarettes, only the mutations of the strong survive. The weak, the anonymous, the defeated leave few marks: field-pattern axe-heads, folk-tales, broken pitches, burial mounds, the fading memory of their youthful beauty. (*Shame* 124)

For Rushdie, history is an act of interpretation, or the product of it. The question is: who remembers? Why does she/he remember? If history is what is remembered, where is the location of amnesia? Rushdie remembers the forgotten. Mohit K. Ray is true in his observation of Rushdie. "He is a dreamer in a visionary world. But dreams create a nightmarish reality in *Shame*" (141).

Fantasy

It is one of the strategies that Rushdie used in *Shame*. As I have already stated before, there is a strong undercurrent of fantasy in Rushdie's treatment of historical reality. In an interview, he tells Rani Dharker "I have always thought of fantasy as only being useful as a way of enriching realism and not as an end in itself". The shore of fantasy, he admits, is "the one and only shore upon which I might be safe for ever". The issues that he takes up for treatment in his novels have a universal validity. *Shame*, he reiterates, is not the 'exclusive property of Pakistan'. In its author's estimation, *Shame* is a 'sort of modern fairy tale', in which 'nobody gets upset, or takes anything I say too seriously'. The novelist regards himself as 'a fantasist' and thus, he admits in the following lines: "I build imaginary countries and try to impose them on the ones that exist. I, too, face the problem of history: what to retain, what to dumb, how to hold on to what memory insists on relinquishing, how to deal with change. And...I haven't managed to shake myself of it completely" (*Shame* 88).

Throughout the novel Rushdie depicts the political history and the relationship between two important architects of Pakistan's history—Raza Hyder and Iskander Harappa (who are, in fact, based on General Zia and Zulfikar Ali Bhutto, respectively). He wants to relieve the colonial dominance in the postcolonial era. He even wants to show, how shame is a part of the architecture of the society that the novel describes. People in countries like Pakistan, he observes, grow upon 'a diet of honour and shame'. But shame is like everything else; live with it for long time and it becomes part of the furniture. Fantasy is an interpretation of inner feeling, but his feeling should be legitimatized for critical acceptance. In most of Rushdie's works, we notice Fantasy having a pivotal role especially in *Imaginary Homelands*. He has however, something interesting to say on certain significant points such as migrants' experiences and alienation, the Indian cultural scene, the political scenario of the Indian subcontinent, history and fantasy and their intermingling in the novel, fictional form, the English languages, and of course, on certain writers and their works. Fantasy, according to Rushdie, is an effective way of dealing with problems of less compatible societies. The shadow world, he adds is evidently a good deal, more fascinating than the one most people inhabit. The use of fantasy may also be helpful in creating a distance from actuality, which may help us to take a new look at the 'actual'. Perceiving the interconnection between reality and fantasy, Eric Rabkin has pointed out that fantasy "reveals not only our deepest fear, but also our greatest aspiration; not only our hidden shames, but also our finest hopes" (226). Occasional trips to dream world are, according to Rushdie an essential part of our essence: given the gift of self-consciousness, we can dream versions of ourselves, new selves for old. Waking as well as sleeping, our response to the world is essentially imaginative. This insistence on the mingling of reality and fantasy is the most significant aspect of Rushdie's theory and practice of fiction. Another theme that is so dear to Rushdie's heart is the use of history in fiction and its interrelationship with fantasy. Most of his own fictional works hinge on his concept of the nature and role of socio-political materials pertaining to various periods of history. It is worth remembering that Rushdie has called himself "a fairly political animal". *Midnight's Children* and *Shame* are overtly political in their themes. "It seems to me", Rushdie told his interviewer Gordon Wise, "that everything in both books has to do with politics and with the relationship of the individuals and history" (Pathak 136).

Magical Realism

Magical Realism is a genre where magic elements are a natural part in an otherwise mundane, realistic environment. Although it is most commonly used as a literary genre, magic realism also applies to film and the visual arts. One example of magical realism occurs when a character in the story continues to be alive beyond the normal length of life and this is subtly depicted by the character being present throughout many generations. Or else what the human mind is unable to conceive in the real and physical world becomes a part of it. On the surface the story has no clear magical attributes and everything is conveyed in a real setting, but such a 'reality' breaks the rules of our real world. The author may give precise details of the real world such as the date of birth of a character and the army recruitment age, but such facts help to define the age of the fantastic character of the story that would turn out to be an abnormal occurrence like someone living for two hundred years.

Sufiya's transformation is a fantastic element in the narrative and, following its thread, it is appropriate to discuss magical realism as a tool used to uncover reality. In an interview, Rushdie mentions that the use of magical realism in Gabriel García Márquez is designed to tell the truth about a certain situation, though very often it is a misunderstood term by the public:

> The trouble with the phrase 'Magical Realism' is that when people use it, they tend to hear the 'magic' and not hear the 'realism', whereas in fact, one of the things of going to the world of Garcia Márquez [visiting Latin America] is that you discover he is telling the

> truth (...) these books which people call "fantasies" are actually mild understatements of the truth. (Rushdie in Conversation with Hitchens)

This means that, at first glance, fantastic elements are just a hyperbole for out scaled situations of what happens in real life: an angry person or a mob, yes, but the anger would never turn them into a beast; a woman with many children, yes, but not twenty-seven, and so forth. However, they are not hyperboles because they transcend the border of reality, of what is possible: an exaggeration would portray Naveed with ten children, because it is a rare phenomenon, but it is possible. Therefore, these elements are almost a euphemism of what they are trying to communicate. According to M.H. Abraham,

> the term magical realism originally applied in the 1920s to a school of painters, used to describe the prose fiction of Jorge Luis Borges in Argentina, as well as the work of writers such as Gabriel Garcia Marquez in Colombia, Gunter Grass in Germany, and John Fowles in England. These writers interweave, in an ever-shifting pattern, a sharply etched realism in representing ordinary events and describing details together with fantastic and dream-like elements as well as with materials derived from myth and fairy tales. (200)

Now we can locate Salman Rushdie's stand in England as he resides there. Largely, it gives us the view that ordinary things of life can't be taken for granted. It has some spell of magical charm turns things that has never been imagined. A literary mode rather than a distinguishable genre, magical realism aims to seize the paradox of the union of opposites. For instance, it challenges polar opposites like life and death and the pre-colonial past versus the post-industrial present. Magical realism is characterized by two conflicting perspectives, one based on a rational view of reality and the other on the acceptance of the hyper-real as much as of prosaic reality. Magical realism differs from pure fantasy primarily because it is set in a normal, modern world with authentic descriptions of humans and society. According to Angel Flores, magical realism involves the fusion of the real and the fantastic, or as he claims, an amalgamation of realism and fantasy. The presence of the supernatural in magical realism is often connected to the primeval or magical mentality, which exists in conjunction with European rationality. According to Ray Verzasconi, as well as other critics, magical realism is an expression of the New World reality which at once combines the rational elements of the European super-civilization, with the irrational elements of a primitive America. Gonzalez Echchevarria believes that magical realism offers a worldview that is not based on natural or physical laws or objective reality. However, the fictional world is not separated from reality either.

The Supernatural and the Natural

In magical realism, the supernatural is not displayed as questionable. While the reader realizes that the rational and irrational are opposites and conflicting polarities, they are not disconcerted because the supernatural is integrated within the norms of perception of the narrator and the characters in the fictional world.

Magical realism has been a greatest device that Rushdie uses after Gabriel Marquez García and thus, has aptly used this mechanism in *Shame* quite a number of times. In the beginning of the novel, we find the three sisters Chhunny, Bunny and Munny looking alike and conceiving a child without having a husband, they have only a father who is a widower and the question will arise in our mind—how come those sisters became pregnant without having physical contact with any man?

Metafiction

Metafiction is one of the devices that Rushdie uses in *Shame*. Literally "Meta" means beyond. No doubt *Shame* is a meta-fictional novel. As Patricia Waugh points out, "Metafiction lays out the linguistic basis of the alternative worlds constructed in literary fictions" (*Metafiction* 100). Often the narrator in the story reminds the reader of the fictionality of the text and the location. Rushdie says "Here I am instead, inventing what never happened to me." Likewise "The country in this story is not Pakistan or not quite. There are two countries, real and fictional, occupying the same space, or almost the same space. My story, my fictional country exists, like myself, at a slight angle to reality" (*Shame* 29).

The relationships between creator and created, reality and fantasy, between fiction and truth are all open to exposition in meta-fiction. We can't exactly call this type of writing a genre as it is a way of description as much as it is a technique or method. We wouldn't call fictional stories with an interest in boats a genre of writing in the same way we call 'mystery' fiction or 'young adult' fiction genres. Specifically, what are the criteria for a book of fiction to be considered metafiction? Not surprisingly, there is no satisfying criterion for metafiction. If a book contains an element of 'fiction within fiction' such as a story told within a frame story or larger narrative structure, it can be considered as metafiction. The occurrence of stories within stories is about as common as finding oxygen in the air. However, a reasonable narrowing of the parameters has metafiction defined as fiction that purposefully draws attention to its own nature (i.e. fiction, i.e. made-up writing). Now let us take for an instance that Rushdie is narrating the history of Pakistan within the history of colonial aftermath. He goes on delineating the fairy tales of the early age of Pakistan. Sufiya's shame and Omar Khayyam's representation as a peripheral hero in the celebrated personality of Persian poet, Omar Khayyam is the instances of metafictional devices found in the novel.

Mimicry

Mimicry is a representation of a particular image or a character, a repetition of something. Mimicry tips the hand of its non-originality and implies the non-originality of that which it mimics. This specific description of mimicry helps explain numerous examples of mimicry in *Shame*. Rushdie's mimicry is one of the motifs which its place in tact in *Shame*. Mimicry in common sense is imagining the situation and making it your own, it is a sort of repetitious acts which can be pleasant but at the same time ridiculous. Rushdie has rightly realized to project this device in a humorous way. In *Shame*, mimicry has been placed in centre, as we see the delineation of characters and their daily basis, which is suggestive of colonial mimicry.

Rushdie problematizes his own historical narrative by making a mockery of mimicry, especially in the context of colonial mimicry. Colonial mimicry is a consequence of the desire of the colonized to be like the colonizer through the power of decades and centuries of violence and cultural conditioning that enables imperial cultural hegemony.

Homi K. Bhabha explains the 'ambience' of 'colonial mimicry' as the not so benign colonial discourse that describes the natives as 'almost but not quite' which fetishizes the colonizers themselves, and reminds us that the locals are still and always will be *Others*. When we find the three sisters set up the occasion for the purpose of becoming pregnant: oh shame, shame, poppy shame! (*Shame* 16). The sisters then mimic each other and appear as one during the pregnancy, they all appear pregnant, and have morning sickness-ostensibly to avoid the shame that one of them would be forced to endure with an out-of-wedlock pregnancy. It indicates the complexities and potential use of mimicry, in this case to subvert shame (Hart 7).

With the Shakil sisters, Omar, and others, Rushdie writes overt and nuanced parodies. Mimicry has often been an overt goal of imperial policy. For instance, Lord Macaulay's 1835 *Minute to Parliament* derided Oriental learning, and advocated the reproduction of English art and learning in India (most strategically through the teaching of English literature). However, the method by which this mimicry was to be achieved indicated the underlying weakness of imperialism. Macaulay suggested that "the riches of European learning should be impacted by a class of interpreters between us and the millions whom we govern, a class of persons Indian in blood and color, but English in tastes, opinions, in morals, and in intellect" (Macaulay 1835). In other words, not only was the mimicry of European learning to be hybridized and therefore ambivalent, but Macaulay seems to suggest that imperial discourse is compelled to make it so in order for it to work.

As a whole, Rushdie's narrative style can be viewed as a tongue-in-cheek use and 'abuse' of numerous literary narrative conventions and theoretical perspectives that include exaggerated reflections of colonial mimicry, unreliable narrator's fairy tale motifs and intertextuality. *Shame* offers a somewhat mythical interpretation of the contemporary world, more specifically of the obsessions and values of the West and the dilemmas of the liberated Third World nations. Thus, it does by displaying a conflation of genres and forms: metaphor, allegory, autobiography, history, fantasy, satire and so on and so forth.

Works Cited

Abraham, M.H. and Geoffrey, Galt Harpham. *A Handbook of Literary Terms*. Delhi: Cengage Learning Pvt. Ltd., 2011.

Ashliman, D.L. *Folk and Fairy Tales: A Handbook*. Westport: Greenwood, 2004.

Bhabha, Homi K. *The Location of Culture*. London: Routledge, 1994.

Currie, Mark. *Postmodern Narrative Theory*. London: Macmillan Distribution Ltd., 1998.

Hart, David W. "Making a Mockery of Mimicry: Salman Rushdie's *Shame*". Web. 26 March 2014.

Gennet, Gerard. *Narrative Discourse: An Essay in Method*. New York: Cornell University Press, 1983.

Hitchens, Christopher. *A Conversation with Salman Rushdie*. Web. 23 April 2011.

Kuortti, Joel. *Fictions to Live in Narration as an Argument for Fiction in Salman Rushdie's Novels*. New York: Peter Lang, 1998.

Pathak, R.S. *Creative New Literatures Series-28 Modern Indian Novel in English*. New Delhi: Creative Books, 1999.

Prince, Gerald. *Narratology: The Form and Functioning of Narrative*. New York, Amsterdam: Mouton Publishers, 1982.

Rabkin, S. Eric. *The Fantastic in Literature*. New Jersey: Princeton University Press, 1976.

Rajagopalchary, M. and Co. "Historical Element in Salman Rushdie's *Shame*". *Kakatiya Journal of English Studies*, 29 (2010): 75-77.

Rao, M. Madhusudhan. *Salman Rushdie's Fiction: A Study*. New Delhi: Sterling Publishers Private Limited, 1992.

Ray, K. Mohit, Rama Kundu, eds. *Salman Rushdie: Critical Essay*, Vol. II. New Delhi: Atlantic Publishers and Distributors, 2006.

Rushdie, Salman. *Shame*. U.S.A.: Picador, 1983.

———. *Imaginary Homelands*. London: Granta Books India, 1991.

———. An Interview with Rani Dharkar. *Salman Rushdie Interviews: A Sourcebook of His Ideas*. Ed. P.S. Chauhan. London: Greenwood Press, 2001. 47-62.

Thiher, Allan. *Words in Reflection: Modern Language Theory and Postmodern Fiction*. Chicago & London: University of Chicago Press, 1989.

Waugh, Patricia. *Metafiction*. London: Routledge, 1984.

Section–D

Rushdie's Diasporic Passage to the New World: Some Observations

14

Journey Towards the New World in the Selected Novels of Salman Rushdie

Ajit Kumar

> There is the thing I can't let go, which is where I am from. It is where I was born and brought up, where my parents came from, it's my mother tongue, it's all kinds of things obviously and those kinds of things don't change. They are part of what is given, they are part of how I see the world, why I am this kind of writer and not that kind of writer, says Salman Rushdie.
>
> (Mohanty 196)

Diasporic writing captures the two invariables of one's experience: exile and homeland. It involves the variety of experience. In fact, all diasporic literature is an attempt to negotiate between these two polarities. It is an emblem of true spirit of nationalism. It presents the difference between belonging and non-belonging of the human substantial base of living world. The writings of exiled/immigrant writers undertakes two moves one temporal and one spatial. It is as Meena Alexander puts it, "writing in search of a homeland" (Nayar 188). As Rushdie, clarifies, "When the Indian who writes from outside India tries to reflect that world, he is obliged to deal in broken mirrors, some of whose fragments have been irretrievably lost" (*Imaginary* 11). The writer, in fact, tries to capture the both the experiences being at home and outside. He exposes all the hidden aspects which are not known to the world outside. Doing this, he makes his efforts to achieve the lost social and political distinction due to diasporic elements. In *Imaginary Homelands* Rushdie echoes, "Our identity is at once plural and partial. Sometimes we feel that we straddle two cultures, at other time we fall between two stools. But however, ambiguous and shifting this ground may be it is not an infertile territory for a writer to occupy" (15). The constant feeling of insecurity and fear of being weak pave the path for the diasporic literature. It has successfully evolved the world of different cultures and languages.

In the 1980s and 90s, India emerged as a major literary nation. There came many writers who took different aspects of life into literature. They involved human relationship, feminine issues, social concerns, racism, casteism and ambivalence in culturalism and lingualism. But the diasporic element in literature came in the writing of writers like Bharati Mukherjee an author of *Jasmine* (1989) who spent much of her career exploring issues involving immigration and identity with a particular focus upon the U.S. and Canada. Vikram Seth also entered the gate of different cultural barriers in his writing. He not only focused on the diasporic element but social and human elements also. Seth's *The Golden Gate* and *A Suitable Boy* made him the first writer if the Indian Diaspora to enter the sphere of international writers and leave an indelible mark on the global literary scene. Other important writers of Indian Writing in English are Shobha De, Bhabani Bhattacharya, Arun Joshi, Khushwant Singh, Shashi Tharoor, Amitav Ghosh and Upamanya Chatterjee. Salman Rushdie is the most notable among the writers of his age with his famous work, *Midnight's Children* which ushered in a new trend of writing.

The Indian Diaspora literature is considered to be the body of writing in English which is produced by the people who recognize themselves as an Indian but live outside the national state of India in places as Australia, Trinidad, Malaysia or in Western countries like Canada, the United States and Great Britain. Migrants may settle in new places but do not belong there and disqualified from thinking of the new land as their home. Their home seems to be elsewhere, back across the border. G.S. Sharat Chandra, the noted academic and novelist states in *Sari of the Gods*:

> I was twenty-seven when I left India for good since then, I've steered a new course in my life.... Though India is always on my mind, there's no link that connects the sudden stop my life came to there and my new self. I leaped from one life to another, and in between I left nothing but a vacuum. Only imagination and memory, when I need them, act as my bridges. Thus whenever I go back to India, I'm a stranger wandering almost invisibly in familiar neighbourhood. (Singh 37)

These were some of the glimpses of the Indian writings in English. The Indian Diaspora is reflected in the works of Kiran Desai, Bharati Mukherjee, Amitav Ghosh and others. They all have emphasized on the human values under all the worldly circumstances. They all have been very particular about the existential values of human beings which are quite more important than any other material achievement. Kiran Desai captures the experience of migrants and their Diaspora in *The Inheritance of Loss*. Desai's experience of migration from India to U.K., then to U.S. is reflected in *The Inheritance of Loss*. She has sensitively drawn the Indian Diaspora in America and England, and Nepalese Diaspora in India. In her work, she writes about the marginalized community. From her writing it becomes clear that she has read the works of Indian Diasporic writers like Salman Rusdie, V.S. Naipaul, Rohinton Mistry, Amitav Ghosh, and her mother Anita Desai. Diasporic writing is concerned with the immigrants' uprootedness from their homeland, language, culture into an alien language, culture and land:

> Diasporic writings are invariably concerned with the individuals or community's attainment to the centrifugal homeland. But this attachment is countered by a yearning for sense of belonging to the current plays of abode. Caught physically between two worlds, Diasporas are... in the process of moving from one cultural state to existence to another. (Ramraj 216)

Kiran Desai has sensitively drawn the Indian Diaspora in America and England, and Nepalese Diaspora in India. In her work, she writes about the marginalized community. From her writing it becomes clear that she has read Indian Diasporic writers like Salman Rusdie, V.S. Naipaul, Rohinton Mistry, Amitav Ghosh, and her mother Anita Desai. Diasporic writing is concerned with the immigrants' uprootedness from their homeland, language, culture into an alien language, culture and land. The Indian writers whether settled in India or living abroad have made Indian English a form of Indian culture and a voice in which India speaks. Almost all diasporic writers have been well presented in creative writing. The Caribbean Diaspora has V.S. Naipaul as its figurehead. M.G. Vassanji is from African Diaspora. Rohinton Mistry, Vikram Chandra and Bharati Mukherjee are the writers in North America. Living in Diaspora means living in exile which leads to the confusion of identity and identification problems in an alien land full of different cultures. The past few years have been a massive flourishing of Indian English writings in the international market. Amitav Ghosh is also one such writer. Though settled in United States of America, his writings depict the Indian culture and outlook. The narrative technique of his novel *The Shadow Lines* is in the form of Interior Monologue, that's why the characters are studied from the psychological point of view. The novelist has been able to depict the inner thoughts of his narrator through this form and other characters are also probed psychologically. Thus, it can be said that this novel has laid foundations for the future writers who want to write novels portraying the psychology of his characters who have faced the dilemma of Diaspora.

The concept of 'home' performs an important function in our lives. It gives a sense of our place in the world. It tells us where we from are and where we belong. As an idea it stands for shelter, stability, security and comfort; for instance Rushdie who was born in Bombay and then moved to England. Meenu Gupta says in her article, "The Works of Salman Rushdie: A Global Omnibus", that Salman Rushdie "seems confines to his place of imagination but they still have universal appeal. But his more recent novels explore new relations between the global and the particular...where cross cultural dialogues become possible..." (qtd. in Lahiri 301). He says in his novel, "'We are. We are here.' And we are not willing to be excluded from any part of our heritage" (*Imaginary Homelands* 15). One of the main reasons for motivating his writing of his novels was to record the world of his childhood home, distant in both time and space, which Salman Rushdie reveals. It is impossible to return home through process of writing. We feel a sense of loss while leaving home at one time or another. Rushdie argues, "...the writer who is out-of-country and even out-of-language may experience this loss in an intensified form. It is made more concrete for him by the physical fact of discontinuity, of his present being in a different place from his past, of his being "elsewhere" (qtd. in McLeod 211). The sensual appraisal of the psychology of human beings gets transformed with different states of human mind. It tries to capture the holistic and spiritual values of human beings which get affected with the variations of stages.

The novels written by Parsis and the assimilation of the Parsis into the Indian environment have an important aspect that has been found in the works of various Parsis writers. Parsis, who have gone to the west, find discrimination against them. They hold no unique position in the land of the whites. This is an identity that they never considered. This then delays their assimilation into the new expatriate environment. Thus, the Parsi voice in recent Indian English fiction has been raised to assert the Parsi ethnic identity. According to Salman Rushdie, immigrants lose their respect dignity and pride in an alien land, and sometimes find white people's behavior unsocial and inhuman towards them. Thus, immigrants are cut off from their past, roots and culture. Salman Rushdie states the predicament of immigrants in the West. Rushdie remarks that when he thinks about his Bombay childhood, he could recall only fragmentally and partial memories. He records that his reflections were made "in broken mirrors, some of whose fragments have been irretrievably lost" (*Imaginary Homeland* 39). Indian Diaspora could be categorized as colonial and postcolonial with sub-categories within each of these broad divisions. In *Shame*, Rushdie generalizes:

> All migrants leave their pasts behind although some try to pack it into bundles and boxes—but on the journey something seeps out of the treasured mementoes and old photographs, until even their owners fail to recognize them, because it is the fate of migrants to be stripped of history, to stand naked among the scorn of strangers upon whom they see the rich clothing, the brocades of continuity and the eyebrows of belonging. (Singh 42)

Salman Rushdie in *Midnight's Children* has explored the psychological transformation of human mind in the different circumstances. *Midnight's Children,* his tour de force, paved the path for postcolonial literature in India. Rushdie began to decolonize English from the English and his programme is still in furtherance by him as well as from others. Like Salman Rushdie, the protagonist Saleem Sinai wanders among three countries, i.e. India, Pakistan and Bangladesh but is unable to find a proper place to live in. *Midnight's Children* is a narrative of displacement and rootlessness that is caused by relocation. Many of its characters are migrants drifting from shore to shore in search of some "imaginary homelands" and obviously, the author identifies himself with his migrant personae. As Pramod K. Nayar opines, "Much of diasporic writing explores the theme of an original home. This original home as now lost—due to their exile—is constantly worked into the imagination and myth of the displaced individual/community" (191). The migrations enlarge the stifling of human minds which affect the growth level of migrants.

Born at the dawn of Indian independence and destined, upon his death, to break into as many pieces as there are citizens of India, Saleem Sinai manages to represent the entirety of India within his individual self. The notion that a single person could possibly embody a teeming, diverse, multitudinous nation like India encapsulates one of the novel's fundamental concerns: the tension between the single and the many. The dynamic relationship between Saleem's individual life and the collective life of the nation suggests that public and private will always influence one another, but it remains unclear whether they can be completely equated with one another. Throughout the novel, Saleem struggles to contain all of India within himself—to cram his personal story with the themes and stories of his country—only to disintegrate and collapse at the end of his attempt. Politically speaking, the tension between the single and the many also marks the nation of India itself. One of the fastest growing nations in the world, India has always been an incredibly diverse.

Its constitution recognizes twenty-two official languages, and the population practices religions as varied as Hinduism, Islam, Christianity, Sikhism, and Buddhism, among many others. Indian culture is similarly hybrid, having been influenced by countless other cultures over the millennia of its development. At the same time, however, maintaining India's sprawling diversity in a peaceful fashion has often proved difficult: India's division into the Islamic nation of Pakistan and the secular, but mostly Hindu nation of India—a process known as Partition—remains the most striking example of the desire to contain and reduce India's plurality. In *Midnight's Children*, the child Saleem watches as protestors attempt to do divide the city of Bombay along linguistic lines, another attempt to categorize and cordon off multiplicity. Meenu Gupta explains the real eccentric point in the novels of Salman Rushdie:

> In the post-structuralism parlance Rushdie, in his works, privileges a post-modern space or third principle that blends both sides of binaries: east/west, secular/religious, real/fantasy, and colonizer/colonized and foregrounds hybridity over clarity and open endedness over closure. As a result the work becomes adaptable, creative, fluid and imaginative. He himself is the modern diasporic individual with multiple allegiances and identities making him a citizen of many countries, both real and imaginary. He thinks migration is a process of not uprooting but a kind of multiple rooting.... (qtd. in Lahiri 301)

Salman Rushdie's first novel *Grimus* is, in fact, an attempt at alienation in the world of chaos. Flapping Eagle, the young Indian, blessed with the immortality after drinking a magic fluid. He is alienated from the society as he is very fairer in complexion. His mother dies just after his birth. His sister Bird Dog looks after him after his mother's death. Flapping alienates from his people, and moves in the world for centuries in search of his sister and his identity and in this mission, he wanders for many years. The sense of alienation and non-belongingness arise out of the circulated atmosphere. This atmosphere leads all the members towards the search for a better environment for themselves. To obtain this, their attention and enthusiasm get a new plight and attempt which embarks the atmosphere that is human favoured in all means. Because of his eternity, he lands at the preternatural Calf Island. People of this island are consecrated with immortality yet fed up with the monotony of life. In the search of his identity, the novel apparently emerges as a source of exposition for all the migrants who have no future, neither on Mortal Island nor on immortal one. The human desires get stronger everyday with the different circumstances which they have been facing it for a long-time. It finally depicts the reality of the modern world where desires are very much in existence in the heart of the people without knowing or thinking about their consequences. The protagonist of the novel has got what he desired but still he has one more desire that his identity in the world. So, it takes him to the different places in life, however, he remains unsatisfied in the world. Salman Rushdie's influential effect in his first novel *Grimus* involves his masterly skills on diasporic literature. The protagonist Flapping Eagle's wandering of the earth for 777 years 7 months and 7 days explore the human desire for a sensuous home world.

Midnight's Children exposes the circumstances which have played a vital role in the partition of British India. Saleem Sinai narrates the whole situation that emerges during the British rule in India. His birth takes place right at the time of India's independence in 1947. It highlights the various circumstances which curve the political, social and economic atmosphere of the country. However, notably the immigrants start feeling isolated and alienated in the absence of the native culture and the language in the overseas countries. Saleem feels the same, he does not find the peace and comfort in none of the countries like India, Pakistan and Bangladesh. His behaviour and senses get across his nature. Salman Rushdie calls his situation an, "anaesthetized against feeling as well as memories" (*Midnight* 353). He finds himself nowhere attached and related to anything. Clark Blaise concludes the theme of the novel that "it is about to be redrawn.... *Midnight's Children* sounds like a continent finding its voice" (18). Culture, tradition, religion and myths include the global perspective about her novels. As Rajeshwar Mittapalli and Pier Paulo Piciucco put it:

> The imaginative re-working of Indian history in a culturally hybrid environment, the innovative use of literary techniques...together with a supreme command of the English language and a genius for storytelling modeled on the hoary Indian narrative traditions and cultural practices, had established *Midnight's Children* as a trend-setter and classic for all times. (v)

Midnight's Children virtually captures the attention of three generations of the family of Saleem Sinai. Salman Rushdie views regarding the relevance of history to the present, "Reality is a question of perspective; the further you get from the past, the more concrete and plausible it seems—but as you approach the present, it inevitably seems more and more incredible" (*Midnight* 165-66). Salman Rushdie has emphasized on the particular context of imagination and supposition based on the consequences of the past. He illustrates it, "...suppose yourself in a large cinema, sitting at first in the back row, and gradually moving up, row by row, until your nose is almost pressed against the screen. Gradually the stars' faces dissolve into dancing grain; tiny details assume grotesque proportions; the illusion dissolves or rather, it becomes clear that the illusion itself is reality" (*Midnight* 165-66). One learns a lot from the past to constitute the future of the present. Rushdie has not only presented his philosophy on the different elements of diaspora like relations of nativity, blood, nationalism and above all belongingness.

Shame is the novel, which has a wonderful depiction of migration and its impact on the lives of different individuals and communities. "I wanted to talk about the immigrant community in London particularly the South Asian immigrant community, and at that time what I wanted to say about it is, "Here's this enormous community of people who are, it seems, invisible—their concerns their lives you know, their fears, and so on, somehow invisible to the white population" (Herwitz and Varshney 19). The town called 'Q' explores the lives of three sisters (Chunni, Munnee, and Bunny Shakil) who give birth to Omar Khayyám Shakil. However, it is not known who is the real mother of Omar. Because, all the three sisters get pregnant at a house party. Omar behaves in a different manner which is not comfortable for his mothers. Omar Khayyám leaves Q. Later, his contacts with the tutor Eduardo Rodriguez, Iskander Harappa and General Raza Hyder, "I, too, am a translated man. I have been borne across" (*Shame* 29). Throughout his life remains a matter of suspicion over his relationship. He becomes an isolated being even among his own family members. Rege calls his sense of imagination as "a migrant, diasporic, cosmopolitan consciousness" (185). Salman Rushdie says, "I am an emigrant from one country (India) and a newcomer in two (England, where I live and Pakistan to which my family moved against my will)" (85). Minoli Salgado is very much impressed with the diasporic elements in it, he remarks:

> The novel appears to replicate the author's predicament by foregrounding a sense of banishment and impending death, opening and closing the eponymous Moor's narrative with his premature death in exile. Exile and death thus frame the rich narrative collage that constitutes this saga of Catholic-Jews Da-Gama-Zagoiby family, containing the events in a foreclosed temporal register that offers the cultural and historical density of text. (153)

Rushdie validates the value of history in relation to the present. The visionary insight which enables oneself towards the real belonging creates a phenomenon that embarks the way towards essentialism connected with one's history. He himself speculates upon this matter in *Shame,* when he says, "Outsider! Trespasser! You have no right to this subject.... We reject your authority. We know you, with your foreign language wrapped around you like a flag: speaking about us in your forked tongue, what can you tell but lies? I reply with more questions: is history to be considered the property of the participants solely?" (*Shame* 28). However, one may succeed in paving a way which is consequently important keeping the present situation in mind. He not only emphasizes the concept of belongingness which is an inherent phenomenon with every human being. He relates, "I mustn't forget I'm only telling a fairy-story. My dictator will be toppled by goblinish, faery means. 'Makes it pretty easy for you', is the obvious criticism; and I agree, I agree. But add, even if it does sound a little peevish: '*You* try and get rid of a dictator some time'" (*Shame* 257). All different feelings being in different culture have nicely been presented in *Shame.* Living approach seem quite opposite in both country.

The Ground Beneath Her Feet is the novel where Rushdie has presented a beautiful picture of a new world which focuses on the new approach of the people on nationalism. All the three major characters, i.e. Ormus Cama, Vina Apsara and Umeed Merchant have experienced the predicament of migration. They all feel that nationalism has got a new identity. Salman Rushdie shows:

> Ormus, Vina and I: three of us came west and passed through the transforming membrane in the sky. Ormus, the youthful proselytizer of the here and now, the sensualist, great lover, the material man the poet of the actual, saw visions of the otherworld and was transformed into an oracle, a ten-year monk and an Art Decorated recluse. As for me, I must say at last that I passed through a membrane too. I became a foreigner. For all my advantages and privileges of birth, for all my professional aptitude, I was turned by the fact of leaving my place of origin into an honorary member of the ranks of the earth's dispossessed. (*The Ground* 418)

Rai altogether has new feelings when he sees the new house. He exclaims, "So this is what they feel like, I thought: roots. Not the ones we're born with, can't help having, but the ones we put down in our own chosen soil, then you could say radical selections we make for ourselves" (*The Ground* 414). All characters seem quite comfortable in America, "...America below fourteenth Street, loosey-goosey and free as air, gave me more of a sense of belonging that I'd ever felt back home. Also, with the dream America everyone carries round in his head, America the Beautiful, Langston Hughes's country that never existed but needed to exist with that like everyone else, I was thoroughly in love" (*The Ground* 419). Salman Rushdie himself proclaims in his novel *The Ground Beneath Her Feet,* when he bids his farewell to India, "India, fount of my imagination, source of my savagery, breaker of my heart. Goodbye" (*The Ground* 249). However, they have comparison in their minds for both the countries. The different contrasts are realized related to the daily routine life. In fact, people think differently in terms of living life and passing time. In fact, there was a special place for art and nature, "...the day doesn't pass when I don't think of India, when I don't remember childhood scenes. Rushdie says,

> Dara Singh wrestling in an open air stadium, Tony Brent singing, Sherpa Tenzing waving from the back of an open car outside Kamla Nehru Park. The movie *Mughal-e-Azam* bursting into color for the big dance-number. The legendary dancer Anarkali strutting her stuff. The non-stop sensory assault of that country without a middle register, that continuum entirely composed of extremes. Sure I remember it. It's the past my past. (*The Ground* 416)

The difference in the regular and habitual life ethics is exposed at the very outset. The worldly sensations get dominated and people begin realizing their potential being the materialistic.

Rushdie's next novel, *The Enchantress of Florence* presents the social differences which all characters face in the different countries as every country has its own rituals and customs. Salman Rushdie asks in this novel, "You still think that home, at the end of a long journey, is a place where a man finds peace" (*The Enchantress* 231). These are some questions which are encountered by the Indian Diaspora, who suffers from a sense of triple displacement—they lose their native place, they enter into an alien language and find themselves among people whose culture is different. Rushdie says, "Our identity is at once plural and partial. Sometimes we feel that we straddle two cultures; at other times, that we fall between two stools. But however ambiguous and shifting this ground may be, it is not an infertile territory for a writer to occupy" (*Imaginary* 15). In fact, according to Salman Rushdie immigrants lose their respect dignity and pride in an alien land, and sometimes we find white people's behaviour unsocial and inhuman towards them. He reiterates, "To conquer English may be to complete the process of making ourselves free" (*Imaginary* 17). The immigrants are cut off from their past, roots and culture. Salman Rushdie states the predicament of immigrants in the West:

> A full migrant suffers, traditionally, a triple disruptions: He loses his place, he enter into an alien language, and finds himself surrounded by beings whose social behaviour and codes are unliked and sometimes even offensive to his own. And this is what makes a migrant such a pathetic figure, because root, languages and social norms have been three of the most important parts of the definition of what it is to be a human being. (*Imaginary* 67)

Rushdie while focusing on the predicament of the human psychology in terms of social and individual contexts does not forget to analyze the traditional values of a society. Salman Rushdie says very confidently, "...the migrant is, perhaps, the central or defining figure of the Twentieth Century" (*Imaginary* 277). He does not focus on the concept of homelessness, rootlessness, etc. rather he terms it as a process of assimilation, gain and an opportunity to succeed in one's life. For that, the relativity of existentialism and growth both go together. Later on his views about the relation of present and past, he says, "...the past is home, albeit a lost home in a lost city in the mists of lost time" (*Imaginary* 9). He views that in the previous centuries, a large scale population has been replaced due to circumstantial migration, and however the process of globalization has led to an increase in the rate of voluntary migration. Salman Rushdie's focus lies mainly in the concept of gain and rehousing in comparison with the loss and non-rehousing. He dreams of a world which emphasizes both home and relations.

Thus, the concept of Diaspora in the modern world is attached with man's isolation and a desire for achieving distinctive identity. In the history of Indian Literature of English, Salman Rushdie's efforts are well visible to the readers. Right from his first novel *Grimus* to *Midnight's Children, Shame* and *The Enchantress of Florence,* he seems to be an explorer of the psychology of the human being in the modern world where people long for identity and peace but they all seem wandering for it. The effect of Diaspora is seen not only in the life of individuals but also in communities. In the Diasporic writing, characters have their own world to live in. Imagination power of the author is highly realized. Feelings of people towards nations have changed. They anticipate and presume their own world which has a new perception of balance and satisfaction with which characters, however, are not satisfied. Throughout, one thing is sure that Salman Rushdie has been brave enough to think and imagine a new world for his characters so that their desire for a world of peace and spiritual satisfaction is realised. This adventurous effort takes Salman Rushdie to the new height of success in the world literature of English.

Works Cited

Blaise, Clark. "A Novel of India's Coming of Age." Rev. of *Midnight's Children* by Salman Rushdie. *New York Times*. 19 Apr. 1981: 18. Web. 7 Jul. 2014. <http://rushdiedigitalexhibit.blogspot.in/p/framework.html>

Herwitz, Daniel and Ashutosh Varshney. *Midnight's Diaspora: Encounters with Salman Rushdie*. New Delhi: Prestige Books, 2009.

Lahiri, Himadri, (ed.) *Literary Transactions in a Globalised Context: Multi-Ethnicity, Gender and Marketplace*. New Delhi: Worldview Publications, 2011.

McLeod, John. *Beginning Post Colonialism*. United Kingdom: Manchester University Press, 2007.

Mohanty, Niranjan. "Orientalist Construction of Home and/or Nation: A Study in the Poetry of A.K. Ramanujan, Sujata Bhatta and Meena Alexander". *Interpreting Diasporic Experience*. Eds. Kavita A. Sharma, Adesh Pal and Tapas Chakrabarti. New Delhi: Creative Books, 2004. 192-222.

Rajeshwar Mittapalli and Pier Paolo Piciucco, eds. Preface. *Studies in Indian Writing in English*. Vol. 2. New Delhi: Atlantic Publishers & Distributors Pvt. Ltd., 2001. 1-10.

Ramraj, Victor J. "Diasporas and Multiculturalism." *New National Post-Colonial Literatures*. Ed. Bruce King. New York: Oxford University Press, 1996. 214-29.

Rege, Josna E. "Victim into Protagonist? *Midnight's Children* and the Post-Rushdie National Narratives of the Eighties". *Rushdie's Midnights Children: A Book of Readings*. Ed. Meenakshi Mukherjee. Delhi: Pencraft International, 2003. 182-211.

Rushdie, Salman. *Grimus*. London: Vintage Books, 1996.

———. *Midnight's Children*. London: Vintage Books, 2006.

———. *Shame*. London: Vintage Books, 1995.

———. *The Ground Beneath Her Feet*. London: Vintage Books, 2000.

———. *The Enchantress of Florence*. London: Jonathan Cape, 2008.

———. *Imaginary Homelands: Essays and Criticism, 1981-1991*. London: Granta, 1991.

Salgado, Minoli. "The Policies of Palimpsest in *The Moor's Last Sigh*". *The Cambridge Companion to Salman Rushdie*. Ed. Abdulrazak Gurnah. Cambridge: Cambridge University Press, 2007. 153-68.

Singh, Manjit Inder. *Contemporary Diasporic Literature*. New Delhi: Pencraft International, 2007.

15

Diasporic Identity in Salman Rushdie's *Shalimar the Clown*

Vikrant Sehgal

Salman Rushdie has established himself as one of the most powerful modern writers. He is the author of eight previous novels—*Grimus* (1975), *Midnight's Children* (1981), *Shame* (1983), *The Satanic Verses* (1988), *Haroun and the Sea of Stories* (1990), *The Moor's Last Sigh* (1995), *The Ground Beneath Her Feet* (1999) and *Fury* (2001)—and one collection of short stories, entitled *East, West* (1994). He has to his credit four works of non-fiction—*The Jaguar Smile* (1987), *Imaginary Homelands* (1992), *Step Across this Line* (2002) and as co-editor *The Vintage Book of Indian Writing* (1997).

His ninth novel *Shalimar the Clown* (2005) is a welcome addition to the Rushdie canon where he moves across the globe and follows his characters from terrorist camps to the privileged world of Los Angeles, motivated by shades of love, curiosity and burning vengeance. In one of the "Columns" entitled "June 1999: Kashmir" published in *Step Across this Line: Collected Non-Fiction 1992-2002,* he says:

> For over fifty years, India and Pakistan have been arguing and periodically coming to blows over one of the most beautiful places in the world, Kashmir, which the Mughal emperors thought of as Paradise on earth. As a result of this unending quarrel, Paradise has been partitioned, impoverished and made violent. Murder and terrorism now stalk the valleys and mountains of a

> land so famous for its peacefulness that outsiders made jokes about the Kashmiris' supposed lack of fighting spirit. (Rushdie 2002: 305)

The "Kashmir problem must be defused", he says, "or else, in the unthinkable worst-case scenario, it may end in the nuclear destruction of Paradise itself, and of much else besides" (Rushdie 2002: 307). He has also been successful in advancing some of the major themes, concerns and settings of his earlier novels to match the hysterics of the problems of living in the contemporary world. The novel not only reflects the author's sense of "diaspora" but can also be read as a study of his responses to the diasporic predicament in the postcolonial space.

There has been a strong debate over terms like "diasporic difficulties", "postmodernism", "postcolonialism" and "culture studies" in the context of new literatures from various "generic, ethnic and regional traditions" (Rushdie 2002: 5). I refer to Michael Berube's brilliant essay, "Introduction: Worldly English" (2002), published in *Modern Fiction Studies*, in which he makes a mention of Jay Paul's "Beyond Discipline? Globalization and the Future of English" (2001) and significantly argues that "globalization is to be understood as having gotten under way sometime around the death of Chaucer in 1400, but that globalization only started providing really compelling reasons for re-conceiving literary study as post-national sometime around the birth of midnight's children on New Year's Day 1947, as they were reconceived by Salman Rushdie in 1980" (Berube 2002: 9). He goes on to question the appeal to "diasporic" forms of English:

> The very expansion (and, some would say, dereferentialization) of the term beyond its traditional use with regard to Jewish and American peoples is a very recent phenomenon-perhaps, indeed, an important epiphenomenon of the confluence of postmodern and postcolonial ways of thinking about hybridity, identity and global flow. To put this another way: the fact that so many multiple and conflicting forms of ethnic and religious identification are now called "diasporic" seems at once to mark the hegemony

> of and the resistance to postmodern, postcolonial, postnational modes of identification: we who are diasporic are necessarily cosmopolitan, hybrid, scattered and incompletely sutured, and yet we who are diasporic have a common transnational ethnic identity that somehow subtends the vagaries of its many global manifestations. (Berube, 2002: 9-10)

I may also refer to John Oliver Perry's "A Dialysis of Diasporan Difficulties" (2002) published in *Journal of Contemporary Thought* in which he observes that "despite the claims of various types of Diasporan Indians in America and elsewhere, the term, like 'Commonwealth' or 'postcolonial', has no coherent, critically useful referential base; it merely indicates an immigrant from the Indian subcontinent, or a descendant of one. There is no way to select "truly Indian" Diasporans in America—or anywhere else, for that matter" (Perry 2002: 83). He is, however, of the view that the "dominant type of Diasporan Indian obviously does experience frustrating isolation and alienation simply because it attempts to rely so heavily for its identity on maintaining some generally recognizable form of 'Indianness' through a few narrowly operating gestures" (Perry 2002: 108).

Shalimar the Clown, not very much unlike *Haroun and the Sea of Stories* (1990) and *Midnight's Children* (1981), affords a diasporic reading. The earlier works had references to Kashmir in passing and places like Bombay, Pakistan, London and New York had performed central roles. Kashmir, the homeland of Rushdie's maternal grandfather and a favourite location for Rushdie family holidays, appears for the first time as a central backdrop in *Shalimar the Clown*, a novel in which the burning issues of the land feature prominently. Rushdie has long been concerned with rediscovering the past which, as he says in *Imaginary Homelands*, is "a country, from which we have all emigrated, that its loss is part of our common humanity". He further suggests that "the writer who is out-of-country and even out-of-language may experience this loss in an intensified form" and "it is made more concrete for him by the physical fact of discontinuity, of his present being in a different place from his past, of his being 'elsewhere' and "this may enable him to speak properly and concretely on a subject of universal significance and appeal" (12). In one of the questions asked in an Interview to the *Pittsburgh Tribune-Review* (Sunday, September 11, 2005) about the reasons for dedicating the book to the memory of his Kashmiri grandparents and whether he wanted to tell the story of Kashmir especially to the Westerners who are unfamiliar to the region, he says:

> I have cared about Kashmir all my life because of family ties and a lifetime of going there and loving it. And yes, I wanted to tell its (Kashmir's) story, the story of a paradise lost not so much lost as smashed up, and I think western readers will find many resonances with events in other, perhaps more familiar parts of the world, other places in which armies and fanaticisms have marched over people's lives. But above all I wanted to write about beauty, and the tragedy of its loss. (7)

The novel, very early on, states the theme in the words of a character: "Everywhere was now a part of everywhere else. Russia, America, London, Kashmir. Our lives, our stories, flowed into one another's, were no longer our own, individual, discrete. This unsettled people. There were collisions and explosions. The world was no longer calm.... Contentment, contentedness, content; these variant forms were the names of dreams" (61).

The action of the story starts with an assassination of Max Ophuls, an octogenarian French born Jewish-American diplomat who is "slaughtered...like a *halal* chicken dinner, bleeding to death from a deep neck wound caused by a single slash of the assassin's blade" (5). He is murdered by the Kashmiri 'terrorist', nicknamed Shalimar the clown. The murder takes place on the steps of the apartment building Los Angeles where Max's twenty-four-year-old illegitimate daughter, named India, is living. The murderer is his own obedient and loyal chauffeur, Shalimar, whom we later come to know through flashback, was so full of love and laughter; capable of loving and being loved. The day before his murder, Ophuls had given his daughter a De Lorean, "a silver luxury speed mobile with batwing doors, the same futuristic machine in which people were time travelling in the movies that year" (19). The whole story remains in motion on the wheels of the car and Rushdie effectively uses it to move back and forth through the twentieth century giving each and every detail of the lives. Of his four important characters about whom, when he was asked that "All four of the main characters are complicated—they aren't totally likeable, and they do terrible things to one another", he replied in an Interview given to the Atlantic on August 24, 2005: "Yeah, people make bad moral choices. Max is a philanderer and so on, and I just thought, People are like this, aren't they? I didn't want straightforward good people and bad people. I wanted realistic people who had all the qualities that we all unfortunately have." After the murder, the novel circles back in time to Kashmir, where a Hindu girl named Boonyi, the only daughter of Pandit Pyarelal Kaul and a Muslim boy named Shalimar fall in love. Shalimar is a clown, an acrobat whose father had trained him not to think of the "rope as a safety line through space" (88). The parents of both the lovers and the village environment are so liberal that in spite of being Hindu and Muslim it is agreed that the marriage be solemnized by both Hindu and Muslim rituals:

> The lovers were their children and must be supported. Their behaviour was worthy of the strongest censure—it had been licentious and rash and filled with improprieties that were a disappointment to their parents—but they were good children, as everybody knew. That Abdullah then mentioned Kashmiriyat, Kashmiriness, the belief that at the heart of Kashmiri culture there was a common bond that transcended all other differences. Most bhand villages were Muslim but Pachigam was a mixture, with families of pandat background, the Kauls, the Misris and the baritone singer's long-nosed kin-sharga being a local nickname for the nasally elongated and even one family of dancing Jews. "So we have not only Kashmiriness to protect but Pachigaminess as well. We are all brothers and sisters here", said Abdullah. "There is no Hindu Muslim issue. Two Kashmiri—two Pachigami—youngsters wish to marry, that's all.

> A love match is acceptable to both families and so a marriage there will be; both Hindu and Muslim customs will be observed." Pyarelal added, when his turn came, "To defend their love is to defend what is finest in ourselves." (180)

It is a village where Hindus and Muslims live peacefully side by side:

> Today our Muslim village, in the service of our Hindu maharaja, will cook and act in a Mughal—that is to say Muslim-garden, to celebrate the anniversary of the day on which Ram marched against Ravan to rescue Sita. What is more, two plays are to be performed: our traditional Ram Leela and also Budsha, the tale of a Muslim sultan. Who tonight are the Hindus? Who are the Muslims? Here in Kashmir, our stories sit happily side by side on the same double bill, we eat from the same dishes, and we laugh at the same jokes. We will joyfully celebrate the reign of the good king Zain-ul-abidin, and so far our Muslim brothers and sisters, no problem! They all like to see Sita rescued from the demon-king, and besides, there will be fireworks. (115-16)

We at times wonder whether Max has actually been murdered. He has been brought back to life in the coming pages of the book and the events narrate the "seduction of Boonyi Kaul Noman (the name she herself disliked, 'my name is mud', she said, 'it's mud and dirt and stone and I don't want it', and preferred to be called Boonyi, the 'local word for the celestial Kashmiri chinar tree' (72-73)—or, more accurately, the seduction of Max Ophuls by Boonyi—took time. Even for a man of Edgar Wood's unusual aptitudes it was not easy to arrange a private meeting between the Ambassador and a married Kashmiri dancing girl. At the end of the Dachigam hunting lodge festivities Wood voiced the Ambassador's desire to thank personally all those who had given him such a delightful evening, and out they came in a crowd, the poets and *santoor* players, the actors and cooks." Max congratulates Boonyi whose "eyes modestly downcast, felt a breeze on her cheek, as if a door were opening and the air of the outside world were being allowed to enter" (301-02). The result of this relationship, was, as Max had foreseen, "trouble; the biggest Indo-American diplomatic rumpus in history. But for a time the master forger was deceived by the forgery he had bought, deceived and satisfied, as content to possess it as an art collector who discovers a masterpiece concealed in a mound of garbage, as happy to keep it hidden from view as a collector who can't resist buying what he knows to be stolen property. And that was how it came about that a faithless wife from the village of the *bhand pather* [a performing troupe of Hindu Kashmiris] began to influence, to complicate and even to shape, American diplomatic activity regarding the vexed matter of Kashmir" (318-19). The novelist has described the career of Ophuls, a teacher by profession, who comes from Belgium and when Hitler annexes Belgium he escapes to France as a confidante of Gen. de Gaulle. On being tracked by Nazis he slips to England to join his boss. In the resistance movement he meets his future wife whom the novelist calls Grey Rat. Max is a habitual adulterer and later becomes a secret negotiator for American interests around the globe. He is picked up by the administration to replace Galbraith as Ambassador to India. His involvement in Kashmir is registered through his impact upon the lives of Boonyi, whom he seduces, impregnates and abandons. In Delhi Ophuls puts her up in an expensive flat. The luxurious lifestyle and available leisure badly influences Boonyi who gets addicted to drugs and in two years' time becomes what Rushdie describes as a "vegetarian and non-vegetarian, fish- and meat-eating, Hindu, Christian and Muslim, a democratic, secularist omnivore" (333). Her physical appearance is described in the following words: "Inevitably her beauty dimmed. Her hair lost its lustre, her skin coarsened, her teeth rotted, her body odour soured, and her bulk-ah! Her bulk—increased steadily, week by week, day by day, almost hour by hour. Her head rattled with pills, her lungs were full of poppies" (333). Soon she gets pregnant and gives birth to a girl and whispers into the little girl's ears: "Do you hear me?"... "Your name is Kashmira Noman, and I'm going to take you home" (345). Peggy comes to Boonyi, calls the new born India, puts her hand on the young mother's head and says: "You can't keep this little girl. She will drag you down and she will be the death of you and that will be the death of her.—You follow? Whereas with me she can live like a queen" (349). Boonyi is left in an emotionally shattered state: "She did not know if she could live without her little girl.... She closed her eyes and willed her child away. There was no Kashmira. There was only Kashmir" (355). On her return to Pachigam, "she saw them all through the snowstorm, circling her like crows, keeping their distance" and even her "sweet father stopped six feet away and wept, the tears freezing on his cheeks" but immediately said: "nazare-bad-door" (360-61). Shalimar was restrained by both the parents. She finally fell to her knees in the snow with her arms "outspread" and waiting (362). Boonyi was taken by another rape victim of the village named Zoon, the carpenter's daughter to stay with her in a wooden hamlet. Boonyi never goes back to Pachigam. She now realizes that "Only Man wears masks. Only Man is a disappointment to himself" (373).

Shalimar, on the other hand becomes an introvert. He proposes that the "scene in the Anarkali play in which the dancing girl was grabbed by the soldiers who had come to take her to be bricked up in her wall might be sharpened if the soldiers came on in American army uniform and Anarkali donned the flattened straw cone of a Vietnamese peasant woman. The American seizure of Anarkali-as-Vietnam would, he argued, immediately be understood by their audience as a metaphor for the Indian army's presence in Kashmir, which they were forbidden to depict" (377). Himal didn't like the idea and warns him: "Just try seeing straight instead,"..., "Don't look for what's not here, but look at what there is" (377-78). He then wants to meet his brother Anees who had joined a group of freedom fighters. Pachigam was not the old place any more: "These days the two sexagenarians (Abdullah and Pyarelal Kaul) didn't speak much. Abdullah had started mentioning the word *azadi*, but to Pyarelal the word didn't mean freedom but something more like danger, and it made a difficulty between the two old friends" (407). Shalimar the clown "left Pachigam the next morning carrying nothing but the clothes he stood up in and the knife in his waistband and was not seen in the village for fifteen years" (409). His brother Anees, along with the comrades were working for the liberation of Kashmir and it was Bulbul Fakh's responsibility to re-educate all newcomers and Shalimar the clown "sat on a boulder by a frozen mountain stream and listened to the iron mullah as once he had listened to Pandit Pyarelal Kaul while longing for the simple happiness of Boonyi's touch. But that happiness had proved to be an illusion, a deception, and Shalimar the clown's memory of being deceived made the iron mullah's lessons easier for him to accept" (433). Bulbul Fakh announces: "This warrior has put off the garments of lie and put on those of truth. He is ready for the war" (435). His words "the infidel says that a man's character will decide his fate; we say that a man's fate will forge his character anew";.... The infidel speaks of universal truth. We know that the universe is an illusion and that truth lies beyond the illusion, where the infidel cannot see (436) had a strong effect on Shalimar who "almost believed that he was no longer what he was and could indeed leave the past behind" (437). He is now forty years old, completely transformed, "clean shaven and wearing Western clothes", with a pistol, feeling like a "Superman" and for a man like him "there will always be plenty of work" (447, 449).

In Kashmir the liberation struggle entered a militant phase. On the one hand, there were 'freedom fighters' with their internal contradictions as factions asking for an independent Kashmir and those who wanted to follow a religious path and wanted a merger with Pakistan; on the other, they were pitted against a ruthless army headed by General Hammirdev Suryavans Kachhwaha who "despised the fundamentalists, the jihadis, the Hizb, but he despised the secular nationalists more" (488). He had spent all his active life chasing Kashmiri 'freedom fighters'. Pachigam was also affected: "Alas! Not one of the Pachigam contingents of five dancers survived" (497). Rushdie's observation is worth quoting:

> In early 1991, before the spring thaw, Pandit Pyarelal Kaul felt his life detaching itself from his body in a series

> of small painless, inaudible pops...he had nobody to teach any more except himself, and even to himself he no longer had any knowledge to impart.... He...pulled out the English romantics. Now more than ever seems it rich to die, to cease upon the midnight with no pain. Ah! Poor Keats. Only the very young could imagine that death was a proper response to beauty.
>
> He closed his eyes and pictured his Kashmir...it is this, it is this, it is this.... No, he would not ride out into Kashmir, did not want to see her scarred face, the lines of burning oil drums across the roads, the wrecked vehicles, the smoke of explosions, the broken houses, the broken people, the tanks, the anger and fear in every eye. Everyone carries the address in his pocket so that at least his body will reach home. (498-99)

Shalimar was happy when Mullah and his comrades were killed by the Indian forces. He returns to Pachigam, kills his wife and then goes to America through Philippines and Canada and reaches Los Angeles where Max is living after his retirement with India who is angry to the core. She writes to Shalimar who has been sentenced to death but it is she, not the twelve Americans in a jury Box, who will be her judge: "Don't call me your stepdaughter I'm not your stepdaughter I'm my father's daughter and my mother's child and if I'm inside you then so are they. My mother whom you butchered torments you now and my slaughtered father too. I am Maxmillan Ophuls and Boonyi Kaul and you are nothing. I crush you beneath my heel" (618). Shalimar breaks out of the San Quentin prison remembering that "as long as he was held in his father's hand he could not fall" (643). India had been learning archery and Shalimar was there to kill her but "She was ready for him. She was not fire but ice. The golden bowl was drawn back as far as it would go. She felt the taut bowstring pressing against her parted lips, felt the foot of the arrow's shaft against her gritted teeth, allowed the last seconds to tick away, exhaled and let fly.... There was no possibility that she would miss. There was no second chance. There was no India. There was only Kashmira and Shalimar the clown" (649).

The scenario of the novel clearly indicates that Kashmir's problems are nor a result of Hindu-Muslim antipathy but an antipathy that has come to the fore due to our politicians and historians. *Shalimar the Clown* is a very powerful narrative and on many occasions reads like history. The most striking feature of the novel is the effectiveness with which Rushdie conveys his sense of anger at the systematic slaughter carried out in the once peaceful valley of Kashmir. The narrator poses a host of questions:

> There were six hundred thousand troops in Kashmir but the pogrom of the *pandits* was not prevented, why was that. Three and a half lakhs of human beings arrived in Jammu as displaced persons and for many months the government did not provide shelters or relief or even register their names, why was that. When the government finally built camps it only allowed for six thousand families to remain in the state, dispersing the others around the country where they would be invisible and impotent, why was that. The camps at Purkhoo, Muthi, Mishriwallah, Nagrota were built on the banks and beds of nullahs, dry seasonal waterways, and when the water came the camps were flooded, why was that. The ministers of the government made speeches about ethnic cleansing but the civil servants wrote one another memos saying that the *pandits* were simply internal migrants whose displacement had been self-imposed, why was that. The tents provided for the refugees to live in were often uninspected and leaking and the monsoon rains came through, why was that.... There was one bathroom per three hundred persons in many camps why was that and the medical dispensaries lacked basic first-aid materials why was that...and the *pandits* of Kashmir were left to rot in their slum camps, to rot while the army and the insurgency fought over the bloodied and broken valley, to dream of return, to die while dreaming of return, to die after the dream of return died so that they could not even die dreaming of

> it, why was that why was that why was that why was that why was that. (484-85)

The earth, Rushdie had earlier remarked was not a planet. The "earth was the subject" (503). "Pachigam was the earth, the grabbee, helpless" and, therefore the questioning:

> Who lit that fire? Who burned that orchard? Who shot those brothers who laughed their whole lives long? Who killed the sarpanch? Who broke his hands? Who broke his arms? Who broke his ancient neck? Who shackled those men? Who made those men disappear? Who shot those boys? Who shot those girls?... Who killed the children? Who whipped the parents?... Who raped that woman again? Who raped that woman again? Who raped that woman again? Who raped that dead woman? Who raped that dead woman again? (503-04)

Ultimately, the significance of *Shalimar the Clown* lies in the fictional response of Rushdie to the political events of Kashmir. In this context, it is relevant to express what he said in *Imaginary Homelands*:

> It may be that writers in my position, exiles or emigrants or expatriates, are haunted by some sense of loss, some urge to reclaim, to look back even at the risk of being mutated into pillars of salt. But if we do look back, we must also do so in the knowledge—which gives rise to profound uncertainties—that our physical alienation from India almost inevitably means that we will not be capable of reclaiming precisely that thing that we lost, that we will, in short, create fictions, not actual cities or villages, but invisible ones, imaginary homelands, Indias of the mind. (Rushdie 1991: 10)

Where is Kashmir? Have we really lost it? Is there no hope? Yes there is. Religion and race are, of course, manmade and Rushdie seems to be asking all fundamentalists to bring in drastic reforms, become liberal and make this world a better place to live in or else perish. Rushdie through his questioning not only demands attention but also seeks redressal for a peaceful co-existence in a multi-cultural and pluralistic society in the times to come. We should not miss his Shakespearean epigraph to the novel: "A plague on both your houses."

Works Cited

Bacon, Katie. "The Limits of Tolerance: An Interview with Salman Rushdie". Web. 22 Feb. 2013. <www.theatlantic.com/magazine/archive/...limits-of-tolerance/304265/>

Berube, Michael. "Introduction: Worldly English". *Modern Fiction Studies* 48:1 (Spring 2002): 1-17.

Perry, John Oliver. "A Dialogue of Diasporan Difficulties". *Journal of Contemporary Thought* 17 (Winter 2002): 83-115.

Rushdie, Salman. *Imaginary Homelands: Essays and Criticism 1981-91*. New York: Granta, 1991.

———. *Step Across this Line: Collected Non-Fiction 1992-2002*. London: Vintage Books, 2003.

———. *Shalimar the Clown*. Delhi: Random House, 2005.

———. "An Interview." *Pittsburgh Tribune-Review*. Web. 11 Sept. 2005.

16

Indianness and Satire of History in Salman Rushdie's *The Moor's Last Sigh*

Indah Lestari

> Christian, Portuguese and Jews; Chinese tiles promoting godless views; pushy ladies, skirts-not-saris, Spanish shenanigans, Moorish crowns...can this really be India?
>
> (Rushdie 1995: 87)

The Moor's Last Sigh (1995) is often regarded as a historiographic trilogy of Salman Rushdie along with *Midnight's Children* (1981) and *Shame* (1983). Like most of Rushdie's fictions, the setting of this novel is the Indian subcontinent. India, as a nation-state, has been Rushdie's main theme and he is renowned for his brilliant political satire. In this novel, Rushdie narrowed down this theme to, among others, migrant's quest of identity. From the perspective of identity, the family saga in *The Moor's Last Sigh* can be read as historical allegory. The modern Indian history back-dropping this novel—the Independence struggle, the Partition and the Emergency era—are inserted into and mutually affect the characters in this novel. This paper aims to analyze the complexity of India as a nation-state from the aspect of its history as depicted in the novel and how Rushdie satirizes Indian history through intertwining the protagonist's personal life and historical events.

The common technique Rushdie uses in *Midnight's Children* and *The Moor's Last Sigh* is the sophisticated connection between India and the main character's life journey. In the first novel, Saleem Sinai's birth coincides with the birth of the nation, on the Independence Day, while in the latter India's plot movement is in sync with the experience of Moor's family. The story in *The Moor's Last Sigh* covers the life of four generations, from the nineteenth century to the present, and is set in Bombay and Cochin. It is narrated by a Christian Portuguese-Jewish named Moraes ('Moor') Zogoiby. In his narration, the Moor tells about the history of 'India' as he remembers it. History is maintained and modified from time to time. The writing of history in Rushdie's novel more or less resembles what the Moor says about his mother's family conflict, "I tell them as they have come down to me, polished and fantasticated by many re-telling. These are old ghosts, distant shadows, and I tell their tales to be done with them; they are all I have left and so I set them free" (11). So his family story becomes an account that is flexible, it changes as it is transferred from generation to generation.

The play with history is evident in Aurora's paintings. As a child, she is "allowing the torrential reality of India to awaken her soul" (45). When her talent is first discovered by her father, she draws history on the walls, starting from King Gondophares and St Thomas the Apostle, the building of the Taj Mahal, the battle of Srirangapatnam, the modern history including the Congress and Muslim League, to, most importantly Catholic Portuguese Vasco da Gama's first setting his foot in India. Da Gama played a very important role in Indian history. After Vasco da Gama's arrival in 1498 and the domination of European maritime, India was open to significant influences, which peaked in the decline of the Muslim rule and the colonialism of the British Empire. Here it is as if she wants to claim to be a part of historical narrative. Her bloodline as a Da Gama also formed India in the past, thus she possesses the sense of Indianness. Aurora accommodates the long history of the nation using the technique of palimpsest to accommodate the long history of the nation. The palimpsest of her painting contains, in the first layer, the coming of Vasco da Gama in India and, second, the Hindu-Muslim conflict especially the Babri Mosque riot in 1992. Other stories that may also be included are the Moors in Spain and the Jews in India.

Plural India

Indianness is a plural and unstable idea. India is a multilingual, multicultural and multireligious country. Purity of race is rendered as impossible. Anderson states that nation, nationality and nationalism are difficult to define (3). We need to see the historical context of those concepts because the meanings change over time. Flory Zogoiby, a Jew, objects her son's choice of woman, the Portuguese Aurora da Gama because of religion and nationality difference. However, it is later revealed that Flory's bloodline can be traced back to Boabdil the Misfortunate, or in Moorish tongue, El Zogoybi (83). The term 'Moor' itself is difficult to define. 'Moor' is defined, among others, as, formerly a member of the Muslim population in currently Spain and Portugal ("Moor"). It is of mixed Arab, Spanish and Berber origins and settled in North Africa between the 11th and 17th century. It can also refer to Muslims in general, such as that of Sri Lanka and the Philippines. Moor is a loose category in terms of ethnic group, ancient or modern. For Europeans from the Middle Ages to the 17th century, Moors were black and thus the term "white Moors" for non-black Muslims. Besides Hindu, Islam and Christian, other religions in India include Sikh, Buddhism and Jainism.

India is also plural in terms of language. In the novel, the demand of the people for the departure of the British was proclaimed "in Malayalam, Kannada, Tulu, Konkani, Tamil, Telugu and English" (31). The official national language of India is Hindi, but the Constitution recognizes twenty-two "scheduled languages" for official correspondence. These languages comprise Indo-European, Dravidian, Sino-Tibetan and Austro-Asiatic languages. Most importantly, the colonizer's language, English, is an "associate" official language. The large number of language bears the consequence of the people being bilingual or multilingual (Sahgal 299). We can see the complexity of identity in, for example, Francisco. Political preference is only one side of Francisco. Beneath his determination of the end of the British Empire, he loves English literature and can recite Andrew Marvell's 'On a Drop of Dew' with deep sentiment. Thus the colonized builds dilemmatic relationships with the colonizer. The former is both attracted to and loathed by the latter.

Culture that is born out of colonization becomes diverse and rich, due to the dislocation and displacement. The Moorish Spain and modern India societies, which the novel mainly focuses on, depict pluralism which can be defined in different ways according to interpretations.

Family Entity as a Nation

The nation as a family is something that India is familiar with. This can be seen from the term 'Mother India'. First, Mother India is embodied in Isabella, "who loved and betrayed and ate and destroyed and again loved her children, and with whom the children's passionate conjoining and eternal quarrel stretched long beyond the grave" (60-61). Then, the embodiment shifts to her daughter, Aurora. She resembles her mother so much—beautiful and sharp-tongued—that Camoens could not even bear to look at her daughter.

The allegory of nation as a family can also be found in the behaviour of a husband and a wife. Isabella, who then marries Camoen, recites Nehru's speech in May 1922: "Intimidation and terrorism have become the chief instruments of government. Do they imagine that they will thus instill affection for themselves? Affection and loyalty are of the heart. They cannot be extorted at the point of a bayonet" (24). Then she says that the passage depicts Camoen's parents' marriage, which is arranged. This implies that Francisco and Epifania do not and are likely unable to love each other.

The Abraham-Aurora relationship in a way represents India. The couple is full of hatred and vengeance. However, they still love each other. From a letter, Moraes knows that his mother is expecting to be assassinated at any time. Aurora's "The Moor's Last Sigh" palimpsest painting, after a hard job of carefully removing the first layer and using X-ray equipment, reveals that the murderer is Moraes's own father. Moraes admits that "blood-lust was in [his] history, and...[his] bones" (365). The Hindu-Muslim conflict is something that lingers in

Indian history. One of the major incidents is the 16th century Babri Masjid, a heritage of the Islamic Mughal Empire, being demolished only within a few hours by fundamentalist Hindus, following the riots where the Hindus wanted to build a temple in the site. The site is known as Rama's birthplace and the location of an ancient Hindu temple. Moraes comments, "They surge among us, left and right, Hindu and Muslim, knife and pistol, killing, burning, looting, and raising into the smoky air their clenched and bloody fists" (365). Violence is inherent and manifests itself in a family and a nation.

Moraes says that "motherness...is a big idea in India, maybe our biggest: the land as mother, the mother as land, as the firm ground beneath our feet" (137). In discussing Bengali novels particularly Bankimchandra Chatterji's *Anandamath* (1882), Mukherjee argues that the concept of mother goddess is a combination of Hindu religious feeling and patriotic fanaticism, linking to the idea of the nation as a political entity (49). The novel is the origin of Congress Party's national anthem "Bande Mataram" or "Hail to Thee Mother", which accompanied nationalism in Bengal in relation to Partition (Ahmed 88). In relation to motherhood, Rushdie also brings up the mega movie *Mother India,* directed by Mehboob Khan and produced in 1957. The movie portrays poverty in agricultural India. The protagonist, Radha, is a willful mother who ploughs the soil, raising her two sons by herself and being exploited by a moneylender. The movie ends with a tint of technology, symbolized by the opening of a new dam. In *Imaginary Homeland*, Rushdie himself writes about the conflict between Bombay cinema and 'difficult' Satyajit Ray. Satyajit Ray is a Bengali director who well known for the Apu Trilogy. Rushdie quotes the documentary by Andrew Robinson "Satyajit Ray: The Inner Eye". Nargis Dutt, the star in *Mother India*, commented on Ray saying that "if Mr Ray projects Indian poverty abroad, he should also show 'Modern India'. According to her, modern India is "dams..." (Rushdie 1991: 108-09).

However, *The Moor's Last Sigh* does not only speak of modernity with regard to mother. Through Moraes, Rushdie shows the contrast of a woman as mother who produces children and mother who "haunts the fantasy life of Indian males" (139). Indian males here can be the mother's own son. Aurora says that "bad Birju had the hots for his gorgeous ma" (138). The relationship between Birju and Nargis is an example of Freudian Oedipus complex and this is even more obvious in the relation between Moraes and Aurora. The Moor is the mother's object in her series of paintings. She transforms his deformed limb into art. In "To Die upon a Kiss" painting, Aurora is portrayed as Desdemona and the Moor, Othello. The mother-son relationship even becomes more complicated as Aurora is jealous of Moor's lover, Uma. This is also fueled because Uma is a sculptor, thus a rival in art. Aurora rebukes Uma's wish to be a part of Moor's family. After Uma's first visit to his house, Aurora decided to paint a nude picture of him, as if showing off her possession. Here the incest theme is clearly depicted as a great drive in the entity of family.

Mothers' role is glorified in Indian mythology and cultural symbols. A woman is the "benevolent mother goddess, the food-giver but without actual control over external factors which govern the food supply to the home" (Dutta 84). Dutta gives an example of the cultural artifact *Deshmata* that symbolizes the country as motherland. The symbol was confirmed during the nationalist movement. Prime Minister Gandhi was brought to a status of virtual "mother goddess" at home due to the Bangladesh war. In the novel, one of Aurora's traits is her being an ordinary wife, "a woman of her generation" (222). Aurora ignores Abraham for his love affairs because he is the breadwinner of the family. His spice business gives her freedom of creation. She is allowed to go into arts and become very famous.

Intertwining history and personal life is also made possible by creating larger-than-life characters and placing them to actual time and place. Aurora is an apt example. She has several affairs, even with 'Pandit Nehru', the Prime Minister of India. Further, it is suggested that Moraes is his son. Aurora, according to Moraes, is "too bright a star, look at her too hard and you'd be blinded" (136). Moreover, Moraes is a descendant of Vasco da Gama, Portuguese navigator who came to India and introduced pepper that he brought from Lisbon to Malabar Coast, first to Calicut then to Cochin.

Moraes, as the narrator, mentions the historical milestones related to India, from the Spanish reconquista of Granada and the expulsion of the Moors, the foundling of the spice trade between Europe and India, Português colonial expansion, political events of twentieth-century India. The manipulation of the narrative is aimed at telling the history of India fictitiously. The nation's politics come in bits and pieces and are put as the backdrop of the novel's story.

Identity and India's Secularism

Moraes in a way represents India. He is a big man, six feet and a half. In terms of size, India is vast and is a subcontinent. Moraes has asthmatic condition, misshapen right hand. Moreover, his greatest anomaly is that his body appears twice as old as his real age. Rushdie shows that identity is a creative process of retelling and reinventing oneself through time and space. The Moor's body is built of two worlds, the Da Gama's Christian and European bloodline and the Zogoiby's Indian Jewish family. He represents India's heterogeneous and ambiguous identity. This complicates the notion of purity of race and political views that are based on religious ties.

Looking at the age, Gediman compares Moraes to India and says that the two grow too fast. The Moor is a four-month premature-born child. This is in line with the occurrence of the Partition, which was soon after Indian independence in August 15, 1947. The subcontinent was divided into two: India with a majority of Hindus, and Pakistan of Muslims. Jammu and Kashmir states were the trigger of India-Pakistan war only two months after the Independence due to the privilege given to the princes. Further, the eastern part of Pakistan then separated and became Bangladesh. This issue will bring us to the next idea, nationalism.

Indianness can also be built by the sense of nationalism. Critics view that Rushdie's nationalism tends to be that of Jawaharlal Nehru. The Da Gamas support secularity for

"Mother India". Francisco, Camoens and Abraham seem to fall in the same group. Francisco believes that the British must go, while Epifania thinks that the British have been doing some good to the 'Empire's children'. She believes the British have given civilization, law and order. Aires is on his mother's side and he even names a bulldog Jawaharlal to provoke Camoens. On the other hand, Camoens is "for Nehru, not Gandhi—for business and technology and progress and modernity, for the city, and against all that sentimental clap-trap of spinning your own cotton and travelling third-class on the train" (54). However, India is divided into two ideologies, Nehru's and Gandhi's. Camoens tells Belle that 'in the city we are for secular India but the village is for Ram' (55). Camoens foresees that in those kinds of village, the people will fight the non-Hindus. India is still seen as a Hindu country, and as we can see in the novel, Camoens' prophecy begins to come true. The catastrophe of the Babri Mosque at Ayodhya battered down by some fanatical Hindus takes place during Moraes' lifetime.

The character Raman Fielding is based on India's Hindu fanatic politician Bal Thackeray—an anti-Muslim, anti-immigrant, pro-caste, pro-segregation and pro-sati Hindu nationalist—is contrasted with Abraham, who is for secularism. Fielding is on Indira Gandhi's side in terms of preferring the Hindu god Rama. He is:

> against unions, in favour of breaking strikes, against working women, in favour of sati, against poverty and in favour of wealth. He was against 'immigrants' to the city.... He derided the Marxist analysis of society as class struggle and lauded the Hindu preference for the eternal stability of caste. (298-99)

This means the plurality of Bombay is pushed to the edge. He is longing for Bombay's past, "the golden age 'before the invasions' when good Hindu men and women could roam free" (299). Again this brings us to the Babri Masjid riot and demolition. Thus it can be seen that Rushdie tries to propagate humanism. In spite of social differences we are all humans. Our true identity is the 'unity of the flesh' (414). This is also what

Aurora believes in and practices in her paintings. Her concept of secular India is national identity that is constructed out of cultural pluralism and freedom of expression.

In the meantime, Bombay—Rushdie's hometown—can be regarded as a microcosm for India. Bombay is the heart of India. Bombay is central geographically. It is "the bastard child of a Portuguese-English wedding, and yet the most Indian of Indian cities" (350). It is the melting pot of India. The multifarious cultural experience derived from colonial past forms India. As the city develops, people from all over the world come there for business. It is the location of Abraham Zogoiby's company and talcum powder business which disguises the underworld business including heroines, nuclear weapons and human trafficking. In his article, Rushdie acknowledged that to be an Indian of his generation was to believe in Nehru's vision of a secular India as secularism for India means survival. In India, 'communalism' or sectarian religious politics must not take place because they are too dangerous (404).

The ambiguity of India's secularism can be seen in the speech of ultra right Shiv Sena chief Raman Fielding that every community—Christians, Parsis, Jains, Sikhs, Buddhists—must have its own place. This is acceptable to the majority Hindus, as it is part of the ideology of Ram Rajya. However, if Hindu places are disturbed, or 'when minority seeks to dictate to majority, then we say that the small also must accept to bend and move before the big' (260). This is in spite of the fact that the Hindus worship so many gods and goddesses. Indianness is continuously redefined as the time goes by. Moraes concludes this by bluntly saying that, "[b]efore the Emergency we were Indians. After it, we were Christian Jews" (234). Identity is formed based on the question of who is one of us and who is the Other. The Emergency Rule became a moment of constructing elements into identity.

Defending one's version of Indianness is taken to the farthest point that it appears to be absurd. *The Moor's Last Sigh* describes this complicated situation:

> (W)hat harmony emerged from that cacophony! In Punjab, Assam, Kashmir, Meerut—in Delhi, in Calcutta —from time to time they slit their neighbors' throats and took warm showers, or red bubble-baths, in all that spuming blood. They killed you for being circumcised and they killed you because your foreskins had been left on. Long hair got you murdered and haircuts too; light skin flayed dark skin and if you spoke the wrong language you could lose your twisted tongue. (350)

The above passage illustrates that Indian identity is plural. Variety is noticeable in terms of skin color and light skin. Beyond that, language, ethnicity and religion also form one's identity. Unfortunately, physical and cultural difference are potential to be justification of taking fellow-citizens' lives. Later the narrator compares this to Bombay, where those are more unlikely to happen. This is because its ports and exchanges are pillars for the nation's wealth. Rushdie is as if suggesting that the economy is the new faith that can unite people.

Writing Identity

Like Gup City and the great Story Sea in *Haroun and the Sea of Stories,* Bombay is portrayed as "an ocean of stories; we were all its narrators, and everybody talked at once" (350). As a immigrant, Rushdie writes his novels with a sense of loss and displacement from India. He is of a middle-class Muslim family and educated in England. His family moved to Karachi in 1964 during the India-Pakistan war. He was in exile because of the fatwa issued by Iranian Ayatollah Khomeini for his controversial novel *The Satanic Verses* (1988). His vision of India, like any other person's, is fragmented. Speaking on behalf of Indian migrant writers, he says that his fictions are imaginary homelands, Indias of the mind (Rushdie 1991: 10).

As in his other works, Rushdie plays with language. He confuses figures of speech, makes puns and other verbal inventions, for example Aurora's talk "One day you will killofy my heart" (8) and "it stickofies too far out" (12). He puts English, Portuguese and Hindi words in the story, undercutting syntax or normality of language. The presence of Aoi Uë in Vasco

Miranda's nightmarish fortress whom the Moor meets signifies Rushdie's challenging the notion of significance. As the Moor's search for identity is deferred by Vasco Miranda's disclosure of Abraham's involvement in Aurora's death, Aoi brings up to his mind that: "We were consonants without vowels: jagged, lacking shape. Perhaps if we'd had her to orchestrate us, our lady of the vowels.[...] There is in us, in all of us, some measure of brightness, of possibility" (428).

Aoi's all-vowel name means the element that makes signification possible when grouped. Identity is a complicated construction of notions.

Multiculturalism, which celebrates cultural diversity, implies that there is an easily defined culture of a group, culture that is original. This essentialism holds on the belief that cultural difference is built from biological differences in race, gender, etc. Talking about hybridity and the act of writing, Rushdie occupies what Homi K. Bhabha called 'the Third Space'. This space represents, "both the general conditions of language and the specific implication of the utterance in a performative and institutional strategy of which it cannot 'in itself' are conscious" (208). This means the 'other' cultures are defined in a ways employing mythologies and exoticism. Thus these cultures, often referred to as the subaltern, are embedded with identity that is seen from the outside, rather than what they possess themselves.

Culture is always fragmentary and complicated in forming an identity. Rushdie's "in-betweenness" in terms of cultural identity makes him concern about Indianness and nation-state issues. As Homi Bhabha says, cultural diversity can be used to compare categories of ethics, aesthetics, or ethnology. Cultural forms are recognized as pre-given in our consciousness. However, cultural diversity also reminds us of "the separation of totalized cultures that live unsullied by the intertextuality of their historical locations" (206). Moraes feels that "[he] was nobody from nowhere, like no-one, belonging to nothing" (388). He feels the tension between the Self and the Other.

In the end of the novel, Moraes departs to Granada in search of his mother's painting "The Moor's Last Sigh". He feels that he detaches the "place, language, people and customs [he] knew [...]; and these, for most of us, are the four anchors of the soul" (383). The language in the novel is not quite English: there are indigenous languages and colloquial conversations. This also shows postcolonial impact on India in connection with English as the language that unites the nation. Moraes does not either speak Spanish or know the places. Arriving in Andalusia, his world becomes "absurd" (385). He feels being invisible to people. He also questions the goal of his "trans-global pilgrimage" (387), if his journey can be called one. When he reaches the Streets of Parasites, he finds it to be un-Spanish; there are international boutiques and expatriates speaking different languages. This shakes his expectation and conception of the Moors. To go back to Bhabha, Moraes' cultural identity is depicted as unstable. Moraes is longing for authenticity, as can be seen in his dream of peeling off his skin and enter the world naked, free from the categorizations of color, race and clan. Within a timeframe, the past and tradition are translated into the present and this involves historical memory and authorship.

Indianness can be nothing but multicultural. Aurora's paintings being palimpsests is Rushdie's metaphor of India, where the past always stands: Moorish Spain has to make room for modern India yet the past creates Moraes' multicultural identity. His Indianness is never fixed and it needs to be redefined over time. Blending personal experience and historical events, the paintings also allow the untold secrets of the past to be revealed.

The focus on personal experience also portrays the symbolization of family as a nation. The role of mother is contextualized in the scope of nation-state. Mother is not only the homeland, but also a woman with sexual appeal. Furthermore, family affairs show sensitive issues, such as incest.

Rendering history from the arrival of Vasco da Gama to Babri Masjid riot and the Moraes' four-generation family story, Rushdie is peppering history, so to speak. He blends the realist with the magical. Rushdie's *The Moor's Last Sigh* is like Aurora's painting—influenced by both Vasco Miranda's "imaginary worlds whose only natural laws was his own sovereign whimsicality" and Abraham's "clear-sighted naturalism that would help India describe herself to herself" (173).

Works Cited

Ahmed, Salahuddin. *Bangladesh: Past and Present*. Web. 5 August 2013.

Anderson, Benedict Richard O'Gorman. *Imagined Communities: Reflections on the Origin and Spread of Nationalism*. London: Verso, 2003.

Bhabha, Homi K. "Cultural Diversity and Cultural Differences."

Bill Ashcroft, Gareth Griffiths, Helen Tiffin, Eds. *The Post Colonial Studies Reader*. London: Routledge, 1995: 155-57.

Dutta, Sangeeta 1990. "Relinquishing the Halo: Portrayal of Mother in Indian Writing in English." *Economic and Political Weekly* 25 (42/43): WS84-WS94, 1990.

Gediman, Paul. "The Moor's Last Sigh." *Boston Review*. Web. 20 April 2010.

"Moor." *Encyclopaedia Britannica*. Chicago: Encyclopaedia Britannica, 2010. CD-ROM.

Mukherjee, Meenakshi. *Realism and Reality: The Novel and Society in India*. Delhi: Oxford University Press, 1985.

Narain, Mona. "Re-imagined Histories: Rewriting the Early Modern in Rushdie's *The Moor's Last Sigh*." *The Journal for Early Modern Cultural Studies* 6.2, 2006.

Rushdie, Salman. *Imaginary Homelands*. New Delhi: Penguin India, 1991.

———. *The Moor's Last Sigh*. London: Jonathan Cape, 1995.

Sahgal, Anju. "Patterns of Language Use in a Bilingual Setting in India". *English Around the World: Sociolinguistic Perspectives*. Jenny Chesire, Ed. Cambridge: Cambridge University Press, 1991. Web. 5 Aug. 2013.

17

(W)hole in the Transition: The Problematique of Terrorism in *Shalimar the Clown*

Javaid Iqbal Bhat

> Terror: extreme fear, a person or thing that causes terror, a formidable person, a troublesome person or thing, the use of organized intimidation. [Based on Latin *terrere* 'to frighten'.]
>
> [Metcalf 859]

> I think anybody who's been at all engaged with Kashmir knows that it's been essentially trampled over twice from opposite directions. First, the Indian army behaved shockingly there, and still does. That alienated a lot of people. Then the arrival of Islamic fundamentalism, sponsored by Pakistan, destroyed their lives in a quite different way.
>
> [Rushdie Interview]

Shalimar the Clown is, inter alia, a book on "Terrorism". As the novel proceeds towards an engaging Kashmir portion, the innocent rhythms of the village Pachigam are brought to the fore. The villagers live a self-sufficient life in which their needs are easily fulfilled within the local economy. The beginnings of change become visible when the village gradually rises to a new consciousness. This is in the context of the rather ignominious withdrawal of British and the coming into being of two independent states of India and Pakistan. The villagers come upon a new discovery. Their loyalties are now tempted by the newly sovereign entities. In the confusion, which follows, a new reality is born. There are those who want and demand a world unto themselves, an independent state free of any unnecessary meddling from the either country. Some others lured by the zealous pan-Islamists, work towards an accession with Pakistan. The consequence of both these strands of thought running at cross purposes is the inevitable violence or as the Indian state puts it "terrorism". The youth take up arms, initially against the state agencies and later, very ironically, against each other. However, what is irking in all this minute depiction of the rise of violence is the sloppy and slipshod manner in which the enterprise of the construction of a "terrorist" has been undertaken. Be it in the case of Anees Noman or his pan-Islamist brother Shalimar, the way in which they become "terrorists" is unconvincing. This process, which is very briefly delineated, is provocative and reeking with problems.

Rushdie and Kashmir

Salman Rushdie's engagement with Kashmir is not new. In the early part of *Midnight's Children*, a very prominent character Dr. Aadam Aziz is seen in Kashmir. He has received his five years doctoral training from Germany and on his return faces an acute cultural crisis, a sense of alienation from his former belief. Doctor Aziz who "does not feel Indian" (31), leaves the valley along with his wife Naseem Ghani, the landowner's wife, and he reaches Mumbai after travelling through the northern parts of India. Saleem Sinai, grandson of Aadam Aziz and the protagonist of the Novel, takes birth on the eve of India's Independence from the British. The early sections of the novel fictionalize his actual "personal connection" (Brians 141) with Kashmir from where his ancestors had migrated.

Haroun and the Sea of Stories is an "exciting, fanciful story for children" (Coppola 3). In *Haroun and the Sea of Stories* (1990), the reader is returned to Kashmir and through a myriad literary touches, ["the Sea of Stories" part of this title is reminiscent of Kathasaritsagara. This compendium of stories compiled by the ancient Kashmiri Hindu scholar Soma Dev Bhat makes the famed *Arabian Nights* look like a novella] is reminded of the vast literary heritage of this relatively small place to which Rushdie owes no little gratitude. Rashid and his son Haroun travel to K which bears an "unmistakable" (4) resemblance to Kashmir. There the duo is put in a splendid boat in Kashmir. This allegorical narration dramatizes the relationship between those espousing freedom of speech and the power of stories, and those who ask "what is the use of stories that aren't even true"? The fairy tale was published soon after edict of death against Salman Rushdie by Iranian Ayatollah Khomeini. The tale clearly celebrates "the triumph of story-telling and imagination over raw power and dogmatism" (Aji 103).

In *Shalimar the Clown* (2005), a novel for the most part set in Kashmir, he gives some form to the secessionist narrative behind the cycle of violence. A close reader of Rushdie would note a glimpse of that form in the *Midnight's Children* in the mystery-brimmed character of Tai, in addition to his observations in the interviews.[1] A comprehensive treatment of the form is made in this Novel. Earlier in the narrative, with a rich complexity of the Kashmir conflict, he brings out his firm grip over the numerous dimensions of the problem. Yet, surprisingly, is able to maintain attitude favoring the predominant perception. Because very few passages, amid the reams and reams of paper written, are as prescient and provocative, I feel tempted to quote in full:

> The key to understanding this position was the word *integral* and its associated concepts. Elasticnagar was integral to the Indian effort and the Indian effort was to preserve the integrity of the nation. Integrity was a quality to be honoured and an attack on the integrity of the nation was an attack on its honour and was not to be tolerated. Therefore Elasticnagar was to be honoured and all other attitudes were dishonourable and consequently illegal. Kashmir was an integral part of India. An integer was a whole and India was an integer and fractions were illegal. Fractions caused fractures in the integer and were thus not integral. Not to accept this was to lack integrity and implicitly or explicitly to question the unquestionable integrity of those who did

> accept it. Not to accept this was latently or patently to favor disintegration. This was subversive. Subversion leading to disintegration was not to be tolerated and it was right to come down on it heavily whether it was of the overt or covert kind. (96)

Just a page after the dedication words, there is a long quote from the famous Kashmiri English poet Agha Shahid Ali (1949-2001) poem "The Country without a post office" [*I am rowed through paradise on a river of hell...*].[2]

In addition to the novels, there is a short story "The Prophet's Hair" (1981) which was published in the context of mysterious disappearance of the Holy Relic of the Prophet Muhammad from Hazratbal Shrine in Kashmir in 1963.

Kashmir: A Brief Modern Historical Background

Immediate causes on one side, there were older grouses for the people. The roots of these grouses lay in the exit of the Britishers and the Partition of the subcontinent. The princely state of Jammu and Kashmir with a Muslim majority population but a Hindu Maharaja as the ruler, was in a peculiar position regarding accession with India or Pakistan. He chose neither and harbored the desire of an independent state. Meanwhile Pakistani non regular tribesmen, believed that as per the logic of partition J and K must go with Pakistan, invaded the state after hearing of atrocities against Muslims in other parts under the control of the Maharaja (Stephen). India on the other side led by Jawaharlal Nehru, the first Prime Minister of independent India and an ethnic Kashmiri by origin, got the Instrument of Accession signed by the ruling Maharaja and dispatched the Army to defend the state from the invaders. They managed to push back the militiaman to the existing Line of Control (LOC). In the process the former state of Jammu and Kashmir got sliced into two territorial regions viz. Pakistan Administered Kashmir (PAK) also named as Azad (Free) Kashmir and Indian Administered Kashmir (IAK). It is the IAK, which bore the brunt of the armed conflict. The important point to remember here without explaining further the labyrinthine intricacies of the origin of this dispute is that even as the Indian Army consolidated its feet on the soil of Kashmir, Nehru made some solemn promises of plebiscite which have never ceased to haunt post-Independent India (Varshney 1008) and has put India in what some believe to be a "terminal colonial situation" (Mathur) in Kashmir. Exactly at the moment when Kashmir was attacked Prime Minister Nehru dashed a letter to the British Prime Minister Clement Richard Attlee (1883-1967) in which he outlined the context of the assistance given to the maharaja against the invaders, and clearly maintained that the presence of India in the valley is provisional, and the permanent decision would be scripted by the people themselves. "Ultimately—I say this with all deference to this Parliament" he said, "the decision will be made in the hearts and minds of the men and women of Kashmir; neither in this Parliament, nor in the United Nations nor by anybody else" (qtd. by Noorani).

The mystique of Pandit Jawaharlal Nehru's relationship with Kashmir has never ceased to absorb people. Why did a person of his high stature with impressive democratic credentials create such a mess in Kashmir through a series of unredeemed promises? Was the redemption of promises forestalled by the nefarious designs of Pakistan? Or where they merely part of a time-buying tactic? The predominant point of view in the disputed region is easily inclined to bend towards the latter. For the special constitutional guarantees enshrined in the Indian constitution under Article 370 were also gradually eroded under various Delhi-imposed regimes in Srinagar and Jammu. The elections were for the most part stage managed as those were selected who would bend backwards in serving the interests of Delhi. Therefore, the promises made earnestly in the years immediately succeeding the invasion by the Pakistan-backed tribal militiamen remained merely on paper. Just four years after the tribal invasion, Pandit Nehru again reminded his countrymen of the provisional accession of Kashmir with India. This time round he was more forthright:

> And I say with all respect to your constitution that it just does not matter what your constitution say; if the people of Kashmir do not want it, it will not go there. Because what is the alternative? The alternative

> is compulsion and coercion...the decision ultimately lies with the few million people in Kashmir, not even with this parliament...that is the important thing. And if we seek to gain their goodwill we should act accordingly. Do not think you are dealing with a part of U.P. or Bihar or Gujarat. You are dealing with an area, historically and geographically and in all manner of things with a certain background. We have to be men of vision and there has to be a broadminded acceptance of facts in order to integrate really. And real integration comes of the mind and the heart and not of some clause which you may impose on other people.... (Nehru 418-19)

All these historical details densely resonated through the years of armed insurgency. There was an acute consciousness of the accumulated disgruntlement over the past half-a-century. The catchy, popular slogans, (most of them ironically in Urdu and not in Kashmiri) the media of rebellious communication, the code signals, the code names of the underground insurgents etc. all testified to the same consciousness and a sense of vengeance nurtured against the humiliation heaped upon the people. The bonfire of the Indian flag was a common sight. It was during these years that Abdullah's (Lion of Kashmir as *Pandit* Jawaharlal Nehru used to hail him) grave was protected by state as defilement was threatened by the secessionist forces. The threat was resoundingly symbolic. For in the years around the momentous 1947, it was the then popular leader S.M. Abdullah who stood by Nehru. The threat thus carried a deep sense of revivalism against the bonhomie between the duo, and also against the Shimla accord (1975), signed by him in the presence of Prime Minister Indira Gandhi (Nehru's daughter). The accord put the final seal on Accession with India and made it nearly irrevocable.

SC and Terrorism

Pachigam is in many ways a microcosm of the global condition. In this village a relatively peaceful ethos is disturbed under the combined impact of a polarized world. Therefore the two houses mentioned in the quote by Mercutio[3] do refer to the feud between the two families of Romeo and Juliet, as they do, of course, to the acute animosity between the two houses on the global scale. Call those two houses Cross and the Crescent or Terrorism and State Terrorism, Capitalism and Socialism or Fundamentalists and the Modernists, or whichever two faces you produce, the author does perceive a violent friction between them in which our civilization is coming under increasing threat of decimation.

However, the immediate context of these two houses is the squabble over Kashmir between the estranged neighbors India and Pakistan. Between these states, the ancient manuscript of this valley, the garden of the *Pirs*, *Rishis* and *Sufis*, "resource rich but cash poor, perched thousands of feet up in the mountains like a tasty green sweetmeat caught in a giant's teeth" (253) is socially, economically and culturally torn apart. The conflict which grew into a low-intensity war in the early 1990's due to the self-recruitment of Kashmiri youth into the ranks of numerous Guerilla groups has pierced through the heart of what Kashmir represented before the world and before its own people. The relocation of Shakespeare's line and placing it in the context of Kashmir distills the nature and the irreversible ramifications of the dual onslaught on the Kashmir valley. "Plague" is what the poetic voice wishes them for what the two sovereign entities have wrought in the valley. Till this stage in the narrative no perceptive observer of the violence will dispute with the author.

However, where the novelist flounders is in the delineation of the psyche of a "terrorist". We are not given convincing answers to a series of cardinal questions. Like, why an ordinary Kashmiri tightrope walker, carrying on the family tradition, entertaining a mixed audience, turns into a "terrorist". Why does *Shalimar the Clown* become a "terrorist"? How does he become a "terrorist"? The "why" side of the investigation gives out two branches: one is ridden by ambiguities and the other very ridiculously, hints at the possible realization of impotence on account of his failure to keep Boonyi Kaul. In other words, the charismatic American Ambassador, the "Resistance hero" and the "architect of the post-Second World War world" took Boonyi, forced Shalimar to join the "terrorist" groups for he believed "honor ranked above everything else" (258). Not motivated by history, not goaded by the pecking albatross of bilateralism between the two warring countries, not indoctrination for any noble goal, Shalimar plunges into the jaws of death "the most present of absences" because Maximillian Ophuls, the Jewish ambassador, originally from Alsace-Lorraine—a region with close historical resemblance with Kashmir—in Europe, flew away with his sweet heart.[4] Such a description of the migration of heart from the beloved to "terrorism" is unconvincing. Such depoliticisation in the shift of commitment will not stand the test of facts on ground. When Shalimar is seen by his mother, Firdous Noman or Firdous Bhat, for the last time before he enters the circle of pan-Islamism accompanied by rampant violence, he is clearly vague about his objectives and the motivation behind his decision. To his mother, dumbfound by the inexplicable shift in his behavior, he gives out the reason for setting out on this dangerous track. The speech is at once misty, magisterial and laden with intense personal rage:

> "Be glad you are not a man," he retorted. "Because once we stop being asleep we can see that there are only enemies for us in this world, the enemies pretending to defend us who stand before us made of guns and khaki and greed and death, and behind them the enemies pretending to rescue us in the name of God except that they are made of death and greed as well, and behind them the enemies who live among us bearing ungodly names, who seduce and then betray us, enemies for whom death is too lenient a punishment, and behind them the enemies who never see, the ones who pull the strings of our lives. The last enemy in the invisible room in the foreign country far away: that is the one I want to face, and if I have to work my way through all the others to get to him then that that is what i'll do." (248-49)

Shalimar's language is driven more by his private animosity than any historical political feeling of resentment. Here the private sentiment pervades over the contextual political substance. Something which taken at his face value befuddles the very nature of the origin of violent conflict and only reinforces the idea of what William A. Doghlass and Joseba Zulaika describe as the "mythography" of terrorism in which the media circulated images are perpetuated as well as recreated in the novelistic imagination. Contrary to the "mythography" beginning of violence had an immediate as well as a long-term cause.

The text provides the immediate reason for "terrorism". We are given a detailed account of the happenings of the late 1980s to which you do not need to be a Kashmir specialist to testify. The resentment nursed till then eventually boiled over when a massive rigging took place in the state legislative assembly elections. The newly formed party Muslim United Front (MUF), an umbrella political formation composed of strong political dissidents was shown as having been defeated though it had managed to sway the popular feeling and was believed to have swept the elections. The MUF got defeated but the people reasonably believed otherwise. Then electricity was apprehended in the air. The rage was writ hard on the eyes. Just a spark was needed to set the paradise alight. It was not hard to come by. The people like Maulana Bulbul Fakh with the "knife like clarity" (126) and his counterfoil Colonel Hammirdev Kachhwaha, had already prepared the ground. Interestingly and quite symbolically, these Maulanas rose from the metallic refuse of the army:

> The Indian army had poured military hardware of all kinds into the valley, and scrap metal junkyards sprang up everywhere, scarring the valley's pristine beauty, like small mountain ranges made up of malfunctioning truck exhausts, jammed weaponry and broken tank treads. The one day by the grace of the God the junk began to stir. It came to life and took on human form. The men who were miraculously born from these rusting war metals, who went out into the valley to preach resistance and revenge, were saints of an entirely different kind. They were the iron mullahs.... (115)

Kashmir descended into chaos, for many, a splendid chaos, for others a soul shaking catastrophe. The *Pandits* who had illuminated the valley with their learning and knowledge fled under darkness when the guns began to boom. Since then blood is flowing and the cold hearted gods atop the ancient Sanskritised mountains are watching with deep indifference. Going back to the author, it is not hard to agree when in a plain statement of facts he portrays the picture of what immediately preceded the onset of "terrorism":

> But it was the just concluded polls that changed everything. This was the year 1987, and the Indian government had held state elections in Kashmir. Farooq Abdullah, the Sheikh's son, was the government's preferred choice. The opposition party the Muslim United Front, named as its candidate on Mohammed Yousuf Shah, described by General Hammirdev Kachhwaha as the state's 'most wanted militant'. Unofficially, as the results came out, it became clear that the wrong man was winning. So the election was rigged. MUF supporters and electoral agents were seized and tortured. Mohammed Yousuf Shah went underground, and Syed Slaheddin became the chief of the militant group Hizb-ul Mujaheddin. His closest aides the so called HAJY group (Abdul *Hamid* Shaikh, *Ashfaq* Majid Wani, *Javed* Ahmed Mir and Mohammad Yasin Malik), crossed the mountains and joined the JKLF. Thousands of previously law abiding young men took up arms and joined the militants, disillusioned by the electoral process. Pakistan was generous. There were AK 47s for everyone. (2)

However, true to the fictional representation of terrorism, *SC* focuses more on the victims, and steers clear of the politics and the historical motivation for the acts of "terrorism" (Paknadel 2008). Like Philip Roth, Doris Lessing and many other novelists who have made "terrorism" a theme of their novels, Rushdie seems to be more interested less in the political background of the "terrorist" than the actions of which the latter is a part directly or indirectly.

Birth of a "Terrorist" in *Shalimar the Clown*: The Ambiguous Transitions

All these details and incidents are reiterated to refute the idea of a depoliticized and an ambiguous participation in militancy devoid of the immediate historical consciousness by the likes of Shalimar and Anees. It is fallacious to propose that youth became unexpectedly conscious of the problematic of the Kashmir dispute after joining the armed ranks, as is portrayed in the case of Shalimar. On the contrary, the complaints had snowballed and a minor push was required to plunge the valley into Stygian darkness or into a splendid chaos subject to one's perspective about insurgency.

Despite the historical rationale for the youth to rise against the state, why did the writer choose to depoliticize the moment of change in Shalimar? This is a very natural question for one who has not merely witnessed the years of the radicalization of youth but also lived through the turmoil. No doubt Shalimar becomes a pan-Islamist and Anees represents the indigenization of the armed ideology. That idea might arguably come to the rescue of the author. However, the point to be noted here is that Anees's own transition from being an innocuous minded youth who received a substantial quantity of love from his parents, to a "terrorist" espousing liberation from the Indian "hegemony," is also laden with problems not dissimilar from those of his brother Shalimar. Out of the four brothers Hameed, Mahmood, Anees and Shalimar, Anees was born with a natural bend towards artistry. He was bestowed with a pair of gifted hands. His skill of whittling "wood into tiny wonders, such as owls with latticed bodies inside which other tinier owls could be seen" (106) brought him to the attention of the local Liberation Front people. He was perceived as a potential recruit. Crucially in his own moment of transition and something which closely aligns him with his brother's entry into the fear and violence ridden realm, he is shown as hesitant and inarticulate. He does not meet the people who approach him for joining the ranks with any degree of alacrity or evokes any spirited response. He seems to be timid, cowardly and recoiling against their advances:

> ...one star-filled night Anees was brought by two fighters with scarves around their faces to the wooded hill where Nazarebaddoor's old cottage stood rotting and empty. Here he was asked by a man he could not see if he would like to learn to make bombs. Okay, Anees shrugged. At last this meant that his melancholy life was like to be short. When he said this he was wearing his longest and most lugubrious face and the liberation front commander standing in the shadows was mysteriously seized by an inappropriate urge to laugh which he only partially managed to resist. (106-07)

For the writer as well as the reader, Anees, as his picture grows, emerges a little removed from his elder brothers Hameed and Mahmood who are gentle, gregarious fools and whose chief passion in life is to "make each other laugh" (106). Like them, Anees does not appear to be aware of the revolutionary murmurs going around him and is not even remotely inclined to join the revolutionaries. Now, in case of Shalimar such a situation is comparatively understandable for his indoctrinators are not ethnic Kashmiris but foreigners of various hues. But Anees' unwillingness is somewhat hard to believe, because he propagates the localization of the movement and does not see eye to eye with the extreme Right supporting the formation of a non-secular purist state. His idea of the indigenization of the struggle along secular, nationalist lines had a long history. And the people who associated with the ideology were not waiting for any outside signal to rise against the state. They had inherited a legacy of resentment and the massive rigging of elections in the late 1980s was the last straw on the camel's back.

Before evaluating the possible causes of the nature of transition, let me return to another episode in the novel wherein one is struck by the intriguing character of a momentous decision. This is related to Boonyi Kaul. The time is when she makes up her mind to leave the valley. This change of mind comes at a bewildering speed and suddenly urges the reader to ask why. Apparently she wants to train herself further in dancing and polish her subtle, bewitching moves in Delhi under the tutelage of Jayanta Mudgal. This desire springs in her heart after being watched by the American ambassador, Maximillian Ophuls, during a dance performance specially organized for his entertainment on his visit to Kashmir. (An age-old motif of the West as a source of temptation rearises in the novel.) On the face of it Boonyi wants to convert him into a vehicle for the realization of her dancing goals. She is ready to temporarily sacrifice her passion for her beloved Shalimar. The decision, as it subsequently turns out, is a lethal one. It forces Shalimar into a dangerous understanding of betrayal in love, eventually leading to fill his eyes with the murderous rage. A character pushed ahead by a double cause—personal and political, more personal sounding than political. Boonyi too pays a huge price. Before dying she is sequestered as a Living-Dead one, *mritak*, as her father likens to call her condition. The unfortunate life lived by Boonyi after her return from Delhi and the pathos laden death is easily traceable to her momentous transition.

Like her beloved she is not clear about the motivation of her exit from Kashmir. A vague feeling does rounds in her mind about being dissatisfied in her present location. The change in the thinking regarding the relationship with her father, the Muskadoon stream and Shalimar—all part of the emotional covenant she had signed with her childhood sweetheart—is so fast and dramatic as to be unbelievable. She longs to move out and give freer rein to her imagination. In fact an aura of suffocation develops around her:

> Boonyi remained wide awake, staring furiously at the nocturnal ceiling, willing the walls of the house to dissolve so that she could rise up into the night sky and escape. For at very moment in which the village had decided to protect her and *Shalimar the Clown*, to stand by them by forcing them to marry, thus condemning to a lifetime of jail sentence, Boonyi had been overwhelmed by claustrophobia and had seen clearly what she had been too deeply in love with *Shalimar the Clown* to understand before, namely that this life, married life, village life, life with her father chattering away by the Muskadoon and with her friends dancing their *gopi*

> dance, life with all the people amongst whom she had spent every one of her days, was not remotely enough for her, didn't begin to satisfy her hunger, her ravenous longing for something she could not yet name, and that as she grew older life's insufficiency would only grow harder and more painful to bear. (114-15)

There is no concrete and convincing reason for her inner decision. It is only when she is supposed to dance and entertain the American ambassador that she begins to construct the image; a peculiar situation of cause succeeding the effect. The effect is more interior. Psychologically her wings of migration were already outspread; the entertainment dance provides the right amount of incentive for the rebellious wings to take flight. Ironically, during her stay in Delhi, and when she comes back to her village, she quite inanely puts the entire blame on her husband, believing that he could not defend her from the ambassador and also from her own self. This despite her knowledge of the poignant love filled letters Shalimar wrote to her. In short in a narrative unambiguously rich with substantive factual details, one can't help but be struck by the absence of the same in the moments of cardinal transition in some of the most important characters. One is left merely with speculation.

On his part, whatever knowledge Shalimar has about formal Islam comes only after he joins the ranks of "terrorists". Before that he was only a tightrope walker enchanting people with his antics. Therefore one does not derive a psychologically contenting portrayal from *Shalimar the Clown* as it is in the case of *Terrorist* by John Updike or even in case of Alice in *The Good Terrorist* (1985) by Doris Lessing.

This becomes clearer after Shalimar leaves the valley and turns into a globe-trotting undercover terrorist. There are wrenching descriptions of the crimes committed by him. He is now a hardened murderer going around with *Abu Sayyaf* militia-men in South-east Asia and other guerilla groups in the Muslim world. He fights alongside them against the non-Muslims. He transforms into a revenge-machine. However, almost every day the moment he sleeps, he returns to the valley reconstructing the betrayal at the hands of his childhood sweetheart. It becomes more and more clear that he is driven more by his sense of failure in relation to Boonyi and not by any deep seated conviction in the pan Islamic vision. The final proof comes when he eventually lands in the US and begins to aim at Maximillian Ophuls in Los Angeles. Acting as his chauffeur, he ends up killing him. Same is the situation with Hammirdev Kachhwaha. Being a part of the state machinery, he is the central grid of state terrorism. He is also pushed into curbing the rebellious activities more because of his ridiculous defeat at the hands of Boonyi. Instead of giving a cogent presentation in support of his repression policy, he behaves like a failed lover-cum-military man. In such a scenario drawing the terrorist-state sponsored or the anti state—from within, giving his deeper motivation, seems to be out of the question. The characters described begin with apparently strong conviction after their baptism to terrorism but soon turn into animated cartoon characters. Rather, Shalimar and Hammirdev, brutal as they are, are essentially clownish in their execution of terrorism.

Magic Realistic Transition

Shalimar the Clown, a majestic feat on the level of form, is unlike his preceding narratives largely free of what is known as Magic Realism. The compulsions of globalizing the tragic tale of a small place and putting it on a vast canvas are manifest. It is exactly in the moments of transition in which the factual terrain is skipped and recourse taken to a montage of mysteriously assembled feelings that one gets a feel of the particular retreat into the Magic Realist mode as well as the understanding of pressures inherent in converting the tumultuous tempest of a small place into a world defining microcosm. Why does the author take recourse to such a mode in an otherwise predominantly fact laden story? Does such a moment in which the past, present and future coalesce define the impossibility of scripting a global novel? That the time is not yet ripe for such an exposition? That the global reality despite the shrinkage of time and space is not so easily amenable to locating the characters across the board? Or is it, to flip the argument a little, a suggestion towards the inevitability of the usage of such a mode if one is to aspire the creation of a mind boggling global linkages? Surely the author's idea of trying to illuminate a global disaster through a microcosm or putting across a parable of the willing and unwilling subversion of multiculturalism has come unstuck because the link between the microcosm and the macrocosm is weak. Shalimar's relationship with the fighters, for example, in Afghanistan and Philippines is never going to be convincing, particularly when his obsessions are Boonyi and her paramour, Maximillian Ophuls and not the enterprise he is shown to be part of. The macrocosm is a separate world from the microcosm and the 'moment' when the characters decide to make it to the macrocosmic stage has been pretty ordinarily manufactured keeping away the factual record sketched around them in their small world. No doubt the world has become a small place. The stories of 'here' are part of the stories "there". They flow into each other. But the characters like Shalimar, Anees and Boonyi are place in a certain recognizable context. They bear a representative value. Unless this representative and context bound value is part of the mutual flow between the small and the big, the exchange naturally sounds implausible.

Naipaul's recent contention in this context demands attention. The argument runs that post-9/11, novelists ought to come back to reality as it is understood in the conventional sense for their material, and not fly away into the fantastic realm, for what lies there (fantasy) is probably less fictitious than the images spawned by the September 11 and its aftermath. The event read apolitically was a revolt of the reality against the fiction generated by aggressive imagination. It changed the perception of reality for novelists. It sounded a death knell for the novel as it was conceived and written. The reality post-9/11 got more fictionalized than fiction itself. Rushdie's novel, *SC*, demonstrates that despite the occurrence of that cataclysmic event, one still requires the cushion of moments in which fact merges with fiction. Or fiction is made to merge with aesthetically pleasing arrangement of facts. The facts in vogue might have defeated the capacity of the richest imagination to chisel anything uniquely fictitious yet the role of latter is no more absolute than the incorporation of the former. The fiction segment as a welder of the small with the big, spanning the disparate periods in a bewildering speed, helping the writer and the reader to fill the gaps and also providing the [il]logic of geographical mobility to characters. Boonyi and Shalimar, and Anees as well move geographically after the passage through their ambiguity-ridden moments of decision-making.

Not unrelated to this ambiguous moment of metamorphosis is the idea of authorial location. Living in a first world metropolis, the writer has chosen to use a Third World space for explaining the current global condition. The pitfalls of such big project are obvious. On the one hand the eye is fixed on a global audience spread across cultures; on the other the pen strains at the authenticity of representation. The casualty is the middle point, the inevitable connector whose shape is crafted with verbal trickery, stylistic quibbles and out of the world logic. In a sense the artificial cobbling of this mid position posits an internal critique of this wonderful text. Shalimar's father, the awesome *Sarpanch* once advised his son about the inevitable value of change in life. That the heart of life beneath and beyond the exterior signs tastes and sounds is metamorphosis. Metamorphosis is the secret heart of life. Denying or seizing the natural process of metamorphosis was akin to creating a rigor mortis of the heart, the secret throbbing engine of life on earth. The way, however, metamorphosis occurs in Shalimar and others, is not so much as a denial or seizure of the natural motions of life as it is the very denaturalization of the same. Such a process brings to the mind author's peculiar position vis-à-vis his location, subject matter, audience, commitment etc. Or is it that the act of denaturalizing metamorphosis is part of the natural phenomenon? That in order to produce allegories beginning in small crystal clear spaces, and ending on the larger universal scale, it is indispensable to make airy bridges whose existence is reported nowhere but in the fantastic imagination?

End Notes

1. In a freewheeling chat with the television anchor Barkha Dutt, Rushdie spoke about the long running Kashmir problem. His

consistent line of distance from the extremes echoes in the interview. Both the state and anti-state actors are held guilty of devastating the place, and disrupting the calm of the place:

Well, I think there is a terrible amount of oppression of Kashmiri Muslims by this other kind of Islam. That is important, you know. But before and still there was terrible misbehavior by members of the Indian armed forces and you know that is a sad thing to say, but you know, it is true and one creates the other, you know. And I have to say one of the strangest things about this book, given my history as you were saying in India, is that I found myself being praised by both Manmohan Singh and Mr. Advani. (Rushdie, Salman. Interview with Barkha Dutt. January 28, 2007 http://urpushi.blogspot.com/2007/01/salman-rushdie-in-jaipura-friendly-chat.html)

> THE CALAMITY of Kashmir is a wound on a wounded body; it is death arriving in awful majesty in a place where death has become a grubby, ugly, everyday affair. There has been so much man-made dying in Kashmir that if one believed in God one might say that God had become competitive and decided to show the killers, the killers in uniform and the terrorists cloaked in secrecy, what a real killer can do. (*If We Look Away, Kashmir Could Become Worse than a Tsunami.*)

2. It is worth recalling here that the poet's long association with the independence movement is not concealed from anyone. For a corroboration of the same the Foreword to the collection of poems titled *The Country without a Post-office* is a testimony. The collection as per Edward Said (1935-2003) is laden with the "extraordinary formal precision and virtuosity" and "searing imagery" (*Norton Poets Online*.......Online) of the trauma undergone by the population. The lines:

   Drippings from a suspended burning tyre
   Falling on the back of a prisoner
   The naked boy screaming
   I know nothing. (Ali 2002)

   are reverberating with the poets commitment.... More clear than a derivation from Ali is the short quote from *Romeo and Juliet* by the Bard-upon-Avon, William Shakespeare (1564-1616). Mercutio's observation "plague on both your houses" not merely delivers the author's ideological verdict vis-à-vis the simmering Kashmir problem but also creates a broader methodological axis.

3. It is appropriate here to refer to John Updike's novel *Terrorist* (Updike, John. *Terrorist.* New York: Alfred A. Knopf, 2006) by way of a comparison with the characterization of "terrorists" in *Shalimar the Clown.* Terrorist by John Updike is about Ahmad Ashmawy Mulloy, an 18-year-old boy in Northern New Jersey who is devoted to Islam. Ahmad was raised by an Irish-American mother after his Egyptian father disappeared when he was three. Ahmad converts to Islam at age 11 and is instructed in the *Qur'an* by a local imam.... Ahmad is very deep and thoughtful. Unlike Shalimar he has received a formal training in the Arabic language. How important it is to understand the nature of the Arabic language in order to gauge the degree of motivation in a "terrorist" was underscored by the author in an interview.

   "My conscience was pricked by the notion that I was putting into the book something that I can't pronounce," he said, but he added: "Arabic is very twisting, very beautiful. The call to prayer is quite haunting; it almost makes you a believer on the spot. My feeling was, 'This is God's language, and the fact that you don't understand it means you don't know enough about God.'" (Updike, John. Interview with Charles Mc Grath "In "Terrorist," a Cautious Novelist takes on a New Fear." ...May 31, 2006). By bringing out these nuances in the formation of a "terrorist's" mind we get to know about the psychology of a "terrorist".

4. Alsace Lorraine has a past not much different from Kashmir. Perhaps the difference lies only in name. One is Alsace Lorraine, another is Kashmir. The rest is same. A history marred by occupation, rebellion, freedom, re-occupation, re-rebellion, and slavery yet again. Alsace met with Frenchification, de-Frenchification, Germanisation, de-Germanisation. Maximillian Ophuls, a Jew, is from Alsace Lorraine, familiar with its past of betrayals and treacheries. It is during the de-Germanisation in the mid-1940s when, the flying Jew emerges as a great Resistance Hero—a resistance in which one took leave of one's name "one's past, one's future, one lifted oneself away from one's life and existed only in the continuum of the work, borne aloft by necessity and fatalism" (166)—fighting for the de-occupation of his homeland Alsace-

Lorraine. Knowing well the psychology of a conflict zone and the strange parallels between Alsace Lorraine and Kashmir, he is assigned the post of ambassador to India by Lyndon Johnson. He is fully aware of the definition and redefinition of Alsace by shifting frontiers, upheavals and dislocations, flights and returns, conquests and reconquests, the Roman empire followed by the Alemanni, the Alemanni by the Attila's Huns, the Huns by the Alemanni again, the Alemanni by the Franks. For some time it was with the Lotharingia, had been smashed by the Hungarians and reconstructed by the Saxons. And as the author says "Reformation and revolution were in its citizen's blood, which counter-reformation and reaction spilled in its charming streets." (138)

In short a history replicated in Kashmir. Curiously, the men and women resisting in Kashmir by a queer quirk turn into terrorists. Anees—leaving aside Shalimar who has a grand and totalitarian project in mind—is not allowed to be read in terms of Resistance. The interests and compulsions of global politics are immediately brought home, when a place as small as Alsace Lorraine and one almost re-writing the history of that place becomes the bastion of terrorists and the not the Resistance fighters. This despite the fact of Ophuls believing "the loss of one man's dream, one family's home, one family's rights, one woman's life is the loss of all our freedoms: of every life, every home, every hope". This tragedy does not belong to others but only to itself. It does not diminish the other but only itself.

Works Cited

Aji, Aron R. "All Names Mean Something: Salman Rushdie's "Haroun" and the Legacy of Islam." *Contemporary Literature,* 36.1 (Spring, 1995): 103-29.

Ali, Agha Shahid. *Selected Poems*. Srinagar: Agha Shahid Ali Foundation, 2002.

Brians, Paul. *Modern South Asian Literature in English*. West Port: Greenwood Press, 2003.

Coppola, Carlo. "Salman Rushdie's *Haroun And The Sea Of Stories*: Fighting The Good Fight Or Knuckling Under." *Journal of South Asian Literature,* 26. 1/2, Miscellany (Winter 1991): 229-37.

Douglass, William A., and Joseba Zulaika. *Terror and Taboo: The Follies, Fables, and Faces of Terrorism*. New York: Routledge, 1996.

Hussain, Masood. "Kashmir Protest against Anti-Islam Film Passes Peacefully." *Economic Times*, Sep. 12, 2012. Web. 28 Oct. 2012. <http://articles.economictimes.indiatimes.com/2012-09-18/news/33926189_1_kashmir-protest-protest-against-anti-islam-film-kashmir-baramulla-and-sopore>.

Lessing, Doris. *The Good Terrorist*. London: J. Cape, 1985.

Mathur, Shubh. "Terror and Impunity in Kashmir." *Asia Times Online*. May 7, 2014.

Metcalf, Jonathan, ed. *Illustrated Oxford Dictionary*. Oxford: Oxford University Press, 2003.

Nehru, Jawaharlal. *Selected Works of Jawaharlal Nehru* (June 26, 1952). Vol. 18. New Delhi: Orient Longman, 1974.

Noorani, A.G. "Article 370: Law and Politics." *Frontline*, 17.19 September 16-29, 2000.

Paknadel, Alexis and Robert Applebaum. "Terrorism and the Novel, 1970-2001." *Poetics Today*, 29.3 (2008): 387-436.

Rushdie, Salman. *Shalimar the Clown*. London: Random House, 2005.

———. "If We Look Away, Kashmir Could Become Worse than a Tsunami." *Hindu*. November 12, 2005.

———. "The Prophet's Hair." *London Review of Books*. 3.7. 16 April 1981: 19-20.

———. *Midnight's Children*. New York: Penguin, 1980.

Stephens, Ian Melville. *Horned Moon: An Account of a Journey through Pakistan, Kashmir, and Afghanistan*. Bloomington: Indiana University Press, 1955.

Varshney, Ashutosh. "India, Pakistan, and Kashmir: Antinomies of Nationalism." *Asian Survey* 31.11 (1991): 997-1019.

Select Bibliography

Ahmad, Aijaz. In *Theory: Classes, Nations, Literatures*. New Delhi: OUP, 1992.

Ashcroft, Bill et al. *The Empire Writes Back: Theory and Practice in Post-Colonial Literature*. London and New York: Routledge, 1999.

———. *The Postcolonial Studies Reader*. London and New York: Routledge, 1995.

———. *Post-Colonial Transformation*. London: Routledge, 2001.

Bhabha, Homi K. *The Location of Culture*. London: Routledge, 1994.

Bharat, Meenakshi, ed. *Rushdie the Novelist: From Grimus to The Enchantress of Florence*. New Delhi: Pencraft International, 2009.

Boehmer, Elleke. *Colonial and Postcolonial Literature*. New York: OUP, 2005.

Bradford, Richard. *The Novel Now: Contemporary British Fiction*. Blackwell Publishing UK, 2007.

Brah, Avtar. *Cartographies of Diaspora: Contesting Identities*. London and New York: Routledge, 1997.

Brennen, Timothy. *Salman Rushdie and the Third World: Myths of Nation*. London: Macmillan, 1989.

Chakrabarty, Dipesh. *Provincializing Europe: Postcolonial Thought and Historical Difference*. New Delhi: Oxford University Press, 2001.

Dalrymple, William. *White Mughals: Love and Betrayal in Eighteenth-Century India*. New Delhi: Viking, 2002.

Das, B.K. *Twentieth Century Literary Criticism*. New Delhi: Atlantic Publishers, 2004.

Devi, P. Indira. *Salman Rushdie and Magic Realism*. New Delhi: Research India Press, 2011.

Dingwaney, Anuradha. "Salman Rushdie". *A History of Indian Literature in English*. Ed. Arvind Krishna Mehrotra. London: Hurst, 2003. 308-17.

Fanon, Franz. *The Wretched of the Earth*. Trans. Constance Farrington. New York: Grove Press, 1963.

———. *Black Skins, White Masks*. Trans. Charles Lam Markmann. New York: Grove Press, 1967.

Frank, Soren. *Migration and Literature*. New York: Palgrave Macmillan, 2008.

Gandhi, Leela. *Postcolonial Theory: A Critical Introduction*. Delhi: OUP, 1999.

Gilbert, Helen and Joanne Tompkins. *Post-Colonial Drama: Theory, Practice, Politics*. London: Routledge, 1996.

Goonetilleke, D.C.R.A. *Salman Rushdie Modern Novelist Series*. Houndmills: Macmillan India, 1998.

Gopal, Priyamvada. *The Indian English Novel Nation History and Narration*. Delhi: OUP, 2009.

Guha, Ranjit. *Elementary Aspects of Peasant Insurgency in Colonial India*. Delhi: OUP, 1983.

Guerin, Wilfred L. *A Handbook of Critical Approaches to Literature*. New York: OUP, 2005.

Gupta, Meenu. *Salman Rushdie: Re-Telling History Through Fiction*. New Delhi: Prestige Books, 2009.

Gurnah, Abdulrazak, ed. *The Cambridge Companion to Salman Rushdie*. Cambridge: Cambridge University Press, 2007.

Jameson, Fredrick. "Third World Literature in the Era of Multinational Capitalism." *Social Text*, Vol. 15: 65-88.

Lindsay, Alan. "Salman Rushdie, History and the Contemporary Novel." *The Literature of Indian Diaspora: Essays in Criticism*. A.L. McLeod, ed. New Delhi: Sterling Publishers, 2000. 170-87.

Loomba, Ania. *Colonialism/Postcolonialism*. London and New York: Routledge, 2007.

McLeod, John. *Beginning Postcolonialism*. Manchester: Manchester University Press, 2000.

Mendes, Ana Cristina. *Salman Rushdie in Cultural Market Place*. Farnham, UK & Burlington, VT: Ashgate, 2013.

Mishra, Vijay. "Diaspora and Art of Impossible Mourning." *In Diaspora: Theories, Histories, Texts*. Ed. Makarand Pranjape. New Delhi: Indialog Publication, 2001.

———. "Rushdie and Bollywood Cinema." *Cambridge Companion to Salman Rushdie*. Ed. Abdulrazak Gurnah. Cambridge: Cambridge University Press, 2007: 11-28.

———. "Postcolonial Differénd: Diasporic Narratives of Salman Rushdie." *Post-Colonial Theory and English Literature: A Reader*. Ed. Peter Childs. Edinburgh: Edinburgh University Press, 1999: 429-38.

Mondal, Anshuman. "*The Ground Beneath Her Feet* and *Fury*: The Reinvention of Location". *The Cambridge Companion to Salman Rushdie*. Ed. Abdulrazak Gurnah. Cambridge University Press, 2007: 169-83.

Mongia, Padmini. *Contemporary Postcolonial Theory: A Reader*. New Delhi: OUP, 2000.

Mukherjee, Meenakshi. *Rushdie's Midnight's Children: A Book of Readings*. Delhi: Pencraft, 2003.

———. *The Perishable Empire: Essay on Indian Writing in English*. Delhi: Oxford University Press, 2002.

———. *The Twice Born Fiction: Themes and Techniques of the Indian Novel in English*. New Delhi: Heinemann Educational Books, 2000.

Nandi, Ashish. *The Intimate Enemy: Loss and Recovery of Self under Colonialism*. New Delhi: OUP, 1983.

Nayar, Pramod K. *Postcolonial Literature: An Introduction*. Delhi: Pearson Longman, 2008.

Nixon, Rob. "Environmentalism and Postcolonialism." *Postcolonial Studies and Beyond*. Ania Loomba, Eds. New Delhi: Permanent Black, 2006.

Paranjape, Makarand, ed. In *Diaspora: Theories, Histories, Texts.* New Delhi: Indialog Publication, 2001.

Parmeshwaran, Uma. *Salman Rushdie's Early Fiction.* Jaipur: Rawat Publication, 2007.

Quinn, Edward. *A Dictionary of Literary and Thematic Terms.* New York: Checkmark Books, 1999.

Rushdie, Salman. *Imaginary Homelands: Essays and Criticism 1981-1991.* London: Granta, 1991.

Singh, Manjit Inder, ed. *Contemporary Diasporic Literature.* Delhi: Pencraft International, 2010.

Smale, David. *Salman Rushdie-Midnight's Children/The Satanic Verses: Readers' Guides to Essential Criticism.* New York: Palgrave Macmillan, 2001.

Smith, Rowland. *Postcolonizing the Commonwealth: Studies in Literature and Culture.* Waterloo: Wilfred Laurier University Press, 2000.

Teverson, Andrew. *Salman Rushdie: Contemporary World Writers.* Manchester: Manchester University Press, 2007.

Tharoor, Shashi. "Rushdie's 'Overartist' Indianness from Midnight to Millennium." *Midnight's Diaspora. Encounters with Salman Rushdie.* Eds. Daniel Herwitz and Ashutosh Varshney, Delhi: Penguin/Viking, 2009: 122-35.

Thiara, Nicole Weickgenannt. *Salman Rushdie and Indian Historiography.* New York: Palgrave Macmillan, 2009.

Thieme, John. "'So Few Rainbows Any More'? Cinema, Nostalgia and the Concept of 'Home' in Salman Rushdie's Fiction." *SPIEL.* Vol. I. Lucknow, 2005: 23-34.

Trivedi, Harish and Meenakshi Mukherjee, Eds. *Interrogating Postcolonialism: Theory, Text and Context.* Shimla: Indian Institute of Advanced Study, 1996.

Trousdale, Rachel. *Nabokov, Rushdie, and the Transnational Imagination.* New York: Palgrave Macmillan, 2010.

Upstone, Sara. *Spatial Politics in Postcolonial Novel.* England: Ashgate Publishing Limited, 2009.

Vassanji, M.G. "The Postcolonial Writer: Myth Maker and Folk Historian." *A Meeting of Streams: South Asian Canadian Literature*. Toronto: TSAR, 1985: 63-68.

Verma, K. Pavan. *Becoming Indian*. England: Penguin Books, 2010.

Young, Robert. *Colonial Desire: Hybridity in Theory, Culture and Race*. London and New York: Routledge, 1995.

Zaman, Niaz. "Caliban's Children: Salman Rushdie and Shashi Tharoor." *Colonial and Postcolonial Encounters*. Eds. Niaz Zaman *et al.* New Delhi: The University Press Ltd., 2000: 112-24.